Contemporary History

To Jessica Seldon (aged 6 months)
in the hope that she may enjoy
a happy contemporary history

Contemporary History

Practice and Method

Edited by Anthony Seldon

Basil Blackwell

Copyright © Basil Blackwell Ltd 1988

First published 1988

Basil Blackwell Ltd
108 Cowley Road, Oxford OX4 1JF, UK

Basil Blackwell Inc.
432 Park Avenue South, Suite 1503
New York, NY 10016, USA

British Library Cataloguing in Publication Data
Contemporary history : practice and method
   1. Historiography
   I. Seldon, Anthony.
   907′2

   ISBN 0–631–16092–2
   ISBN 0–631–16093–0 Pbk

Library of Congress Cataloging in Publication Data
Contemporary history : practice and method
/ edited by Anthony Seldon.
   p. cm.
Includes index.
ISBN 0–631–16092–2. ISBN 0–631–16093–0 (pbk.)
   1. History—Methodology. 2. History—Research. 3. History.
Modern—20th century. I. Seldon, Anthony.
D16.C584 1988   88–7313
907′.2—dc19   CIP

   Typeset in 10 on 11½pt Times
   by Downdell Ltd., Abingdon, Oxon.
   Printed in Great Britain by Page Bros (Norwich) Ltd

Contents

Preface

Although there is no shortage of publications in the field of contemporary history, there has been a lack of practical guides to the sources on which the contemporary historian must draw. Part I of this volume sets out to remedy this with a series of chapters in which specialists in particular source areas assess their value and offer advice on how to make the best use of them. Part II moves on from methodology to contemporary history in action. It includes a series of contributions on the state of the art in Europe and the United States, on the writing of contemporary history in the ancient Classical world, and on the special role of biography. The overall aim of the book is to place the study of contemporary history on firmer methodological and intellectual foundations, and at the same time to help dispel the prejudice against it still current in some quarters by demonstrating its usefulness and potential.

The editor wishes to express his thanks to the contributors; to Sasha Orley for her help in preparing the book; to David Lawrence for help with research; to Alan Harding, Matthew Teller and Lucy Thane for proof-reading; to Stephanie Maggin, the ICBH's administrator, for her diligence and typing; to Graham Eyre for copy-editing; to Claire Andrews of Basil Blackwell for her typically calm efficiency; to Gill Riordan for preparing the index; and to David Walker for advice on a number of chapters. Special thanks are due to my collaborator and Co-Director, Peter Hennessy, for his stimulus, ideas and enthusiasm.

I would also like to acknowledge my deep gratitude to the following, without whose work the Institute of Contemporary British History would never have got off the ground: Sir Frank Cooper, Sir Kenneth Stowe, Dr David Butler, Lady Wood and David Severn.

Part I

Sources and Methodology

The contemporary historian's raw materials are his sources. The range of possible sources is wide, including oral and written or printed evidence of various kinds. The following seven chapters address the main categories of source material, with comments on their weaknesses, strengths and applications, and advice on how to make the best use of them.

Interviews are perhaps the most controversial source material. There still exists the residual feeling that interviews are the stock-in-trade of journalists and political scientists, but not of historians. The root of this belief would appear to lie in excessive reverence for the document, an attitude held strongly in the nineteenth century and perpetuated in recent years by some historians who should have been more perceptive about the source problems faced by those writing on the contemporary period. Chapter 1, by Anthony Seldon, reacts against this prejudice and argues that the oral evidence of the living witness can be a most valuable resource, though, like all evidence, it must be used with care and discrimination.

The press, as Peter Hennessy shows in chapter 2, is another important source for the contemporary historian. Yet it, too, has been undervalued, to the extent that several of the in-depth studies on the post-war period that have appeared in the 1980s have ignored it. Even some biographers have overlooked contemporary press profiles of their subjects. Yet such profiles are an invaluable repository of information and contemporary perception. The press is perhaps at its strongest in its role as a taker of snapshots, fixed in time: the observations stand, informed by and representative of the spirit of the moment. Not even diaries are immune from subsequent tampering by authors, struck by hindsight. As a provider of current perceptions, of comment from different angles of the political spectrum, and of hard fact, the press is an essential touchstone for the serious contemporary historian.

The great problem with the press as a source, however, is that few of its organs are thoroughly indexed. The position is changing gradually as computer data systems are beginning to index the 'quality' papers, but it is most unlikely that this process will be extended backwards to cover the whole of the period since 1945. Retrieval of information, Hennessy suggests, is also a severe problem for the researcher wishing to study material broadcast on radio or television. Since 1945 the broadcasting companies, notably Granada, Thames Television and BBC Radio, have made some outstanding contemporary-history programmes. Most valuable to the historian, perhaps, are the interviews; but here one faces the additional problem that usually only a small fraction of the material actually recorded is selected for broadcast. In Britain we have only just begun to think seriously about the relationship between academic contemporary historians and the broadcasting media. In consequence, material of priceless historical interest is being lost.

Problems of retrieval are less daunting when working with books and scholarly journals. As John Barnes notes in chapter 3, a variety of bibliographies and source books exist to guide the researcher. So far, the bulk of monographs on the period have been written by journalists and those actively engaged in the processes of making history; only since the early 1980s has it become more common for academic historians and post-graduate students to explore the post-war years.

Published secondary sources are the researcher's usual point of departure and most obvious resource; by comparison, surveys and statistics, discussed by Tom Nossiter in chapter 4, have been something of a backwater. The chapter shows how this type of material has much more to offer the contemporary historian than many might suppose, but only if used with due allowance for its special complexities. Above all, the contemporary historian must beware the seductive temptation of regarding any data as objective and final: there are always vital contextual questions to be asked.

Chapters 5 and 6 discuss deposits of official and private papers. Nicholas Cox, in chapter 5, makes it clear that the researcher in public record offices needs to be thoroughly prepared. Not only does he (or she) need to know what he is looking for, but he also needs to understand why documents have been created and preserved, and how they are filed. Moreover, it is important to realize that the document itself is only a starting point, and that every document has a history. Angela Raspin, discussing the use of private papers (chapter 6), conveys similar messages. However, as private collections are widely scattered and research visits can therefore be costly, in both money and time, even more thought and careful preparation may be required before consulting them than is the case for public records. Chapter 7, by the Deputy Librarian of the House of Commons, Dermot Englefield, draws the survey of sources to a close with a masterly guide through the mass of material thrown up by Parliament.

1

Interviews

Anthony Seldon

Interviewing is the black sheep among the contemporary historian's sources.[1] Many are inclined to agree with A. J. P. Taylor that all it gives us is 'old men drooling about their youth'.[2] Yet Taylor conducted few interviews when writing his many books, and many other critics of interviewing have little experience of it either. To be provocative at the outset of this chapter, contemporary historians who are critical of the value of interviews are often either too busy to conduct them, or lack the confidence or imagination to grasp their function and potential. Blanket condemnation of interviews is evidence of shallow comprehension.

This chapter will discuss those occasions when researchers might find interviews a valuable adjunct to their other sources; the likely problems and benefits of interviewing; methodology; and, finally, how to evaluate reliability and how to use interviews in written work. The term 'interview' will be adhered to throughout, although 'oral history' or 'oral evidence' could have been used in its place. In writing this chapter I have drawn not only on my own experience but also on that of many other practitioners, to broaden the base. Much of what is said applies mainly to interviewing elites, i.e. individuals selected because of who they are or what they did; but the historian collecting oral evidence from 'ordinary' people may also benefit. Further reading on this valuable application of the interviewer's art can be found in Paul Thompson's *Voice of the Past* (1978). Some of the best post-war history, such as Max Hastings' *The Korean War* (1987), has drawn on the oral evidence of both 'high' and 'low'.

When interviews might help

Interviews are almost always an inferior source of information to documents written at the time. But, because neither state nor private institutions nor individuals immediately release their papers for general inspection, interviews can be an essential stop-gap which allows contemporary history to be written. In Britain, scholars must wait till thirty years after the event to see the state papers at the Public Record Office at Kew, and even then some material, especially relating to intelligence matters, is held back.

Interviews have thus allowed numerous highly informative books to be written before the release of official papers. To take two episodes from recent British history, the Suez crisis of 1956 and the Falklands War of 1982, without interviews we should have had to wait until 1987 and 2013 respectively for the inside stories to be made known. But, thanks to works such as Paul Johnson's *The Suez War* (1957) and Hugh Thomas's *Suez Affair* (1967), the inner history of aspects of the Suez crisis such as the secret Anglo-French collusion with Israel and divisions of opinion within ministerial and official ranks became generally known much earlier.[3] When the relevant documents (or most of them) became available in January 1987, surprisingly few 'secrets' remained. Detailed chapter and verse could be added, but the broad story as reconstructed by earlier historians was verified. Much as authors, and rather more their publishers, might claim that post-1987 books relating to Suez were offering, at last, the true story, such statements had a hollow ring, at least to those in the know. Likewise, the spate of books on the Falklands War that have appeared following that episode, in particular Max Hastings' and Simon Jenkins' *The Battle for the Falklands* (1983) and Lawrence Freedman's *Britain and the Falklands War* (1988), have probably left few, if any, secrets about it for future revelation.[4]

But, even if the researcher has some or most of the documents at his – or her – disposal (it would be foolhardy to claim one had access to all extant documentation), there may still be gaps that interviewing can help fill. Martin Gilbert, for example, when conducting research for the volume of his Churchill biography covering the years 1914–16 (published in 1971), found that by 'conversation and correspondence with those who knew Churchill during this period . . . I have been able to include reminiscences of Churchill's moods, and of the atmosphere of events not always obvious from the documents, and have been able to describe several incidents not recorded in any contemporary source.'[5] Interviews can be particularly helpful in fleshing out documents when it comes to reconstructing the roles and methods of personalities, and their relationships with others. As the historian of the Royal Air Force, Denis Richards, has commented, information on relationships often 'does not get into the official records'.[6] Such relationships may not only be complex, but also be veiled to contemporaries. To take an example: a Secretary of State may not be very close to his Permanent Secretary, and may rely far more heavily on advice from more junior civil servants; he may be scornful of Deputy Secretary A, but intimate with Deputy Secretary B. Such relationships can critically affect the unravelling of the history; and but for interviews we might never know of them.

Interviews can also be valuable in helping researchers gain an overall grasp of available documentation. The American author David J. Mitchell has written, 'the oppressive weight of the himalayas of paper found in modern archives can be the greatest obstacle to the biographer interested in encapsulating the experiences and expression of his subject in a single book'.[7] Interviews can help identify which documents are important, which were read and acted upon. 'Records have a history of their own', writes John Barnes trenchantly. Some papers are ignored, others widely read and discussed; the historian without recollections to aid him may not know which is which.[8] Lewis Namier noted in the Preface to his *Diplomatic Prelude 1938–39* (1948), 'Even more important than direct information has been . . . guidance [from interviews]. . . . A great many profound secrets are somewhere in print, but are more easily detected when one knows what to see'.[9] Interviews can help the researcher order seemingly confusing documents. 'It may be', Martin Gilbert has said, 'that in a crisis there is no way that an historian can reconstruct the sequence of events from documents alone.'[10]

Interviews can also fill gaps in documentation. Regarding scientific history, Nicholas Kurti has observed that 'in scientific research the false starts are very often not recorded in contemporary documentation'.[11] Biographers are another group to find frequent gaps in documents. Roger Berthoud estimates that between 20 and 25 per cent of the material for his biography of the artist Graham Sutherland came from interviews, including many with the subject himself (who died before the research was completed).[12] The decline in letter-writing (and possibly diary-keeping) has played a role, if one that has been exaggerated, in creating gaps in contemporary documentation.

Interviews can also assist by revealing the assumptions and motives lying behind documents. Reports of meetings often fail to reveal the full picture: convenient rather than real reasons may be given, or underlying philosophies and approaches might have been so taken for granted by participants that no need was felt to elucidate them in the written record. Interviews can 'make positive what was latent', as Michael Holroyd has put it.[13]

Potential problems

All research requires careful evaluation of evidence. There has been a tendency for some to regard some types of evidence, notably material in the Public Record Office, as above suspicion, and for interviews to be treated as uniquely unreliable. Interviews do certainly require very careful treatment, and the problems associated with them can be divided into three main categories.

The first, and perhaps the most significant, relates to the interviewee's own limitations, and especially those of memory. Almost all who have conducted interviews would agree with Roy Jenkins that, 'If detailed work on the events of a period a number of decades ago is followed by the opportunity to talk to someone who was there at the time, the only too common result is that his recollections, not only of the dates, but of the sequence of events, do not fit the framework of the firmly established written facts'.[14] Anthony Howard in his life of R. A. Butler (1987) is another who has found interviews highly misleading, especially with regard to sequence.[15]

A common finding is that the older the witness, and the more distant the events under discussion, the less valuable his evidence. David Marquand, in interviews for his biography of Ramsay MacDonald, found 'memories amazingly short and amazingly fallible', which he suggested might have been because 'most of the people whom I interviewed were elderly and many were very old indeed'.[16] Robert Rhodes James, however, suggests that there are equal difficulties in interviewing people soon after events: recollections of busy, younger witnesses can be 'clouded by personal impressions and, oddly enough, by the very *recentness* of the episode'. He continues, 'It seems to be the case that it is only after a period of time that the mind can put matters in perspective and differentiate between similar occasions which, in the aftermath, tend to merge into one'.[17]

Anxieties about memory are not eased by the mystery that attaches to its workings. Stuart Sutherland, a professor of experimental psychology, wrote in 1983, 'the relation between short-term and long-term memory remains obscure. Nor do we know with any certainty what causes forgetting. . . . Above all, we do not understand how memories are indexed'.[18]

The interviewee may, of course, deliberately set out to falsify or mislead, but this difficulty can be exaggerated. More worrying is *unintentional* inaccuracy. Excessive discretion can be a problem, not least in the time it wastes, and is usually encountered where the interviewee is suspicious of the use to which the interviewer will put the material. Thus, before entering on an interview, one should do everything possible to establish one's credentials and integrity. Account need also be taken of other possible distortions in an interviewee's evidence: oversimplification of events; exaggeration of his own or his organization's role and importance; a partisan perspective; and the influence of hindsight. Philip Williams has noted that 'Politicians subconsciously adapt their views about the past to fit a stance they had adopted later'.[19] Beware too of interviewees who let their personal likings (as opposed to animosities) colour their evidence: for example, an interviewee asked about his friends' actions is likely to be charitable, even if he remembers feeling rather differently at the time.

The interviewer can do more to guard against the second category of problems associated with interviewing: those deriving from his own methodology. Unrepresentative sampling is an obvious error that can be avoided by drawing up systematic lists of potential interviewees from a wide variety of different organizations, backgrounds, sympathies, or whatever distinctions may be relevant. Surprisingly, few experienced authors appear to seek a representative sample when preparing interview lists. Biographers, for example, do not always interview enemies as well as friends of their subject, in some cases because those antipathetic to the subject are unwilling to discuss him or her. The Great Reaper may make unrepresentative sampling inevitable to some extent by gathering up certain partisans and leaving others free to roam the stage to guide (or mislead) historians. Loaded questioning is another avoidable error. It is all too easy to leave an interview having heard exactly what one wanted to hear, because one has asked only certain questions, or phrased them in a certain way. This subtle point requires particular attention, and is a trap into which many of the most experienced contemporary historians and biographers have fallen.

Younger researchers are particularly vulnerable to the danger of being too deferential to interviewees. The risks have been well described by Donald C. Watt:

> It has seduced some of the best-known historians of our day, Sir Lewis Namier being the outstanding example and John Wheeler-Bennett running him a close second. The seduction of being placed on the inside track, being made accessory to the non-written history, is extraordinarily difficult for anyone to resist and I must say most of all for the young researcher fired as he is with the hope of discovering something sensationally new.[20]

It can indeed be very awkward to be unpleasant about or critical of someone at whose hands one has received kindness and hospitality. Getting to know someone can be extraordinarily unbalancing if one is trying to write dispassionate history.

The final category of problems has to do with the nature of the interviewing exercise itself. A whole day can be spent preparing for an interview, travelling, being entertained, conducting the interview, and writing or typing it up afterwards. The same time might well have been better spent reading books, newspapers or documents. Interviews are also expensive in financial terms: the cost of travelling, subsistence, tapes and typing can be heavy. Grant-giving bodies have not, in the past, proved especially friendly to applications to help defray such expenditure.

Where interviewing is considered, a host of unpredictable factors combine to put off many researchers used to the hard certainty of documents. No piece of written evidence will change between visits to archives, but interviewees asked about the same event can and do say different things at different interviews. Worse, they can even change their mind in the course of a single interview. What they say in the morning may be at variance with what they say in the afternoon, and they change again after a drink in the evening. Interviewees may be much more forthcoming in their own home than in a neutral meeting place, and be far more open to a female interviewer than a male, or *vice versa*. Which is the individual's *real* testimony? One often doesn't know and is forced to rely on one's own judgement.

Other inherently unsatisfactory aspects of interviews are the fact that some individuals do not communicate well in such exchanges, and the difficulty of representing exactly what the interviewee said, or meant, including the *way* he said it. Francis King has written, 'As every journalist, psychiatrist and detective knows, what people say is often less revealing than the manner in which they say it. . . . This is the drawback of interviews. . . . The final product is a wholly accurate record of what has been in the speaker's tongue but rarely in his mind or heart.'[21]

With all these snags of interviewing – and there are many more that could have been mentioned – one could be forgiven for wondering whether it would not be better to dispense with it altogether. To do so, however, would be an error, for it would deprive one of much insight and information, as well as sheer enjoyment.

Potential benefits

Some benefits of interviewing have already been alluded to earlier in the chapter, and can be dealt with briefly. The range of benefits can be divided into four main categories.

First, one can gain information not recorded in documents. This may be about events, but is more likely to be about individuals, and organizational and personal relationships. J. A. G. Griffith found when writing his study (with T. C. Hartley) on central–local government relations in Britain that 'we were engaged on a highly *political* exercise – trying to find out the nature of the relationship in practice. There was no other way of doing it but to conduct interviews. The information we sought was nowhere written down. It was a matter of personalities and relationships.'[22]

Secondly, interviews may help one interpret personalities and events. Here the aim is not objective fact, but gaining the interviewee's perspective on people, events and processes. Ben Pimlott wrote that interviews gave him 'a series of free tutorials or seminars in which I could begin to understand a particular area that was puzzling me'.[23] (It is indicative of a changing climate that Pimlott, author of *Hugh Dalton*, one of the most distinguished recent British political biographies, is one of many younger historians who is an enthusiastic supporter of the interview.) Obtaining an interviewee's comments can thus help clarify and explain areas that might otherwise remain baffling.

Thirdly, interviews can help one interpret documents, either by providing an overview that explains underlying motives and assumptions, or by filling gaps or helping to clear up confusion over facts. Finally, there are what one might term the incidental benefits of interviews, a random but significant array of gains. Interviewees might well produce documents to be inspected, although one had no thought of seeing any such material when requesting an interview. Martin Gilbert finds that at least one-third of those he interviews produce documents for him to see[24] – although it would be an error to bank on such windfalls. Interviews can open the door to a fruitful relationship with someone personally connected with the subject of one's research: one can go back to that person for further material, or can send him drafts for comment. Someone whom one may have found unforth-coming or awkward in interview may turn out to be an admirable source of information when reading and commenting upon one's written work in the seclusion of his own home. Even very senior people, especially if retired, are often more than willing to read and comment on passages of text.

'The atmosphere of the time often does not appear in the documents', says Norman Chester.[25] Peter Hennessy describes in the following chapter how the press can be a fertile source of mood and contemporary colour; so too can interviews. Nigel Nicolson found when writing his biography of Alexander of Tunis that interviews gave him insight into 'the atmosphere of a headquarters, what Alex talked about in his mess', as well as 'how he arrived at decisions, his relations with Monty and Patton etc.'[26] This gain is all the more important because, as David J. Mitchell has observed, 'increasingly large volumes of papers found in archives, official or otherwise, can be colourless and impersonal collections of documents'.[27] Insight into a subject's personality and thought processes, and enrichment of one's own experience and understanding through *meeting*, instead of just reading about, living people who made or witnessed great events, are further benefits. Warm, vivid contemporary history has almost always been written by authors who have conducted interviews; dull, clinical history is often produced by those who have buried themselves away in libraries and archives.

Conducting interviews

The advice that follows, based upon my own experience and that of other practitioners, may appear unnecessarily rigid, but space precludes a full explanation of the rationale behind each of the steps suggested here. I am not, moreover, recommending that one slavishly follow this advice, but rather offering food for thought: each researcher will discover in practice how to modify the process to suit his or her own style and needs.

The first question to tackle is *when* to interview. The advantages of interviewing early in one's research are that profitable avenues of discovery are opened up and an overview of one's subject obtained. There is also less chance that key witnesses will die or become too ill to see strangers before one can visit them. Asa Briggs has said, 'In my experience, you have to watch age above all: I've lost some notable people through not seeking them in time'.[28] On the other hand, if one conducts interviews in mid-research, or towards the end, one knows much better what questions to ask, and how far to trust the answers one receives. Much depends on the judgement of the researcher, who must consider questions of timing and availability in the context of a research programme. Time permitting, major figures can be seen twice, at the beginning and near the end of research.

At an early stage one needs to draw up lists of potential interviewees. The latest volume of David Butler's *British Political Facts* can be useful for uncovering names of ministers, and the *Imperial Calendar and Civil Service List* for civil servants. If organizations other than central government are being researched, then they will usually have produced magazines, reports or catalogues which can be consulted for names. Biographers have no short cut, and must proceed piecemeal, asking family, friends and commentators for lists of people to see. Usually, once lists have been drawn up, some selection has to be made: it is rare for authors to exceed 200 interviews for a book, and 25 to 100 is common. Who then to leave out? Surprisingly, those at the very top – who may well have published their memoirs – may be less helpful than those more junior. 'It is almost axiomatic', Beatrice Webb wrote in her classic brief text on interviewing, 'that the mind of the subordinate in any organisation will yield richer deposits of fact than the mind of the principal.' John Campbell, a seasoned political biographer, makes a similar point: he finds most useful 'the recollections of civil servants and second-rank figures who may not have written memoirs, and whose evidence may be less distorted by the urge to self-gratification'.[29]

Some groups, then, may prove better than others. Nikolai Tolstoi finds that 'soldiers are very good interviewees'[30] and H. Montgomery Hyde that 'lawyers were the most reliable [witnesses] because their memories of facts and cases are so good'.[31] There is broad agreement that the least satisfactory class of interviewees is current or retired politicans, who often encounter pathological difficulties in distinguishing the truth, so set have their minds become by long experience of partisan thought. Conversely, civil servants can be the best interviewees, with former principal private secretaries perhaps the best of all. Civil servants tend to be dispassionate creatures by nature and profession: cat-like, they observe action, storing the information in mental boxes that can yield a rich harvest to those who take the trouble to prise them open.

Having drawn up one's lists of targets, the next stage is the approach. Letters are the best method, setting out clearly one's status, the nature of one's research, and the likely end product. Letters should sound enthusiastic about the possibility of seeing the interviewee: 'Flattery is at the root of most successful interviews', writes Paul Ferris.[32] It can be helpful to send out letters in 'batches' of ten to twenty, to avoid being swamped. If uncertain how to address 'top people', consult the latest edition of *Titles and Forms of Address*. One's chance of a favourable response is much higher if one is an established author rather than a doctoral student or unknown journalist. Mention in a letter of a supervisor or other mentor may help, but never offer money as an incentive. Remember that no one does anything for nothing, so if you can subtly suggest that remarks made in an interview will see the light of day in print, that could be a carrot (although, equally, it could deter the more faint-hearted). It is a problematic business, interviewing.

Seeing a subject in his home environment is usually an advantage: he will be more relaxed, with fewer likely distractions, and his papers will be at hand. Not that everyone would agree with even that statement. Bernard Crick, for example, found interviewees 'much more discursive and difficult to keep to the point' in their homes.[33] Wherever the interview takes place, it is essential to be thoroughly prepared. Interviewees, especially if still working, tire very easily of those who have not done their homework. Their frustration, which is fully justified, has been admirably articulated by Quentin Bell:

> I am frequently interviewed by complete strangers; they tend to ask for information I have already supplied, and they talk so much that I barely have a chance to answer them. They do not have enough background information to use any material that I do supply. I usually ask interviewers to list information they seek in advance. They then discover that the information is already available in printed form or that they have no notion of what it is they want to discover. This saves us all from wasting our time.[34]

The least one can do, where relevant, is to consult entries in the latest edition of *Who's Who*. Sending questions in advance can be helpful in preparing the ground and allowing the interviewee the opportunity to reflect and dredge up memories, where relevant consulting his papers (beware, though, if he has read up *other people's* books, or has been concocting elaborate defences or smokescreens!).

So to the interview itself. Three main methods exist of storing the information: memory, notes and tape recorder. It is common to hear authors decry two of the systems as ineffective, and only one, their favoured method, as reliable. In reality, they are commenting less on interview methods than on themselves. All the methods have benefits and drawbacks: no one way is foolproof or 'correct'. The advantages of using memory are that the conversation can flow swiftly, even over a meal, and the interviewee is not distracted by recording devices. The main disadvantage is that one can forget exactly what was said, and consequently write incorrect notes. Method two, taking notes, improves accuracy and gives a fuller record, but can be distracting and slow (unless one has shorthand). 'Hang on a minute' can be a disconcerting interruption to any interviewee exploring the deeper reaches of his memory. The third method is the tape recorder. The bonus is its accuracy and relative invisibility: the snags are that it may put people off, especially the elderly (although this drawback can be exaggerated), and it can take a long time to transcribe tape into a form that one can readily use. If using tape, employ a lapel microphone, and take batteries in case there is no convenient power point. In general, the researcher would be wise to experiment with all three methods, and then settle on the one he finds most helpful.

Practitioners also have strong feelings about the best way to structure questions. Some favour a rigid questionnaire approach, others more a play-it-by-ear or lucky-dip style. The best advice here is to come to an interview with a list of questions carefully prepared (possibly one that has been sent to the interviewee beforehand) but to allow for flexibility. What interviewees have to say unprompted, the way and order in which they say what they say, can all be enlightening. David Marquand found that

> for political biography interviewing, a highly structured interview would have been disastrous. . . . I had a general idea of the things I wanted to talk about before I started the interview, but it often happened that my original inclinations turned out to be wrong, and that the person I was interviewing led me into quite different areas, to my immense profit.[35]

The conduct of the interview very much depends upon individual circumstances. If the interviewee is very elderly, get the main questions in early, because he may well tire after thirty minutes or so. Interviews should seldom last longer than two hours – at least, not without a break. Generally, the older the subject, the longer will need to be spent with him before and after the interview. Margaret Morris found, when interviewing for *The General Strike* (1976), that 'usually I spent at least half a day and frequently a whole day with the subjects. I do not think this could have been shortened. The whole process of achieving a relaxed and friendly atmosphere and sparking off reminiscences among elderly people cannot be rushed.'[36] Clearly, the younger the interviewee, especially if still in harness, the less the time required and likely to be available. Also, the crisper will need to be the style in which questions are put.

Now for some controversial advice: before you leave the interview, or by post subsequently, ask the interviewee to sign a form governing access to the interview record: this will not only guard your own security, but also benefit other researchers in the future. If you reach no agreement, then your records will join the countless others which researchers have collected in the course of their work, with no idea what to do with them after their books or studies have been written. If they deposit the records in libraries for others to see, they could be breaching confidentiality; if they destroy them priceless historical records could be lost. So, awkward though it may be, ask the interviewee to sign a form permitting use of the record under specified conditions. The most convenient method is to ask the interviewee to select from a series of options such as the following, which may be listed on the one form.

1 Record freely available for interviewer and for others to use without further permission.
2 Available to all, but permission for researchers other than the interviewer required before citing or quoting.
3 Available to interviewer only, and permission required before citing or quoting.
4 Available to others only with prior written approval of interviewee. After death, record to be generally available.

One can play around with the categories, but to miss the opportunity of clarifying the basis of the interview can only lead to problems in the future.

If you have relied on memory or taken notes, set to work as soon as possible after leaving the interviewee at making a record or fleshing it out. Also write a thank-you letter, however the interview went, since such courtesy should at least make the subject more willing to see others in the future. If possible, interview records should be typed, clearly headed with details of who the interview was with, where it took place, how it was recorded, and how long the session lasted. Also make a precise record of your questions together with the answers, rather than trying to convert the interviewee's comments into a consecutive whole, which can be very misleading. One can never know how important historically the record may prove to be.

Using oral archives

The warnings sounded throughout this chapter apply with still greater force to the use of interviews recorded by others and stored in an archive. One is having to take a great deal on trust, and is denied the opportunity of asking one's own questions or of assessing the reliability of the interviewee face to face. Archive interviews may, however, be the only source on particular subjects – in which case there is no alternative to them, despite their imperfections.

In the United Kingdom there are few oral archives outside the broadcasting companies' holdings. The British Sound Archive is the nearest thing in Britain to a national archive, and is certainly worth contacting for possible leads, since it is beginning to expand the interviews in its records. The Oral History Society publishes the *Directory of British Oral Collections*, an invaluable guide, especially for social history. Political history is less well served. Some valuable work was conducted by the

Granada Historical Trust and the British Oral Archive of Political and Economic History, the latter based at the British Library of Political and Economic Science, but both projects were terminated prematurely. Valuable interviews relating to colonial history are available at the Bodleian Library's Rhodes House, Oxford (Colonial Records Project), at the India Office Library in London and at the Centre for South East Asia Studies at Cambridge. Military history is another area better served than many: the Imperial War Museum, in particular, has conducted some outstanding oral history work.

On the whole, though, there remain in the late 1980s some major gaps that require filling through careful and thorough oral history programmes. It is most unfortunate there is still little systematic recording of the recollections of senior civil servants and ministers, who ideally should be interviewed shortly after retirement. Regrettably, there are few bodies in the United Kingdom willing to fund programmes in such areas.[37]

Evaluation and use of interview records

How far should one trust interview records? To begin with, one should recognize them for what they are: the memories or impressions of *individuals*, often many years after the events discussed. One must ask why the interviewee has said what he has, whether he was an eyewitness or participant or is repeating hearsay, and what his precise position was at the time and what access to information he had. Junior figures tend to glorify and glamourize; senior people to be cynical and egocentric. Consider subsequent careers and predispositions. Christopher Thorne has written,

> No matter how self-critical and objective witnesses may be (and obviously they vary enormously in these respects) they cannot 'unlearn' what they've come to know subsequently of what came after the moment or period about which they're being questioned. Their evidence may be first-hand, but it isn't contemporary.[38]

In order to assess reliability during an interview, it may be found useful to ask, where appropriate, 'Is that what you thought at the time?' (or some suitable variant); to prepare in advance some specific factual questions – for example, on dates and names – to gain an overall idea of the witness's reliability; and to return to the same issue from different angles in the course of the interview. After the interview, it is vital to check the information remorselessly against other sources; and when there is no other source one should say so in any published account using the evidence.

Whenever interview evidence is employed in published work, it should be acknowledged as meticulously as other sources, giving the name of the interviewee, the date of the interview, and possibly also the place. If the interview has been located in an archive, the source note should state which. If alluding to information obtained in an interview that one has not received permission to cite, one should be as discreet as possible and give the source as 'private information'.

The more rigorous the interviewer's procedures, and the more discriminating his use of oral evidence, the sounder will be the conclusions drawn from it. Only in this way can the residual antipathy to such evidence be reduced, and its rightful status as a valuable, if problematic, source of information be recognized.

Notes

1 The argument in this chapter is based closely upon Anthony Seldon and Joanna Pappworth, *By Word of Mouth* (Methuen, 1983). The 'oral history questionnaires' referred to belong to the background research material for this book. See also Paul Thompson, *Voice of the Past*, (Oxford University Press, 1978).
2 A. J. P. Taylor, quoted in Brian Harrison's valuable article 'Oral history and recent political history', *Oral History*, 3 (1972), p. 46.
3 Paul Johnson, *The Suez War* (Macgibbon and Kee, 1957); Hugh Thomas, *The Suez Affair* (Weidenfeld and Nicolson, 1967).
4 Simon Jenkins and Max Hastings, *The Battle for the Falklands* (Michael Joseph, 1983); Lawrence Freedman, *Britain and the Falklands War* (Basil Blackwell, 1988). See also review article by Freedman on the Falklands literature in *Contemporary Record*, 1, no. 2 (1987).
5 Martin Gilbert, *Winston S. Churchill*, vol. III: *1914–1916* (Heinemann, 1971), p. xxvi.
6 Denis Richards, responses to oral history questionnaire, quoted in Seldon and Pappworth, *By Word of Mouth*, p. 40.
7 David J. Mitchell, 'Living documents: oral history and biography', *Biography*, 3 (Winter 1980), p. 284.
8 John Barnes, 'Teaching and research in contemporary British history', in Donald C. Watt (ed.), *Contemporary History in Europe* (Allen and Unwin, 1969), pp. 41–2.
9 L.A. Namier, *Diplomatic Prelude 1938–39* (Macmillan, 1948), p.v.
10 Interview with Martin Gilbert, 5 November 1981, quoted in Seldon and Pappworth, *By Word of Mouth*, p. 44.
11 Interview with Professor Nicholas Kurti, 4 December 1981, quoted ibid., p. 38.
12 Interview with Roger Berthoud, 17 September 1981, cited ibid., p. 45.
13 Interview with Michael Holroyd, 11 September 1981, quoted ibid., p. 45.
14 Roy Jenkins, *The Development of Modern Political Biography 1945–70*, Don Carlos Coloma Memorial Lecture, 1971.
15 Anthony Howard, *RAB: the life of R. A. Butler* (Jonathan Cape, 1987). Also interview with Howard in *Contemporary Record*, 1, no. 1 (1987).
16 Letter from David Marquand to author, 9 November 1981, cited in Seldon and Pappworth, *By Word of Mouth*, p. 17.
17 Robert Rhodes James, quoted by Harrison in *Oral History*, 3, p. 34.

18 Stuart Sutherland, 'All in the mind', *Sunday Telegraph*, 2 January 1983.
19 Philip Williams, 'Interviewing politicians', *Political Quarterly*, 51, no. 3 (1980), p. 311.
20 Donald C. Watt, quoted by Harrison in *Oral History*, 3, p. 37.
21 Francis King, *Sunday Telegraph*, 3 January 1982.
22 Interview with J. A. G. Griffith, 3 November 1981.
23 Ben Pimlott, responses to oral history questionnaire, September 1981. See also interview with Pimlott in *Contemporary Record*, 1, no. 3 (1987).
24 Interview with Martin Gilbert, 3 November 1981.
25 Interview with Sir Norman Chester, 28 November 1981.
26 Nigel Nicolson, responses to oral history questionnaire, August 1981.
27 Mitchell, in *Biography*, 3, p. 284.
28 Interview with Lord Briggs, 27 November 1981.
29 'The method of the interview', a four-page appendix in Beatrice Webb's *My Apprenticeship* (Longman, 1926), pp. 423–6; interview with John Campbell, *Contemporary Record*, 1, no. 2 (1987).
30 Nikolai Tolstoi, responses to oral history questionnaire, October 1981.
31 H. Montgomery Hyde, responses to oral history questionnaire, September 1981.
32 Paul Ferris, responses to oral history questionnaire, August 1981.
33 Bernard Crick, responses to oral history questionnaire, December 1981.
34 Quentin Bell, responses to oral history questionnaire, August 1981.
35 Letter from David Marquand to Seldon and Pappworth, 9 September 1981.
36 Margaret Morris, responses to oral history questionnaire, November 1981.
37 For further information about oral archives, see Seldon and Pappworth, *By Word of Mouth*, pp. 197–229 or contact the National Sound Archive.
38 Christopher Thorne, 'Talking about Vietnam', BBC Radio 3 broadcast, transmitted 9 January 1987, transcript pp. 10–11.

2

The Press and Broadcasting

Peter Hennessy

Historians, or the documents men and women among their ranks, suffer from an occupational disease. It's called archivitis. It normally strikes in the mid-afternoon in places such as the Public Record Office at Kew or the British Library's newspaper library at Colindale. Its symptoms are lethargy, blurred vision, a certain numbing of the brain cells. The cause is a combination of biorhythms and information overload. For the newspaper reader, however, archivitis can be a boon not a blight. The eye, in wandering away from the column on the political or economic crisis the historian is attempting to reconstruct, often alights on items – the name of a sporting hero, perhaps, or advertisements for clothes or travel – which convey the smell and feel of a period, themselves important ingredients of history if it is to convey, as it must, the spirit of time and place. Few of these fringe but significant benefits accrue to an archivitis sufferer whose eyes are glazing over before an official file. If a press cutting is included among the memos and the letters – the universal instruments of bureaucracy – it deals only with the single issue at hand. The magic ingredient of serendipity is absent.

Let me give an example from personal experience. I put in a long stint on the newspapers at Colindale when preparing a clutch of case-studies for two books on the performance of the British press as an information provider.[1] The technique was to pick an issue from the past for which both the official and the newspaper record was available and to see how close the press came to reporting things as they really were. I called it a 'What the Papers Never Said' exercise and even devoted to it the whole of one edition of Granada Television's *What the Papers Say* in January 1985.

One of the case-studies was press treatment of the Attlee Government's announcement of its intention to manufacture a British atomic bomb. The announcement was made in the quietest way possible, through a planted parliamentary question, on 12 May 1948. The 'quality' papers confined themselves to a straight report on the parliamentary answer (though the

Financial Times ignored it). The *Daily Mirror*, typical of the popular press, did not carry the story at all the day after or at any stage during the following week. But one could not fail to notice in its edition of 14 May a marvellous unwitting scoop in the security field, in the shape of a picture story about a visit to the Foreign Office by the boys of Kingston-upon-Thames Technical School. There were entertained to tea by the Minister of State, Hector McNeil, and photographed in his office. 'What about your spies, sir?' one boy asked. McNeil replied, 'Ah, yes, I have them working for me. But I get more information from a good reporter.'[2] McNeil's private secretary was none other than Guy Burgess, who defected to Moscow with Donald Maclean almost exactly three years later. Sadly, he was not in the picture. He may well have been in earshot. Given the irreverence of his character, he would have loved every nuance of the ironic scene.

Equally ironic in its own way was a coincidence in the second case-study I undertook, on the press coverage of the 1949 sterling crisis, which culminated in a devaluation of the pound in September the same year. The *Financial Times* apart, the quality of coverage was lamentable, because much of the tone and content was set by unattributable briefings given by the Government to the Westminster Lobby correspondents. By a delicious coincidence the Royal Commission on the Press, chaired by Sir David Ross, reported in the middle of the crisis and, naturally, was given extensive coverage in *The Times*, then the trade paper of the British establishment. One passage leapt at the reader from the page:

> The evidence put before us does not suggest that up to now any harmful influence is being exerted on the Press through the medium of the Government information services; but if newspapers get out of the habit of finding their own news, and into the habit of taking all or most of it unquestioningly from a Government department, they are obviously in some danger of falling into totalitarian paths. Future developments, therefore, need to be carefully watched.[3]

Another eye-catching item in that particularly hot summer was a letter and a picture, also in *The Times*, about what was called Manchester University's 'mechanical brain' or 'computing machine'. The computer era was upon us.[4]

Serendipity, atmospherics and irony apart, the historian ignores newspapers at his or her peril. For all my uncharitable remarks about the quality of much political reportage, I have always remembered what a modern historian who taught me a great deal, Dr Henry Pelling of St John's College, Cambridge, had to say about the depth and detail of many newspaper accounts. For the contemporary historian picking his way through the most recent period without the benefit of official documents to guide him, newspapers are a primary raw material, not an ancillary aid to understanding. This fact imposes a sober and serious duty on journalists, particularly at the quality end of the written medium.

When he acquired the magazine *Newsweek* in 1961, the American publisher Philip Graham said he wanted the magazine to be 'the first rough draft of history'.[5] The ambition may or may not have been realized in *Newsweek*. It has not been comprehensive. Inevitably its values have been those of liberal-minded desk editors looking at the world through the eyes of Manhattan or Washington.

The Americans have thought about the journalistic calling. I. F. Stone, the idiosyncratic political commentator and creator of the legendary *I. F. Stone's Weekly* has claimed, 'we are sort of historians on a low level. This is the role that Jefferson gave us: he gave American journalists a status that journalists in the United Kingdom just don't have. Because of the First Amendment.'[6] The claim is valid. Journalists such as Theodore White and David S. Broder have half-consciously been writing their nation's history. Their work is full of historical analogy. It is rounded because their self-appointed task has been to place contemporary politics within a 200-year flow. The trouble has occasionally been that in their self-conscious role as historians they have graced trivial events and ephemeral personalities with a weight they did not deserve.

The British newspaper press and history

Does the British newspaper press offer such a 'first rough draft'? Let us import the Graham–Stone rubric, and immediately acknowledge that, apart from *The Times*, with its traditional claim to be a 'journal of record', no British paper has ever entertained such an ambition. British newspapers matter to the historian both for their reportage of politics and for their role as political participants. Failing to realize that the two functions influence each other could be dangerous.

First, let us charitably acknowledge what the papers do well. They are strong on personality – who's up and who's down. Some excel at profiles which catch careers in mid-flight: these can be far more revealing than obituaries, which tend to be reverential. No political biographer will be able to ignore a Terry Coleman interview with his subject in the *Guardian*,[7] or the like coverage from John Mortimer in the *Sunday Times*, or from the *Observer* in one of its regular, anonymous profiles, or from Susan Barnes (who sometimes writes under the name of Susan Crosland),[8] or, especially in the 1950s, from the *New Statesman*.[9] Of late, the *Listener* profile has acquired a depth and a consistency to match any other examples of the genre. The problem for the historian is that this cornucopia of mini-biography is not catalogued.

The researcher is well served, too, by the intricate political geography charted in the daily press through constant opinion polls, which may, as Aneurin Bevan said they would, have taken the poetry out of politics, but, in the era of three-party politics and tactical voting, have acquired a significance of their own as a kind of share index in the political market, a genuine guide to electoral choice. Equally intricate and consistent is press coverage of faction fighting within and between parties. Indeed, even when the official archive is opened, the press remains the best source on party politics, which, owing to the antiseptic rules of political neutrality which govern the Civil Service, rarely find their way into departmental papers.

The utility of newspaper profiles or reports as sources ought to be gauged in the knowledge that much political information in Britain reaches the public after refraction through the Westminster Lobby, a semi-secret journalist organization that functions as an information cartel and possibly also as an adjunct to the Prime Minister's Press Office. The reporting of Parliament itself is a debased art nowadays: such reporting as there is often misses the exchanges that take place within the specialist committees, which are not covered on a regular basis. Political reporting is the province of journalists in the Lobby. The rules of their game specify non-attribution of sources, which seems to have become a convenient mask for the utterances of prime ministers and prime-ministerial officials who would rather not have a source cited for the items of political news they dangle. A good rule of thumb is to distrust reports bearing the by-line 'By our Political Editor' unless there is independent confirmation (though there are glowing exceptions to this harsh recommendation, such as Peter Riddell of the *Financial Times*). The caveat does not now apply to the *Guardian* or the *Independent*, which have no part in the collective briefing offered the Lobby by officials and which gather their political intelligence in a more pluralistic way.[10]

All political intelligence also has to be weighed by the historian on the scales of newspapers' declared and covert political attachments. The myths of neutral reportage – sacred facts, free opinions – are now as prevalent yet as useless to the historian as when C. P. Scott rolled them on their way with that dictum.[11]

The value of any report or piece of commentary has to be judged in the light of a paper's editorial predilections as well as the writer's own biases. The fairmindedness which ought to characterize the historian's work cannot be assumed to govern that of journalists. The *Daily Express* and even the *Daily Telegraph* have been partisans of the right. Similarly, the *Daily Mirror* has been partisan on the Left, and the *Guardian* has taken an anti-Conservative line for much of the post-war period. Historians of the Left seeking sharp contemporary political comment will, in general, find themselves much less well served, especially after the demise of the pro-labour *Daily Herald* in 1964, than students of the Right. Those interested in the fortunes of the Liberals lost a valuable source with the disappearance in 1960 of the *News Chronicle*.

The British press has its political commentators, a permanent Greek chorus interpreting events and people. Many are acute witnesses. Most also have their political side – Peter Jenkins of the *Independent* an individualistic occupier of the centre ground, Ronald Butt of *The Times* pro-Conservative, and so on. They belong to a parade of able practitioners in which stand Hugh Massingham of the *Observer*, James Margach of the *Sunday Times*, Wilfred Sendall of the *Daily Telegraph*, Sir Harry Boyne of the *Glasgow Herald* and *Daily Telegraph*. But outstanding commentators though these writers were on much of the post-war period, it must be stressed that their articles need always to be seen in the context of the wider political projects of their newspapers. A writer for the *Observer* when it was owned by Astor may have engaged a rather different process of political appraisal from one writing during the Lonrho ownership. Lord Thomson of Fleet gave the *Sunday Times* considerably more leeway for liberalism than Rupert Murdoch. No responsible historian should utilize, say, the *Daily/Sunday Express* or the London *Evening Standard* for the period 1969–79 without first consulting *The Fall in the House of Beaverbrook*.[12]

Newspapers excel at reporting the surface phenomena on the political pond – the people and their impressions – but are usually poor guides to the construction of public policy. Specialist writing is a late-twentieth-century phenomenon. Before 1939 there were some specialists – for example, in farming and agriculture – but the ranks of writers who could call on some expertise and experience grew only in the later 1950s. One specialist area, colonial policy in Africa, was particularly well covered by Colin Legum on the *Observer* and Oliver Woods on *The Times*. Serious newspapers nowadays have education correspondents and defence writers. There are none the less great gaps in their maps of the world. The burgeoning expenditure of the state on training the young has, for example, not been followed. Newspapers are traditional in their interests: the activities of many institutions, such as the Manpower Services Commission, that history may deem more important are often overlooked if not regarded as of sufficient general interest.

Despite the activities of individuals, 'the secret places of British politics', as Richard Crossman called them, are not covered consistently.[13] Regular coverage of the Civil Service is to be found today only in the *The Times*, the *Independent* and the *Guardian*. The problem is that Whitehall, with its secretive culture and protective layers of statute, remains a hard target. With Whitehall's lavish recourse to the Security Service to track down leakers, journalists assigned to it have to operate like intelligence officers in the field.

Through its political, economic, defence, diplomatic and Whitehall correspondents, a quality newspaper's readership, the contemporary historian and the political scientist should ideally be provided, as a matter of routine, with information about the analysis and the choices going forward for discussion in the Cabinet and its committees. Cabinet committees – the engine room of central government – are particularly important.[14] Yet we do not have anything approaching a complete list of these, let alone regular coverage of what they are up to. This is a very hard target to penetrate, but it should be a priority and is one that requires combined operations by a paper's specialists, who in too many cases work in isolation and are sometimes even rivals. If the press were truly fulfilling its function of providing a first rough draft of history, there would be precious little left to discover when journalists congregate at the Public Record Office in thirty-one years' time to unearth today's delayed scoops.

Great efforts to penetrate the best protected targets were made by the Sunday papers in the 1960s and 1970s, during the heyday of the British version of investigative journalism, a genre associated particularly with the *Sunday Times* Insight team when Harold Evans was the paper's editor. By the mid-1980s this type of journalism had been reduced to a small but determined and, occasionally, very important redoubt on the *Observer*, where its spirit was kept alive by David Leigh and his colleagues. Hugo Young wrote in 1986, 'The interest of newspapers in ambitious retrospective inquiries into the recent past was always unpredictable. But the growth of titles and of profits has been accompanied by a withdrawal of resources and commitment from this class of work.'[15] There are tides and cycles in such matters, especially in a fashion-prone industry such as the press. The picture is not static. It would be wrong to assume that the newspaper pendulum will not one day swing back towards a greater emphasis upon policy analysis.

For the duration, however, historians are likely to find newspapers poor witnesses to much contemporary history. Take Britain's relationship with the European Economic Community as an illustration. Newspapers may have diplomatic correspondents. They may have agricultural specialists. But rarely do the twain speak. And the space in between them is not covered. If a paper has a man in Brussels, it probably will not even have thought of having a London-based EEC specialist – someone, in other words, to map the growing accommodation of British policy and administrative practice to European models. The significance, actual or potential, of such joint projects as EUREKA is rarely discussed in newspaper pages.

The other persistent shortcoming of the press as a source of history is bigger but less specific and less easy to define. It relates to those issues which are not the stuff of today's political discourse but should be. The trouble is that it is only with hindsight that one can easily single them out. Brian Wenham, an immensely seasoned news gatherer and BBC executive, delineated the problem when he wrote,

> Over the years big issues ranging from the emerging crisis in Northern Ireland in the 1960s, to the need to pull back from East of Suez, to the growing de-

industrialisation of the North, and then to the growing racial tensions in inner cities, have been either openly evaded or effectively by-passed, side-lined from politics to the realms of economics or sociology, only to force themselves back eventually on to the harsh world of politics to general shock and surprise.[16]

All too often even the best newspapers have followed the political agenda rather than the hidden agenda. It's all very human. It has to do with the tyranny of today's news list prepared for the morning editorial conference and a desire not to have to scramble to catch up with stories rival papers are carrying when first editions flop onto the night editor's desk around about 11.30 p.m. Again, mapping benchmarks that will look significant to the political, economic and social historians of the twenty-first century is easier said than done. But it should, it must, be attempted.

Before leaving newspapers, mention should be made of the provincial press. Often it will have little to add to the coverage of national politics in the national press. But there are exceptions – in particular, where a newspaper's Lobby correspondent had an intimate working relationship with a top politician, as Trevor Lloyd-Hughes of the *Liverpool Daily Post* had until 1964 with Harold Wilson. In the main, however, the provincial press is valuable more to the biographer tracing information on a locality's favourite son, or to students of local politics. Two clear exceptions to this should, however, be mentioned: the *Scotsman* and the *Glasgow Herald*, whose political coverage and comment often exceed the best of the London-based national papers.

Such background to events might be sought in the weekly magazines, for at their best the weeklies do provide a kind of 'first rough draft'. On occasion, they can stimulate and sustain a great debate, as the *New Statesman* did on Labour's future in the run-up to the 1987 general election. Apart from the *Economist* with its huge sale of 300,000 copies (80,000 in Britain, 220,000 in the rest of the world), the weeklies have relatively tiny circulations, despite a mid-eighties renaissance which by the spring of 1987 had taken the *Listener* to a weekly sale of 35,000, the *Spectator* to 31,000 and the *New Statesman* to 27,000.[17] Their influence among the political nation, or the 'chattering classes' as the *Observer*'s Alan Watkins liked to call them, is out of all proportion to circulation in terms of opinion formation within a wider political debate.

The category 'weekly newspaper/magazine' is broad. Historians of institutions will delve into the 'trade press'. *The Times Higher Education Supplement*, for example, has since 1972 been a faithful chronicler of events in the village of higher education – births and deaths, arrivals and departures: sooner or later they make their way into its pages.[18] The *British Medical Journal*, besides being a forum for professional debate, provides a news service about the National Health Service and medical politics in general; its standpoint is that of the medical practitioner but its standards and fairmindedness are evident, too. The persistent under-reporting of science and technology in the daily newspapers makes the *New Scientist* or *Nature* essential reading for those concerned with these areas.

Off the beaten track, the printed press takes many forms. The historian of politics will have to follow such newspapers as *Tribune* and such magazines as the monthly *London Labour Briefing* – essential for understanding the evolution of ideology on the left of the Labour Party from 1980.

Newspapers are a dual feeder of history. Beyond their actual and potential contribution as newspapers, they may stimulate their producers, the journalists themselves, to develop their observations elsewhere. Some of them write good books shortly after the events they have been reporting from their privileged observation post, and these too can be processed with profit through the historical blender. Stephen Fay and Hugo Young were particularly skilled practitioners in the 1970s, with *The Fall of Heath*[19] and *The Day the Pound Nearly Died*.[20] In the 1980s the market leaders have been Max Hastings and Simon Jenkins on the Falklands War,[21] John Lloyd and Martin Adeney on the miners' strike,[22] and Richard Norton-Taylor on the Ponting affair.[23] The genre was pioneered in France in the 1950s with the Brombergers' volume on Suez[24] and provides a spasmodic if revealing flow of instant history whose occasional breathlessness and immediacy should not cause it to be dismissed or underestimated.

Finding newspaper sources

Only *The Times* and, since 1986, the *Guardian* compile and produce a full index of their contents. For the rest, it is a matter of chronology and painstaking search for items. The British Library's newspaper library at Colindale offers its readers most British newspaper titles, together with periodicals and a selection of the foreign press. It provides an excellent information service for the inquirer who wishes to know what is available before making the journey to the north-west suburbs of London.

Back copies of *The Times* are widely available on microfilm in principal public libraries, though disruptions to the paper's production from the mid-seventies onward have produced gaps in the record. Bound copies of older newspapers – invaluable for giving the 'feel' of an era – are less readily available. Newspapers mostly have their own intelligence departments and archives, and historians should not be put off by possible initial resistance to their use by the public.

Runs of magazines can be difficult to track down. Interest groups can be a good source for cuttings relevant to them, and an appeal to journalists' vanity can sometimes secure access to cuttings of their work.

Sound and vision

The BBC and the independent producers of radio and television programmes have their own private policies about the collection of materials; for the outsider these often seem to amount to a lottery in which chance determines whether a programme survives, either in transcript or broadcast form. This is a shame, as much output is of high value to the historian. BBC Radio 4 continuously updates and embellishes a sound picture of institutions, individuals and groups. In collaboration with the producer Anne Sloman, Hugo Young and Simon Jenkins have recently created rich accounts of the contemporary Civil Service,[25] Treasury[26] and Foreign Office[27] which should serve as staples of the politics and history diet in schools and universities for a decade at least. Radio, too, has been a self-aware provider of contemporary history. Anthony Moncrieff's *Suez Ten Years After*, based on the BBC Third Programme series he produced in 1966, put a great deal of new material in the public domain.[28] With Mark Laity I wrote and presented the follow-up based on the declassified archive – *A Canal Too Far*, broadcast by BBC Radio 3 in January 1987.[29] Michael Charlton's *The Price of Victory*, on Britain and Europe 1945–63, will endure as a valuable source and a rich oral archive as long as the EEC remains a subject of interest of historians, political scientists and economists.[30] His series on the Falklands War, broadcast in 1987, also makes excellent use of eyewitness accounts.

Television is less satisfactory than radio as a medium for deep contemporary history, as the old truism that the need for pictures distorts the message is, well, true. There have, however, been certain glowing exceptions, particularly the programmes associated with two gifted historians who happen also to be television producers, Phillip Whitehead and Brian Lapping. Whitehead's series on Britain 1945–63 for Thames Television in 1970, captured for posterity in Alan Thompson's book *The Day before Yesterday*,[31] remains an excellent source. Whitehead's own volume *The Writing on the Wall*,[32] based on Brook Productions' Channel 4 television series on the seventies, will have a long shelf-life.

Brian Lapping's *End of Empire*[33], companion volume to Granada Television's series of the same name broadcast in 1985, is a rich supplement to the hefty scholarly literature on the subject. Granada Television's reconstructions of crises in Cabinet, beginning with *Chrysler and the Cabinet*, broadcast in February 1976, will also prove uniquely valuable sources for contemporary historians. Another outstanding television contribution to recent history, Peter Pagnamenta and Richard Overy's *All our Working Lives*,[34] commands a place on any roll of honour. Television has given us many series such as *Yesterday's Witness* and *Ireland: a television history* which, through their broadcast interviews, and even more those 'off-cut' interview extracts which were not screened, should have abundant value for historians in the future. But as yet we lack a full critical evaluation of the medium, still more a listing and categorization of sources.[35]

As a genre, political film is underdeveloped in Britain, but the contributions of the cinema in expressing, sometimes even defining, a mood are remarkable. I suspect that Alan Bennett's *A Private Function* will never be surpassed as an evocation of 1940s rationing and austerity. The film *I'm All Right Jack* is a useful companion to the Goldthorpe and Lockwood series on the affluent worker. The nether regions of semiotics do not have to be plumbed to make *The Ploughman's Lunch* a stimulating addition to the materials of a student of Mrs Thatcher's first term, or *Local Hero* a point of reference in a study of the impact of oil upon Scotland in the 1970s and 1980s.

While there is no Colindale for radio and television, there is the British Film Institute's considerable archive of both film and television materials. The most recent and thorough survey of what is available and where it can be found is Anthony Seldon and Joanna Pappworth's *By Word of Mouth* (1983). The coming of the video machine has helped matters, particularly if a record is wanted of regular current-affairs flagships such as the BBC's *Panorama*, Granada's *World in Action*, Thames Television's *This Week* or London Weekend's *Weekend World*. Producers of radio and television programmes are often sympathetic to requests for transcripts if a serious case can be made by letter, though they are busy people and compliance cannot be guaranteed. Here the *Listener* can be a boon, especially as, since 1929, it has been indexed. Very often it will carry either an extract of an important programme or an article based upon it during the week of transmission. And its reach extends to the best of independent television as well as the BBC's in-house productions.

The practitioners

The producers of the press and broadcasting output can themselves be important figures in the political and historical processes of their eras. This tends to be appreciated at the time but can fade from view unless they write themselves up for posterity, as it were. Newspaper men or broadcasters as memoir writers or diarists can refract familiar events and personalities through a different, sometimes revealing, prism. I discovered this as a research student interested in the Cold War, when I read Howard K. Smith's *The State of Europe*[36] and Murray Kempton's *Part of our Time*[37] and rummaged through Arthur Krock's papers in the superb archive at Princeton University Library. And the foreign correspondent based in Britain can often throw fresh light on British domestic history, as Howard

Smith did for late-forties Britain and Cyrus Sulzberger managed to do on occasional post-war forays with masterly vignettes of Cripps, Bevan, Churchill and Eden.[38] Biographers of such firemen reporters can, at one stage removed, perform a similar service, a striking example from wartime Britain being A. M. Sperber's life of Ed Murrow.[39]

Home-grown reporters have written a pile of memoirs. The best combine an acute historical eye with a good journalist's ability to coin a ringing phrase. *The Times* of old produced superb practitioners of the craft such as Iverach McDonald[40] and Louis Heren.[41] The autobiographies of Hugh Cudlipp,[42] James Cameron,[43] and Tom Hopkinson[44] are essential reading for anyone who needs to understand the centre Left and its journalistic outlets, as is the collected edition of the incomparable *Picture Post*.[45] But in many ways the most valuable books of all are those penned by James Margach, whose political reporting from the inside track spanned the years between the premierships of Ramsay MacDonald and James Callaghan, in three short years before his untimely death in 1979. Not only are *The Abuse of Power*[46] and *The Anatomy of Power*[47] revealingly autobiographical about one of the most important post-war political journalists, but they also provide pen portraits of other significant figures, such as Hugh Massingham of the *Observer* and David Wood of *The Times*. *The Anatomy of Power* is important, too, for its insider history of that crucial and controversial institution, the Westminster Lobby correspondents' group.[48] Two valuable studies have also emerged from the Prime Minister's press secretaries at Number 10: Harold Evans' *Downing Street Diaries*, covering the period from 1957 to 1963, and Joe Haines's *Politics of Power*, on his period as Harold Wilson's press secretary from 1969 to 1976.[49]

Finally, there is hidden ore to be mined – the notebooks and files of specialist journalists. I have kept many but not all of mine from *Times, Independent, Economist* and *Financial Times* days – records of non-attributable chats and lunches with the mighty, the once-mighty and the would-be-mighty. Not until their subjects perish or give me permission to attribute can I offer them for general consumption. My journalistic colleagues vary enormously in how much they keep. But I am sure that in old filing cabinets there lies the buried treasure of contemporary history – the quiet word over the dining table, the enraged outburst at the private privileged occasion, all recorded in the heat of the moment. Someday, somebody will unearth it.

Notes

1 Michael Cockerell, Peter Hennessy and David Walker, *Sources Close to the Prime Minister* (Macmillan, 1984; Papermac, 1985); Peter Hennessy, *What the Papers Never Said* (Portcullis, 1985), available from the Politics Association, 24 Stretton Road, Great Glen, Leics LE8 0GN. I am grateful for the comments of David Walker on an earlier draft of the chapter.

2 Hennessy, *What the Papers Never Said*, pp. 25–6.

3 *The Times*, 30 June 1949.

4 *The Times*, 14 June 1949.

5 David Halberstam, *The Powers That Be* (Chatto and Windus, 1979), p. 161.

6 John Lloyd, 'Busy Izzy in Search of Truth', *New Statesman*, 15 August 1986.

7 A selection of these interviews can be found in Terry Coleman, *The Scented Brawl* (Elm Tree Books, 1978); and Terry Coleman, *Movers and Shakers* (Andre Deutsch, 1987).

8 Susan Barnes, *Behind the Image* (Jonathan Cape, 1974).

9 *New Statesman Profiles* (Readers Union, 1958).

10 Peter Hennessy, 'The quality of political journalism', *Royal Society of Arts Journal*, CXXXV, no. 5376 (Nov 1987), pp. 926–41.

11 Alastair Hetherington, *The Guardian Years* (Chatto and Windus, 1981), p. 36.

12 Lewis Chester and Jonathan Fenby, *The Fall of the House of Beaverbrook* (André Deutsch, 1979).

13 Richard Crossman, *Diaries of a Cabinet Minister*, vol. I: *Minister of Housing and Local Government, 1946–66* (Hamish Hamilton and Jonathan Cape, 1975), p. 12.

14 See Peter Hennessy, *Cabinet* (Basil Blackwell, 1986), chapter 1: 'The Cabinet machine'.

15 Hugo Young, from 'Consigning more history to the dustbin', *Guardian*, 30 October 1986.

16 Brian Wenham, 'Political certainties and a doubtful truce', *Financial Times*, 27 August 1986.

17 Richard Brooks, 'Weeklies wage a war of words', *Observer*, 19 April 1987.

18 David Walker, 'Creating the "Community" of Higher Education: The role of the *THES*', *New University Quarterly*, Spring 1979.

19 Stephen Fay and Hugo Young, *The Fall of Heath* (Sunday Times Publications, 1976).

20 Stephen Fay and Hugo Young, *The Day the Pound Nearly Died* (Sunday Times Publications, 1977).

21 Max Hastings and Simon Jenkins, *The Battle for the Falklands* (Michael Joseph, 1983).

22 Martin Adeney and John Lloyd, *The Miners' Strike 1984–85: loss without limit* (Routledge and Kegan Paul, 1986).

23 Richard Norton-Taylor, *The Ponting Affair* (Cecil Woolf, 1985).

24 Merry and Serge Bromberger, *Les Secrets de Suez* (Editions des Quatre Fils Aymon, 1957).

25 Hugo Young and Anne Sloman, *No, Minister: an inquiry into the Civil Service* (BBC, 1982).

26 Hugo Young and Anne Sloman, *But, Chancellor: an inquiry into the Treasury* (BBC, 1984).

27 Simon Jenkins and Anne Sloman, *With Respect, Ambassador: an Inquiry into the Foreign Office* (BBC, 1985).

28 Anthony Moncreiff (ed.), *Suez Ten Years After* (BBC, 1967).

29 The script of *A Canal Too Far* can be read in the Reference Room at the Public Record Office. An article based on it, Peter Hennessy and Mark Laity, 'Suez – what the papers say', was published in *Contemporary Record*, 1, no. 1 (Spring 1987), pp. 2–8.

30 Michael Charlton, *The Price of Victory* (BBC, 1983).
31 Alan Thompson, *The Day before Yesterday* (Sidgwick and Jackson, 1971).
32 Phillip Whitehead, *The Writing on the Wall* (Michael Joseph/Channel 4, 1985).
33 Brian Lapping, *End of Empire* (Granada and Channel 4, 1985).
34 Peter Pagnamenta and Richard Overy, *All our Working Lives* (BBC, 1984). The Chrysler programme was published in pamphlet form: *Chrysler and the Cabinet: how the deal was done* (Granada, 1976).
35 A full chapter on radio and television history was written by Anthony Seldon and Joanna Pappworth for their *By Word of Mouth: oral and contemporary history* (Methuen, 1983), but omitted from the published version (see chapter 12).
36 Howard K. Smith, *The State of Europe* (Cresset, 1950).
37 Murray Kempton, *Part of our Time* (Delta, 1967).
38 C. L. Sulzberger, *A Long Row of Candles: memoirs and diaries 1934–54* (Macdonald, 1969).
39 A. M. Sperber, *Murrow, his Life and Times* (Michael Joseph, 1987).
40 Iverach McDonald, *A Man of The Times* (Hamish Hamilton, 1976).
41 Louis Heren, *Growing up on 'The Times'* (Hamish Hamilton, 1978).
42 Hugh Cudlipp, *Walking on the Water* (Bodley Head, 1976).
43 James Cameron, *Point of Departure* (Arthur Barker, 1967).
44 Tom Hopkinson, *Of this our Time* (Hutchinson, 1982).
45 Tom Hopkinson (ed.), *Picture Post 1938–50* (Penguin, 1970).
46 James Margach, *The Abuse of Power* (W. H. Allen, 1978).
47 James Margach, *The Anatomy of Power* (W. H. Allen, 1979).
48 Ibid., chapter 9.
49 Harold Evans, *Downing Street Diaries: the Macmillan years 1957–63* (Hodder and Stoughton, 1981); Joe Haines, *Politics of Power* (Jonathan Cape, 1977).

3

Books and Journals
John Barnes

Contemporary history has never been defined in a way that is universally acceptable. The Institute of Contemporary British History, however, has set a *terminus ab quo* at the end of the Second World War. I have suggested elsewhere that contemporary history is best concerned with that period in which there can be profitable interaction between oral testimony and at least some documentation.[1] Given the existence of the thirty-year rule governing the great majority of official records, that may well seem too purist. Certainly economic and social history can be written successfully from published sources much sooner than that, and it may be wise not to leave the writing of political history to journalists and political scientists. There is, in fact, a good deal of material available in printed form from which the contemporary historian can establish at least a preliminary narrative and provide an explanatory framework. This chapter is concerned with all printed materials other than newspapers and news periodicals, which are covered in chapter 2.

The contemporary historian never begins in a void, although he (or she) might be forgiven for thinking that he does so. His own memories lend some shape to his subject, but very often the framework of fact has yet to be properly established; the division of the period, the topics to be discussed, the major themes to be pursued, have very often not been settled at all. The obvious question is where to begin.

Annuals, almanacs and guides

Establishing the raw framework of what happened in the years in question is relatively easy. *Whitaker's Almanack*, for example, has a section on the events of the year, and does not confine itself to politics or to Britain. *The Times*, like other quality newspapers, publishes a review of the year, and in addition publishes a comprehensive index. This not only enables the student to find his way around *The Times*, but also gives a fair idea of what news stories will be found in the other newspapers, and when. However, it cannot provide any guide to the existence of feature articles elsewhere. The *Annual Register* published by Longman tries to put the year into some kind of focus, digests a good deal of useful information, and has its own table of dates – rather less useful than *Whitaker's* for British politics, but affording a good guide to the international context. The opening section on events in Britain has a considerably broader scope than it did pre-war, and in the hands of recent authors such as James Margach and H. V. Hodson it is a good deal less idiosyncratic than it was in the 1950s and early 1960s, when D. C. Somervell was the author. The section on the British economy has also improved with the years. The *Annual Register* also contains good reviews of the work of international institutions and of the politics of other countries, many of which touch on Britain's international role, and the work is usefully indexed. Finally, mention must be made of another invaluable short cut, *Keesing's Contemporary Archives*, which digests the news and has a full set of cumulative indexes.

Tracking down the personalities of political actors other than the most important is always difficult. Basic biographical information in most cases can be obtained from *Who's Who* and its ten-year supplements *Who Was Who*, which contain entries for those who have died in the intervening period. There is also a useful *Who's Who of British Members of Parliament*, edited by M. Stenton and S. Lees, the fourth volume of which covers the years 1945–79.[2] The successive volumes of *The Times Guide to the House of Commons* published after each election may also prove useful, and current politicians can be pursued in *Dod's Parliamentary Companion* and *Vacher's Parliamentary Companion*, both of which also provide a good deal of information on the organization and personnel of government departments. Such information can be pursued from a number of other sources, but the major annual publications are the *Civil Service Yearbook* and the *Diplomatic List*. These replaced a single publication, the *Imperial Calendar and Civil Service List*, in 1973. *Burke's Peerage* and *New Extinct Peerages* should also be mentioned here.

The Times, as part of its annual summary of the year, prints a useful list of those who have died in the course of it. This helps the historian to track down obituaries, which will assist him in fleshing out the bare biographical details derived from the sources mentioned in the previous paragraph. *The Times* has also republished some of the most important of its obituaries in volume form.[3] Apart from *The Times*, the *Daily Telegraph* has proved a useful source of obituaries; the *Guardian* is disappointing and the *Independent*, on the evidence so far, distinctly patchy. Provincial newspapers, particularly where there was local activity, may also prove rewarding, although currently there is an understandable but regrettable tendency simply to reprint an obituary which is already available elsewhere. Bodies such as the British Academy print fuller obituaries of members in their proceedings and these are always worth consulting, as indeed are some of the records published annually by Oxford and Cambridge colleges. Finally, although not without some considerable delay, most but not all of those with whom history is concerned will find a place in the decennial supplements to the *Dictionary of National Biography*. But the entries are all too brief: few point to useful sources of information beyond the obituary columns, other than those ubiquitous categories 'personal knowledge' and 'private information'. Where they were personally involved with the subject, however, the authors of an entry may, when approached, be willing and able to point to further sources of information. Most entries give some flavour of personality as well as the basic biographical information. However, there has been a disappointing tendency recently to use as authors those who have already written about their subjects elsewhere, and there seem to be fewer lives written by those who had some personal or professional relationship with the person concerned. No doubt this leads to fewer laggards and a more consistent standard of writing, but there is some loss to the historian in his pursuit of the elusive subject of personality and personal relationships.

One or two other guides should perhaps be mentioned at this point. The first is a guide to reference works themselves. The most useful in my experience has been the second volume of A. J. Walford's *Guide to Reference Material*, now in its fourth edition and dating already since it was last published, in 1982. Walford has also published a *Guide to Current British Periodicals in the Humanities and Social Sciences*, which is one of a number of useful publications by the Library Association. Other guides, with more reference to the specific historical content of particular articles and books, will be referred to below, but mention should be made here of the *British Humanities Index*. Fuller than Walford and dealing also with periodicals now defunct is the *British Union Catalogue of Periodicals*, which Butterworth publishes for the British Library.

Finally, there are a few reference books to which the contemporary historian can refer for accurate information and which may save him a good deal of time. David Butler compiled the first edition of *British Political Facts* with that object in view. The most recent edition covers the years 1900 to 1985, and has some useful bibliographical references.[4] The most convenient detailed summary of election outcomes has been put together by F. W. S. Craig in three volumes under the title *British Parliamentary Election Results*, while the elections themselves can be followed in the Nuffield College series, which has devoted a separate volume to each election since 1945, and also to the 1975 referendum. R. B. McCallum and Alison Readman pioneered with the 1945 volume; H. G. Nicholas took over for 1950; and thereafter David Butler with a series of associates has continued to produce these valuable surveys, which have much to say also of the period between elections.[5]

More recent elections have also been well covered in a series of volumes edited by Howard K. Penniman and Austin Ranney, *Britain at the Polls*.[6] Since 1970 the Nuffield series has provided some valuable indications of the social structures of each constituency and these can be pursued in the successive editions of Robert Waller's *Almanac of British Politics*,[7] which David Butler aptly compared to Wisden, and for 1983 and to some extent 1987 in the BBC publication *British Parliamentary Constituencies*, by Ivor Crewe and Anthony Fox.[8]

The line between contemporary history and political science is a fine one, as the Nuffield election surveys demonstrate, and the student can profit from much of the material generated by those who study contemporary politics. Some of this material is in the public domain, particularly the regular surveys of opinion made by the polling organizations. There is no need to mention these further in this chapter since Tom Nossiter deals with them fully in chapter 4. However, it is worth noting that, while their earlier findings were published only in the press, Social Surveys (Gallup Poll) Ltd have published their *Gallup Political Index* monthly since 1960, and this, along with the annual surveys that have been based upon it,[9] throws considerable light on public attitudes and the movement of opinion.

Memoirs and autobiographies

A. J. P. Taylor once described memoirs as 'a form of oral history set down to mislead historians'.[10] While there are examples which justify the cynicism, most memoirs have something to offer the historian. Often they provide the first structuring of a period of history, identifying the major problems, at least as seen through the eyes of a leading participant, and offering some evidence on intention which can be assessed against performance. Dalton's characterization of the 1945–50 Attlee Government, with 1947 seen as the turning point, may now look fairly obvious,[11] and it certainly initiated what has become the accepted way of viewing the period.[12] Someone, however, has to be the first to structure the narrative and lend coherence to the story, and in this case it was Dalton, not uninfluenced, perhaps, by the fluctuation in his personal fortunes.

The modern tendency is to blur the traditional distinction between memoirs and autobiography. Harold Wilson's massive volume *The Labour Government 1964–70*[13] is a clear example of the memoir at its best, though distinctly short on the introspective insight which would have turned it into a valuable piece of autobiography as well.[14] Like most prime-ministerial memoirs, it is extensively based on papers, both private and official, and there are references scattered throughout the text to diary notes dictated at the time. By comparison, Wilson's account of his second period at No. 10, *Final Term*,[15] though written when he had more leisure, reads more like a catalogue of events and shows very little perception.

Most post-war prime ministers have chosen to write autobiography rather than memoirs, although in some cases with so little personal material that their work might almost fall into the latter category. Eden's *Full Circle*[16] is a good example of memoirs intended as such, but Macmillan, claiming to write autobiography, in fact revealed surprisingly little of his personality, except, perhaps, in the telling remark that as a boy he had learnt books before people.[17] In all, he wrote six volumes, three of them covering his premiership, which are of considerable value to the historian, but only the first, from which the remark just cited is taken, provides any insight into the mainspring of his character. Lord Home's account of his life is, if anything, even less revealing.[18]

Attlee offered both a very laconic autobiography and a hybrid volume based on interviews conducted by his former press adviser, Francis Williams,[19] which affords slightly more insight into this late Victorian. Churchill, no doubt the victim of old age, wrote nothing about his peace-time premiership except for a brief introduction to a one-volume abridgement of his war memoirs. Of his successors at No. 10, only Margaret Thatcher (for obvious reasons) has yet to write some kind of autobiography, although Edward Heath's reminiscences have so far been confined to some readable but rather lightweight volumes on music, sailing and travel. The last of these has the occasional political reference buried away in its text. Sir James Callaghan's substantial volume, written, as is often now the case, with the help of two able researchers, is the latest to appear[20] and it has been treated rightly as a serious contribution to our knowledge of the period.

Other senior figures have been as productive: excluding those who are still in Parliament (Denis Healey, David Owen and Geoffrey Howe) only five Foreign Secretaries out of fifteen (Bevin, Gordon Walker, Crosland, Carrington and Pym) have not written memoirs, and two of those died prematurely.[21] Former Chancellors of the Exchequer have been rather less forthcoming. While Hugh Dalton, Rab Butler, Harold Macmillan, Reginald Maudling and James Callaghan have written accounts of their stewardship, Stafford Cripps, Hugh Gaitskell, Peter Thorneycroft, Derick Heathcoat Amory, Selwyn Lloyd, Anthony Barber and Roy Jenkins have not, and only three of them are still alive to tell their tale to earnest researchers. Perhaps the most illuminating account of economic policy-making in government comes from the Chief Secretary in the 1974–9 Labour Government, Joel Barnett, and it is an object lesson in how much can be put on record, within a very short time of a government's fall with reasonable propriety and with no real political fall-out which might cause damage to party or to former colleagues, within a very short time of a government's fall.[22]

While many, if not most, politicians are tempted to write their memoirs, not all can find a publisher. This is particularly true of relatively minor figures, and some, such as Sir Douglas Dodds Parker, a junior Foreign Office minister in the 1950s, are driven to private publication. Other memoirs never see the light of day and can later be found in an archive alongside private papers. But a surprising number of reminiscences, including those of ordinary backbenchers, do find their way into print, and it always pays to check just what is available. The memoirs of a relatively junior minister such as Reginald Bevins[23] can prove to be not only entertaining but also extremely illuminating. Even those of a backbench figure can throw a good deal of light on, for example, a particular episode, or on the way in which a prime minister manages his or her party. Nigel Nicolson's account of his constituency's reaction to revolt over the Suez affair[24] has already been put to good use by historians, and even so slight a memoir as Sir William Teeling's has useful material on both the campaign for the Channel Tunnel in the 1960s and the campaign against integrating Malta into the United Kingdom. More interesting still in the light of what followed is his evident lack of confidence in Edward Heath's leadership.[25] To take another example, Humphry Berkeley's picture of Macmillan reassuring his backbenchers while the process of granting independence to Northern Rhodesia and Nyasaland was in train deserves to be better known.[26] Changes in the techniques of printing and the resultant proliferation of small publishing houses may well help to put more politicians into print.[27] In earlier years even ministers sometimes found it difficult to find a publisher if they waited too long: they had simply ceased to be news.

Civil servants, perhaps because of their natural reticence, seem more reluctant to contribute to historical knowledge by way of memoirs. Possibly publishers also find their recollections too bland to be worthy of publication. Diplomats provide the major exception to the rule of reticence, though not necessarily to the danger of blandness. Even so, only three permanent secretaries to the Foreign Office have written their memoirs. Civil servants disposed to contribute to our historical knowledge but reluctant to contemplate autobiography could profit from the example of the late Lord Garner, who in his relatively frank and well-informed history of the Commonwealth Relations Office, has provided us with a truly valuable piece of work.[28] No Cabinet secretary since Hankey and no permanent secretary to the Treasury has written any form of memoir;[29] indeed Lord Redcliffe-Maud appears to be the only permanent secretary of a home department to have written his autobiography.[30] That is not to say that there are no other recollections from public servants in print, but they are intended less as autobiography than simply as illustrations of points the author wants to make about aspects of government; as such they overlap with the writings of political scientists. Both Sir Richard Clarke and Sir Leo

Pliatsky, for example, have written studies of the changes in the machinery to control public expenditure,[31] and the former has also written about the need to reform the machinery of government. Lord Bridges has published a number of useful lectures, and in his book on the Treasury reflects on the role of a permanent secretary.[32] Sir Antony Part has written similarly about the Department of Trade and Industry.[33] Such examples could be multiplied, and they emphasize that direct reminiscence is not the only evidence available to the historian from civil servants.

The usefulness of memoirs, as Donald Watt has emphasized, must depend in the first place on whether their author has preferred 'frankness to discretion',[34] but that is far from the only test. Efforts have been made to distinguish between the various types of memoir: those based on privileged access to public archives, serious non-archival memoirs, and the merely anecdotal. In practice there is a more extensive spectrum, and even such memoirs as James Stuart's,[35] clearly written to entertain and 'largely undocumented', have useful glimpses of character and personality and make an occasional contribution to knowledge. It may be that more will come to light about the attempted coup in 1947 by senior Conservatives anxious to replace Churchill as leader of the Conservative Party, but, even if this chances to correct Stuart's narrative, the research will have been triggered by his account.[36] Much in party politics can only be documented from memoirs, and this is likely to remain the case even when the party archives and all the relevant diaries and private papers become available. It might be thought that the historian of government policy would be in a different position, with memoirs useful only while other sources were not available, but in fact this is far from true. Not everything gets onto the record, nor do ministers always record their reasons for taking the decisions they do. Even apparently slight autobiographies such as Reginald Maudling's or Richard Marsh's[37] can tell us a good deal about their personal attitude to policies and suggest their precise part in determining the course of events – for example (in Marsh's case), in creating an organizing committee to help in the nationalization of steel in 1966 and in ensuring that its members were paid appropriately when they became the board of the new Steel Corporation.

The value of memoirs, however well documented, inevitably diminishes once the historian has access to the relevant source materials. Even then, however, they often retain some value as a guide to sources, and, particularly where there are few if any diaries, they will remain important as the source of a good deal of material which never found its way on to paper, and occasionally some that did but is no longer extant. There may be accounts of conversations and meetings which were not minuted. Selwyn Lloyd's account of Suez, for example, contains the only available record of three ministerial meetings which took place during the period 21–4 October 1956. Unless a further record comes to light, perhaps in the form of an entry in Macmillan's diary, this will remain the historian's only written evidence that the meetings took place and thus of their importance in the genesis of the Suez operation. Even where memoirs do not retain their importance for such reasons, they remain invaluable as evidence for motivation, atmosphere, perspectives and relationships; and they frequently have to serve as a substitute for biographies which may never be written.

If memoirs are a key source for the contemporary historian, they are also a very dangerous one. He should try by every means possible to assess the way in which they were put together and what sources were used. Memory, even when assisted by press cuttings, Hansard and private correspondence, can be highly fallible. Trivial mistakes are frequent. Often a researcher is used, and in some cases – Peter Goldman's work on Rab Butler's auto-biography was said to be one – he is all but the author of the book in question. He may nevertheless be able to catch the flavour of genuine reminiscence, particularly if he has often heard the nominal author talk about the past. The dangers of using a researcher are obvious. He may establish a framework of fact that owes little to the author's memory, but which could prompt the author to amend his own recollection. Very often politicians reminiscing have a touching faith in the accuracy of those historians who have already offered a preliminary view of what took place. In this way myths can be perpetuated for years.

Politicians themselves are apt to magnify their own role, and nearly all will exaggerate the centrality of the events in which they were involved. It is important to remember that only the historian can hope to see the whole picture. Frequently people vividly recollect events that in fact they only learnt about by hearsay, or, in recalling a conversation, include views and details actually learnt second-hand. It is always wise to be wary of those who repeat long conversations verbatim, though a striking phrase may lodge in the memory. No one, in any case, can recall past events as if nothing had happened in the intervening years to affect his recollection. None of this is meant to decry the value of memoirs, simply to remind those who use them as evidence that they need to be checked as rigorously as possible.

Biographies

At least three types of biography may be distinguished: biographies written with full access to the subject's papers and, ideally, to other documentary material as well; those constructed mainly from the public record but with some degree of co-operation from the subject or his intimates; and finally the more instant type of biography which rests largely on a good press-cuttings library, but which may also contain some interview material. One is tempted to add a fourth category, the biography which, although scholarly, is based to a quite disproportionate extent on interviews. George W. Jones and Bernard Donoughue in their biography of Herbert Morrison showed how much could be achieved in this way, but their use of the technique was out of necessity rather than from choice, and there do not seem to be any further British examples of the type.[38]

From the contemporary historian's point of view, each of these types of biography has its uses, although the third is basically a stop-gap and, like the putative fourth category, contains a good deal that has to be taken very much on trust unless transcripts of the original interviews have been preserved and can be made available. However, as time passes, such 'instant' biographies when taken with other contemporary sources can tell us something about the way in which their subject was viewed at the time. It is wise to consult reviews of these books to see how contemporaries judged them.

The fuller the biography, the more useful it is likely to be, with documents and interviews referred to in detail or even quoted extensively. Biographers who have had access to a subject's papers are likely to have made use of private papers that might otherwise have remained unknown. Even where all the papers in question have come into the public domain (and it is possible that not all of them will), such a biography will remain useful not only as a guide but also as a synthesis of what is to be found in them. Not all biographies in these days of high publishing costs are adequately referenced, however, and this is particularly to be regretted when the work is of the importance of Robert Rhodes James's *Anthony Eden*.[39] The author has evidently made good use of much new source material but provides no notes to guide future students to the collections he has used. Inevitably the authors of biographies written after their subject's death have rather less personal testimony to draw on than might have been the case had they been writing in the subject's lifetime. However, comment is usually fuller and a good deal less discreet. Frequently *nil nisi bonum* does not apply. However, where a widow is alive the full truth may not be told without doing damage to her feelings, and it is evident that both Eden's biographer and Butler's have preserved a decent reticence on occasions where an unauthorized biographer might have wished to probe a little further.

One advantage of the authorized study written in the subject's lifetime is that it does preserve for the historian a good deal of oral evidence which might not otherwise survive. For example, much of Kenneth Young's study *Sir Alec Douglas-Home*[40] is based on tape-recorded interviews with Home himself, and these are often quoted verbatim. Leslie Smith's somewhat hagiographical account of Harold Wilson's pre-prime-ministerial career is likewise based on tape-recorded interviews with his subject and those who knew him, and it is likely to remain a valued source for later studies.[41] Both Home and Wilson have subsequently written memoirs, but the material accumulated earlier retains independent value. That is certainly the case where no memoir is yet available. Both George Hutchinson and Margaret Laing have put on record a good deal of material on Edward Heath's earlier career, most valuably where it can be specifically attributed, and Laing used so few oral sources for her account of the earlier years of Heath's premiership that one can sometimes make an educated guess at the source even where a comment is anonymous.[42] Several useful if hagiographical studies of the making of Margaret Thatcher[43] have also appeared, and Hugo Young, to his credit, persuaded a great many of her contemporaries to offer their current assessment, on the record, for his study *The Thatcher Phenomenon*.[44] For the most part the biographies mentioned above have been sympathetic in tone, but less friendly or even hostile studies may also preserve valuable evidence. Peter Kellner and Christopher Hitchens perhaps wrote too brief a life to help us much with James Callaghan,[45] but Paul Foot's remarkable study, *The Politics of Harold Wilson*[46] and Nicholas Wapshott and George Brock's *Thatcher*[47] are likely to retain their value. Even where one cannot disentangle exactly who said what, the list of those interviewed for such studies gives a good clue to the amount of authority which can be accorded to them. Wherever possible, however, what is said should be cross-checked. The use of press cuttings can preserve myth as well as fact, and those looking back in interview do not always know where the myth ends and the truth begins.

The biographer's task is, of course, the telling of the subject's life and the illumination of his (or her) personality. His main aim should be to make his subject walk and talk again for his readers. In this sense biography is one of the black arts, and it is not essential to the creation of a good biography that the subject should be important: it is sufficient that he made a vivid impression on people. For such reasons, historians such as Geoffrey Elton have been critical of the prevailing taste for biography, claiming that it is not a good way to write history. It may, however, be an essential preliminary to the writing of history, and this is particularly true where the major motive for writing is the fact that the subject played a crucial part in the history of his own time. It can also be true that his activities illustrate in a peculiarly vivid way a theme which the historian wishes to highlight. Often the biographer produces the first detailed study of a particular episode in political history. At other times his command of fresh evidence may cause him to revise the accepted story, or even to show how the prevailing account was deliberately nurtured. It is always disappointing, therefore, where a relatively short life appears, although it should be said in fairness that this may well be more accessible to the general reader. Unless it is lavishly referenced, however, the historian may well feel in some doubt about the reasoning behind some quite major points of interpretation, and he may even feel that too little has been added to the existing stock of knowledge to justify the writing of a biography at all. Almost certainly such a view would be wrong. Any biography must tell us something of the subject, the forces driving him and the themes which inspired him, and, where politicians are concerned, it is bound also to offer some illumination of the interplay between colleagues and rivals that is at the heart of political life.

It is precisely because of this interplay that Maurice Cowling believes that 'biography is almost always misleading. . . . It abstracts a man whose public action should not be abstracted. It implies linear connections between one situation and the next.' He argues that politicians cannot be studied as individuals but only as part of a continuously interacting network of leading actors on the political stage whose decisions and strategies can only be understood as contingent upon the moves made by their rivals in the political game. He argues that the 'system was a circular relationship: a shift in one element changed the position of all the others in relation to the rest'.[48] But, if we believe that human motives and expectations have a part to play in the causal process – and there are few historians who would deny them any role – the relevance of biography to our understanding is clear. The actions of an individual can be understood only in the light of his make-up, his thoughts and his prejudices, and the biographer who has studied the way in which these developed over the individual's lifetime has a far better chance to understand him and to explore successfully the ways in which he may have deceived himself as well as others about his motivation.

There are obvious dangers in biography as a source. The author may propel his subject to the centre of events when he does not properly belong there – at least, not at the time in question. The subject's conduct is all too often defended rather than explained and an interpretation of the course of events given which might well be modified if we had similar studies of the other actors involved. Although it has been done for earlier periods, no one has yet explored for the post-war period the possibility of studying two or more individuals in a group biography, which might resolve some of these problems and the doubts raised by Cowling. But, if the obvious pitfalls are borne in mind, biographies remain a valuable source, not least because, where the relevant archives are closed to access, they may be the only source readily available to students.

Diaries

Perhaps the most useful source for a biographer is his subject's diary, if one was kept, although it is crucial for him to know or at least be able to infer why his subject chose to talk to himself in this way. Diaries can take many different forms, some more self-conscious than others. Macmillan's diary began as letters to his wife, but ended as a form of *aide-memoire*, useful to his continuing political career and available, it seems, not only to himself but also to his trusted band of private secretaries. No doubt the intention was to keep them informed not only of what was happening in the world of No. 10 but also of Macmillan's thoughts about it.[49] Dalton, on the other hand, let few know that he was keeping a diary until the last decade of his life. Perhaps it was always intended to be the basis for memoirs. The driving force, his editor and biographer, Ben Pimlott, speculates, might well have been the need for money.[50] Dalton would have been neither the first nor the last politican to guard against the needs of his declining years in this way. Gaitskell apparently had a more altruistic desire: his purpose was to record the inside story of those events which he thought history would want to know about, and his diary contains little of his private life.[51] In making his own diary notes, Butler, perhaps with less self-deception than most of his fellow political diarists, evidently felt the need to explain and justify himself; and Eden too, like Lord Curzon, seems to have been conscious of a waiting biographer.[52] Crossman's motive was unique, though none the less self-serving. He desired to be the Bagehot of twentieth-century British government, and his diary was to provide him with material for his study.[53]

Given these very varying motives, the first thing that a student of contemporary history needs to establish is the way in which a diary was written and preserved. If, for example, it was dictated or typed up later by anyone other than the original author, it is unlikely that the author will ever be taken off guard. However, unless he subsequently revises the entry or writes it when the outcome of the events he is describing is already clear, hindsight will not be a major problem. Sometimes, as with Churchill's physician, Lord Moran,[54] it is clear that the author was writing for posterity, but, even where the main subject is not the author but the man whom he served, we cannot always be sure that the motive for keeping the diary was altruistic. After all, Boswell is remembered as well as Johnson. Nevertheless, no student of Eden or of Conservative governments in the 1950s will be able to neglect Sir Evelyn Shuckburgh's diary or that of William Clark.[55] Sometimes the diary is used as a safety valve and that lends credibility to the entries but may distort the picture of some of the relationships described, as Alanbrooke pointed out in the case of his wartime diaries. John Colville would not commit the unforgivable but far from unknown sin of correcting his text, but admits that he believes that he exaggerated the cold hatred which Churchill felt for Eden towards the end of his premiership.[56] It could well be so, but how are we to know which version is correct?

Charles Mowat, pioneer of the contemporary history of inter-war Britain, thought that 'much of the value of the diary is in conveying atmosphere',[57] but diaries also add substantially to the information at our disposal. Of course the diarist sees what he wants to see and hears what he wants to hear, but it is not difficult to make allowance for his own sense of self-importance. It is harder to assess his opinions of others and still more difficult to establish the truth of the gossip he hears. However, without the diary we might not know what the gossip was, still less be able to guess its significance. It is good advice never to take diaries at face value and wherever possible to find other evidence to support what is said.

Good editing will make it clear what has been left out, how much and why. It will also indicate omissions, at least within passages, and will try to identify the date of any subsequent additions or amendments. However, it is generally unrealistic to expect modern editors to cross-check the diary they are editing with others in the same field, to draw attention to the discrepancies in testimony and the problems to be resolved. Only if the project had substantial private endowment or was virtually certain to become a best-seller would a publisher be willing to allow editors the space for such refinements. It has to be enough for us that the diary has seen the light of day and that we can exercise our own critical instincts on it. With all its pitfalls, unless there was later tampering or rewriting, the diary remains a more reliable source than the memoir, however well rooted the latter in private papers and the public record, since it is not a vehicle for refighting old battles.

Diaries themselves can often be an excellent check on the official record and are a constant reminder that this should never be taken at face value. In his recent biography of Eden, Robert Rhodes James questions the late Lord Butler's account of the Cabinet's deliberations on 4 November 1956,[58] and he uses the Cabinet minutes to do so. They present a remarkably urbane account of what was evidently a troubled Cabinet, and their tone and accuracy could be queried even on the basis of the diary entry made by Lady Eden, which Rhodes James himself quotes. He has good reason for dismissing Butler's account – Eden had questioned it on publication – but to do so from the standpoint that the official minutes of what took place are a full and invariably accurate record is to ignore a great deal of evidence to the contrary. No doubt when we have the actual notebooks of the Cabinet Secretariat we shall be able to get far closer to the truth, but they are not likely to be available for decades. Hankey's notebooks, even for the First World War, have still to be released.

Butler's biographer[59] does not tell us whether Butler's recollection of the meeting in question was based on some kind of diary note made immediately or shortly after the event, although it seems likely. It was evidently Butler's practice to make such a record, and, even if it no longer survives, that does not mean that it was not there to be consulted when Butler wrote his memoirs. The process of drafting, particularly if others are involved, can often lead to the accidental displacement of material and perhaps to its temporary or permanent loss.[60] What can be said is that Butler's account seems to accord better with Lady Eden's diary and the recollections of some of those present than it does with the official record. There are some ministers still alive who could throw some light on the subject, but, in the absence of other published diary records, the conflict of evidence is unlikely to be resolved for a good many years to come.

Official publications

If students want to know the precise terms in which a decision has been embodied, they will often have to resort to the public record, and not to private papers. Indeed, it could be argued that anyone wishing to know the reasons why a particular policy was adopted should look first at those which were given publicly, notably in Parliament, and this is unavoidable while the relevant government papers are closed to access under the thirty-year rule. No politician will go any further in laying bare his political calculations than absolute necessity dictates, although his opponents, being knowledgeable about such matters, will seek to expose them and may provoke useful comment in reply. But much of the reasoning that the Civil Service has used to convince ministers will be used, naturally enough, to convince others. In argument to a variety of audiences, politicians will tend to use those reasons which have proved to be most persuasive in their own case, so long as the reasons are respectable – an important qualification – and the student can further explore both the factual basis for policy and the reasons for it in a much under-used source, the reports of the various parliamentary Select Committees. These papers may even reveal lack of calculation and simple drift in a way which the official papers in the Public Record Office seldom make clear. The Select Committee on Nationalized Industries, for example, provided a devastating exposé of the decision to electrify the railway link with the West Midlands and illuminated much about the way in which the Ministry of Transport reached its decisions in the late fifties. More recently, both the Defence Select Committee and that on trade and industry have teased their way through the Westland affair in a way which is likely to prove of permanent value to historians.

Hansard itself has often been criticized as a source, and it is true that, while it is well indexed, it takes a fair amount of reading. Nevertheless, it contains an enormous amount of useful information. The reports of debates and parliamentary questions in the *Annual Register* and the much fuller reports in *The Times* can be used as a relatively quick guide as to where it is most useful to dig deeper.

The most important parliamentary papers up to and including the session 1958–9 can be traced in the *London Bibliography of the Social Sciences*. From then on they can be traced through the sessional Numerical List and Index, which is printed as the final volume of the session. To trace the most recent papers it is necessary to consult the Stationery Office's annual and monthly lists. Non-HMSO British Government publications from 1980 onwards can be found by reference to the *Catalogue of British Official Publications not Published by HMSO*. The majority of United Nations and intergovernmental documents which will be held by a major library can usually be traced only through their own published indexes.

Official histories and series of documents

When the late Professor Charles Mowat wrote his study *British History since 1914*,[61] he could point to these sources as being of considerable use. The same cannot really be said today for the period since 1945. There are exceptions, of course, and amongst them are the work of Margaret Gowing and the magnificent series of volumes edited by Nicholas Mansergh, *The Transfer of Power in India 1942–47*.[62] Inevitably where printed documents are concerned the historian has to take on trust the selection made, and he will demand from the editors the fullest possible explanation of how that choice was made. The Mansergh volumes, and those which at long last are appearing in the post-war series on British foreign policy, are admirably edited and very full. Unlike their earlier counterparts, however, they do not anticipate the release of documents under the thirty-year rule. Two series of *Documents on British Policy Overseas*, covering the periods 1945–50 and 1950–5 respectively, are in progress, but, owing to the periods covered, the editors' work is likely to be speedily overtaken by that of zealous research students ferreting out documents whose significance they believe to have been missed. Much the same could be said of the series *British Documents on the End of Empire*, which is being undertaken under the aegis of the Institute of Commonwealth Studies. None of the eight volumes planned for the first module reaches beyond 1957, although that module is not due to be completed until the early 1990s.

None of this is to denigrate the value of such work. The editors of *Documents in British Policy Overseas* have extended their search into departments other than the Foreign Office and have printed much semi-official correspondence. Particularly good examples are afforded by the coverage of documentation relating to the negotiation of the American loan between 3 August and 7 December 1945, and the Schuman Plan. Such compilations offer the contemporary historian an invaluable short cut, if not fresh material. However, there is an obvious danger that, deceived by the wealth of material offered, historians may not for some time use these volumes as guides to the archives, but treat them instead as substitutes for direct recourse to the Public Record Office at Kew. That may not be altogether a bad thing. It will enable the period to be brought into focus more quickly than might otherwise have been the case, and students can only benefit from that. There is also the advantage that such volumes afford the undergraduate student some recourse to primary material, and that too may help stimulate the study of contemporary history.

The organizers of the *British Documents on the End of Empire* series claim 'great merit' for the HMSO project on the transfer of power in India and Burma in making available full documentation rather than creating 'official histories' of the events in question.[63] They may well be right. Official histories often used to be the first considered account of a topic or a period, and to offer a wealth of material which was not otherwise available. That cannot, in general, be claimed for the *History of Peacetime Events* announced by Harold Wilson as long ago as March 1966. Three of the four volumes of *Environmental Planning 1939–69*, by J. B. Cullingworth and Gordon E. Cherry, do extend into the 1960s, and provide some valuable insight into policy-making by the central government; but the greater part of the five-volume study of colonial development and the whole of Sir Norman Chester's volume *The Nationalisation of British Industry 1945–51* offer nothing beyond what one would expect from monographs researched and published by unofficial historians. Perhaps when Donald Watt and Leslie Pressnell publish their long-awaited studies *Defence Organisation since 1945* and *External Economic Policy* it will prove to be a different story. However, the absence of the preliminary team efforts which underpinned the war volumes makes for long gestation periods, and it is difficult to see why discretion could not be afforded under the terms of the thirty-year-rule legislation to allow further scholars to research areas of social policy, at least where official secrecy is not at a premium. But it is now nine years since James Callaghan announced (in July 1978) the latest extensions to the series of peacetime official histories, to include volumes on the British contribution to the Korean campaign and on the health services since 1945. It therefore appears that the whole enterprise has lost some of its direction and purpose.

Instant histories, tracts and party publications

Inevitably, when faced with the mass of available material, the contemporary historian will place considerable reliance on the work of those who have hacked their way through the jungle previously, the 'instant histories' where they are available, whether written by journalists, political scientists or historians. As long as the authors have practised the proper trade of the historian, re-creating, with as much accuracy as the fragmentary evidence available permits, a detailed narrative of what happened and why, all can prove to be good guides. Much, however, both in the press accounts of events on which they have to rely and in their own research, of necessity rests on unattributable testimony. Even where a later historian is able to identify some of the sources used, he cannot check or cross-check them unless some at least of the actors in the events described are still alive. The more professional of these earlier writers may have kept some record of their sources, although these may not be made public immediately. Hugh Thomas, for example, felt able to identify some of his informants when he published the second edition of his account of the Suez crisis, because those who gave him that information had since died.[64] It ought to be standard practice for an author to preserve the original notes of his interviews, but this is by no means common practice; and, even where an author has

preserved his notes, these may not survive his own demise. John
Mackintosh's notes for his book on the British Cabinet,[65] while certainly
preserved during his lifetime, are said to have disappeared subsequently. In
these circumstances it is vital for authors to report accurately the
information they have received, since what is usually defined as a secondary
source may sometimes have to serve in place of primary material. This
phenomenon, already well known to medieval historians, should not
trouble us too greatly, but it underlines the necessity of making as accurate
an assessment as possible of the motives of informants and authors.

Present-day historians need to be alert to possible distortions, which are
usually not deliberate but induced by preconceptions, conscious or unconscious. It may eventually prove possible, for example, to substantiate much
of William Keegan's record of the economic policy-making of the Thatcher
Government from the official record,[66] but, even if it is not, it will still be
possible to make use of his account. His bias is obvious; his sources, even
where anonymous, are clearly insiders; and the historian will simply have to
use his judgement as to precisely how much weight can be placed on what is
certainly a plausible narrative. Since some of the information is not likely to
have been put on record anywhere else, later historians will have to do this
in any case. Precisely the same considerations will apply as do already to the
writings of Henry Brandon and William Davis about the early years of the
1964–70 Labour government.[67] Historians have already begun to make use
of these writers' books, since they contain much that is not yet available
anywhere else and some facts that may never be available elsewhere. We are
fortunate perhaps in Brandon's case to know that the Permanent Secretary
of the Treasury was unable to question the essential accuracy of his
narrative, but must be wary lest this apparent confirmation simply reflects
the fact that Brandon's initial sources were in the Treasury.

However much a contemporary or near-contemporary account purports
to be history, historians will do well to be sceptical. The bogy of the late
Lord Beaverbrook's baleful influence on accounts of the 1916 political
crisis serves as an awful warning of how some of their more distinguished
predecessors have been suborned, sometimes against their will. Even
so good an account of the 1969 crisis over *In Place of Strife* as that
by Peter Jenkins[68] has to be treated for the time being as provisional
history, subject to confirmation from diaries, memoirs and, if possible,
documentary sources. So far it has stood the test well, but there is still
checking to be done. The fact that journalists agree on what has happened
will sometimes seem reassuring, and it can be. The essentials of their
account of the 1976 crisis seem likely to stand the test of time.[69] But stories
can be fed to them in such a way that they all succumb, at least temporarily,
and may perpetuate a myth.

The line between contemporary history and political science is a fine one
and students can profit by reading two or three of the standard texts on the

British political system, comparing them with each other, and making a note of the suggestions offered for further reading. What would now seem dated to contemporary political scientists will still have much to offer the historian, and can throw much light on the development of the political system. Perhaps the most interesting volumes from this point of view are the successive editions of Richard Rose's *Politics in England*.[70]

The advances made in the study of politics since 1945 give the contemporary historian a considerable advantage over his predecessors. However, political scientists' first digestion of much relevant material has to be assessed critically and with a proper regard to its context. It may be possible to infer from the period a study covers to other years, but the historian must be aware of the danger of unconscious anachronism. Historians of the post-war period may find the work done on voting behaviour of particular interest. We are fortunate that the pioneering work done by David Butler and Donald Stokes in the 1960s has been followed up by younger scholars like Ivor Crewe and William Miller.[71] The controversy which has developed between protagonists of class voting, issue voting and the so-called radical model of sectoral voting[72] generates a good deal of light, as well as some heat, to the benefit of the contemporary historian. If the Labour Party is in terminal decline, those studies will enable contemporary historians to explore the reasons why, with tools denied to those concerned to explain its slow rise to power and the process by which the early beneficiary of the Liberal Party's decline was, rather unexpectedly, the Conservative Party. Similar analytical studies could be compiled for other important themes in political history, and the historian needs to have recourse to the valuable bibliographies published in successive editions of R. M. Punnett's textbook *British Government and Politics*, now in its fourth edition, and to study such good recent texts as *The Government of the United Kingdom* by Max Beloff and Gillian Peele[73] and Henry Drucker's *Developments in British Politics*.[74]

There are other contemporary sources available in the form of books and pamphlets on current affairs. Whether these works are descriptive or analytic, advocacy or polemic, they will all contain material of a kind which, if it is not already historical, will shortly become so. Penguin's prescriptive *What's Wrong with Britain* series, for example, was not only an important political publication at the time, but still contains useful material on the state of various organizations and institutions at the start of the 1960s. David Donnison's *Government of Housing*,[75] while it has lost most of its value as a description of current policies, retains all its value for the historian of housing policies in the sixties and the debate which surrounded them. Changes made from one edition to another may themselves provide the historian with clues to the changing nature of the debate in a particular policy area. Pursuing such books is not always easy, but the *London Bibliography of the Social Sciences*, which has been regularly updated by the British Library at the London School of Economics and Political Science, should help. The subject entries in *Whitaker's Cumulative Book List* and the British Library's Subject Index are also useful.

Publications by political parties are potentially valuable because they provide a regular commentary on policies and politics, but due allowance has to be made for their polemical nature. Much of the bias is easily detectable, however. The Conservative Party has perhaps the best series of campaign guides, published for each of the thirteen post-war general elections; these carefully used, can help the historian see what was happening during the term of office of a particular administration. It must be emphasized that the personalities, and above all the policies, which receive most attention are to the fore during the last year before an election. If there has been a sea-change in the course of a Labour administration, that may well be fully exposed if it is to the Conservatives' advantage to do so, but, if it has affected the course of Conservative policies themselves, it is likely to be glossed over even if not totally obscured.

Monographs and articles

The first monographs are only just beginning to appear for the immediate post-war period, and many of them are the result of doctoral theses. Established historians such as Kenneth Morgan and Henry Pelling can do valuable work to bring a whole administration or a period into focus relatively early,[76] but the more general tendency among historians is to wait until the official archives are open and then to tackle a more limited theme. Still more detailed work follows, dovetailing into and supplementing the work already done. At that stage revisionists can begin the necessary and never-ending task of asking whether we have got the general character of the period right and whether we are pursuing the right themes. All this takes time, and there is much to be said for those few courageous historians who take their reputation in their hands and seek to establish a provisional view before the archives are open or many private papers available. Inevitably they depend to an uncomfortable extent on oral testimony, but Anthony Seldon's *Churchill's Indian Summer* shows how much can be achieved.[77] The more recent the period, the less general the readiness to talk frankly. Hugh Thomas's outstanding work on Suez, David Nunnerley's *President Kennedy and Britain*, Malcolm Barnett's account of the 1957 Rent Act, and more recently Martin Holmes's trilogy on the Heath, Wilson–Callaghan and first Thatcher governments are all in their different ways valuable monographs on recent history.[78]

With the resources at their disposal, television companies can often tackle a broader sweep, and the student of contemporary history neglects at his peril those books published to accompany television series on contemporary history – Alan Thompson's *The Day before Yesterday*,[79] Phillip Whitehead's *The Writing on the Wall*,[80] and Brian Lapping's *The End of Empire*,[81] for example. These differ from other, more contemporary accounts since the nature of the medium they reflect means that the bulk of the testimony on which they rely is on the record.

Trying to keep track of monographs and scholarly articles is not an easy task, but a good library should have a number of publications which will help. Perhaps the most convenient is the Royal Historical Society's *Annual Bibliography of British and Irish History*, currently edited by David Palliser. It has a subject index, and is fuller than the annual *Writings on British History* (published by the University of London Institute of Historical Research),[82] which has an appendix devoted to the post-1939 period. The *International Bibliography of Historical Sciences* (published by K. G. Saur Verlag, Munich) may also usefully be consulted.

All monographs are very much a product not only of their time but also of their authors' own background, thoughts and experience. They need to be seen as such and to be placed in a broad context of historical research and writing. This is often best done by a more experienced historian; hence the value of the really authoritative review. Those chosen to review in the 'quality' press will have been picked for many and varied reasons – their ability to entertain being quite high on the list – and, while their reviews may contribute to our knowledge and may be usefully thought-provoking, it is usually best to look elsewhere for a more balanced verdict. Periodicals, and particularly *The Times Literary Supplement*, the *London Review of Books* and its New York counterpart, often contain lengthy reviews of great value, and only the *Economist* maintains the mistaken policy of anonymity.[83] However, the prime source of authoritative reviewing has to be the scholarly journals, particularly the *English Historical Review*, the *Historical Journal, History*, the *American Historical Review* and the *Journal of Modern History*, and the student of contemporary history should always be aware of their verdict on the monographs he is consulting though he may not agree with it. The more technical the subject under discussion, the more worthwhile it will be to see also what opinions are available in the most relevant and authoritative technical or professional journals, though these need to be read critically.

ABC–Clio Information Services publish a regular series of *Historical Abstracts*, Part B of which is concerned with the years since 1914. Dissertations and theses may offer relevant material and can usually be borrowed by one university library from another. Aslib publish a regular *Index to Theses* for the United Kingdom, and the University of London produces a regular listing of its own students' productions. In addition, the Institute of Historical Research lists theses completed and theses in progress. It is worth remembering that much work of historical value is done in faculties and departments that are not primarily concerned with history – accountancy, for example, or medicine. University Microfilms International publish *Dissertation Abstracts*, which is fully indexed.

Scholarly articles are often indicators of major work in progress and the most useful can be traced from the Royal Historical Society's annual publication mentioned above. Both the *English Historical Review* and the *Scottish Historical Review* publish regular lists of articles published elsewhere that are of value to the student of British history, and these lists inevitably save a good deal of personal effort. However, they may not be quite as complete as they appear and the student needs to understand which periodicals have been scanned, and then, Walford in hand, consider what may have been missed that could have a bearing on his field of interest. The political science periodicals, particularly the *Political Quarterly*, the *British Journal of Political Science, Parliamentary Affairs, Political Studies* and *Public Administration*, may contain a good deal of interest, while publications in the fields of sociology, social administration and industrial relations have often proved a fruitful quarry of historical material. Some of the best material on elections has appeared in the *Journal of the Royal Statistical Society. Contemporary Record*, the quarterly journal of the Institute of Contemporary British History, commenced publication in April 1987, and looks as if it will prove a fruitful source for students of contemporary British history.

Fiction

Finally, a brief note about novels, films, plays and other works of fiction. There is no doubt that these can give an insight into the manners, *mores* and ways of thinking of a particular period. They can be dangerous allies, however, and need to be used with great care. No author is typical and most have a message of sorts. In this sense the more commonplace novels may be of more use than great works of literature. By all means read Isabel Colegate on Suez or John Mortimer's account of his slowly developing post-war disillusion, but do not swallow them whole. They are not a substitute for the kind of detailed research a sociologist or anthropologist carries out, or at least should do, but they may nevertheless stimulate imaginative insight into a period and so be of help to the contemporary historian. The genre as a form of evidence deserves a serious study of its own.

Notes

1 John Barnes, 'Teaching and research in contemporary British history', in Donald C. Watt (ed.), *Contemporary History in Europe* (Allen and Unwin, 1969).
2 M. Stenton and S. Lees, *Who's Who of British Members of Parliament*, vol. IV (Harvester, 1981).

3 Times Publishing.
4 David and Gareth Butler, *British Political Facts 1900–85* (Macmillan, 1986).
5 Macmillan publish these studies.
6 Published shortly after each election by the American Enterprise Institute.
7 Robert Waller, *Almanac of British Politics*, 3rd ed (Croom Helm, 1987).
8 Ivor Crewe and Anthony Fox, *British Parliamentary Constituencies* (BBC/Faber, 1984).
9 R. Jowell and C. Airey, *British Social Attitudes* (Gallup, from 1980).
10 Quoted in George Jones, 'The value of recent biographies, autobiographies and diaries', *Parliamentary Affairs*, 34 (1981), p. 335.
11 Hugh Dalton, *High Tide and After* (Muller, 1962).
12 See, for example, K. O. Morgan, *Labour in Power 1945–51* (Oxford, 1986). Note the earlier treatment by Alan Thompson in *The Day before Yesterday* (Sidgwick and Jackson, 1971).
13 Harold Wilson, *The Labour Government 1964–70* (Weidenfeld and Nicolson/ Michael Joseph, 1971).
14 The *Daily Telegraph* carried an excellent review, 'The energetic Mr Wilson', by Patrick Gordon Walker, 26 July 1971.
15 Harold Wilson, *Final Term* (Weidenfeld and Nicolson/Michael Joseph, 1979).
16 Anthony Eden (Earl of Avon), *Full Circle* (Cassell, 1960).
17 Harold Macmillan, *Winds of Change* (Macmillan, 1966).
18 Lord Home, *The Way the Wind Blows* (Collins, 1976).
19 Clement Attlee, *As it Happened* (Heinemann, 1954); Francis Williams, *A Prime Minister Remembers* (Heinemann, 1961).
20 Sir James Callaghan, *Time and Chance* (Collins, 1987).
21 Gordon Walker wrote about Cabinet government, however, and Francis Pym has published reflections on politics with some autobiographical reference. So, among those still in Parliament, has David Owen. See Patrick Gordon Walker, *The Cabinet*, 2nd edn (Fontana, 1972); Francis Pym, *The Politics of Consent* (Sphere, 1985); David Owen, *Face the Future* (Oxford University Press, 1981).
22 Memoirs by Callaghan, Dalton and Macmillan have been listed above. For the others mentioned, see R. A. Butler, *The Art of the Possible* (Hamish Hamilton, 1971); Reginald Maudling, *Memoirs* (Sidgwick and Jackson, 1978); Joel Barnett, *Inside the Treasury* (André Deutsch, 1982).
23 Reginald Bevins, *The Greasy Pole* (Hodder and Stoughton, 1965).
24 Nigel Nicolson, *People and Parliament* (Weidenfeld and Nicolson, 1958).
25 William Teeling, *Corridors of Frustration* (Johnson, 1970).
26 Humphry Berkeley, *Crossing the Floor* (Allen and Unwin, 1972).
27 For instance, Lord Watkinson has published his memoirs, *Turning Points*, with Michael Russell of Salisbury, 1987.
28 Joe Garner, *The Commonwealth Office 1925–68* (Heinemann, 1978). The most valuable of the three memoirs by permanent secretaries is that by Paul Gore-Booth, *With Great Truth and Respect* (Constable, 1974). Lord Strang wrote both memoirs, *Home and Abroad* (André Deutsch, 1956), and a useful history of British foreign policy since the reign of Elizabeth I. Much less useful for his period as Permanent Secretary, perhaps because it was published too soon after the controversial Suez episode, is Sir Ivonne Kirkpatrick's *The Inner Circle* (Macmillan, 1959).

29 Sir George Mallaby, however, who served in the Cabinet Office under Sir Norman Brook, has written about his former chief in *Each in his Office*, (Leo Cooper, 1972). Earlier he had written a brief memoir, *From my Level* (Hutchinson, 1965). Those interested in the role of the Cabinet Office will find Lord Trend's articles on Bridges and Brook in the *Dictionary of National Biography* particularly revealing.

30 Lord Redcliffe-Maud, *Experiences of an Optimist* (Macmillan, 1981).

31 Sir Richard Clarke, *Public Expenditure, Management and Control* (Macmillan, 1968); Sir Leo Pliatsky, *Getting and Spending* (Basil Blackwell, 1982).

32 Lord Bridges, *The Treasury* (Allen and Unwin, 1964).

33 Sir Antony Part, 'Creating and managing a large department', *Management Services in Government*, 34, no. 1 (Sep 1979).

34 Donald C. Watt, *Personalities and Policies* (Longman, 1965).

35 James Stuart, *Within the Fringe* (Bodley Head, 1967).

36 Ibid., pp. 145–7. Cf. Thompson, *The Day before Yesterday*, pp. 86–7.

37 For Maudling see note 20. Richard Marsh, *Off the Rails* (Weidenfeld and Nicolson, 1978).

38 Peter Stursberg's works on two Canadian prime ministers, Diefenbaker and Lester Pearson adopt a rather different format and show clearly what can be done with it.

39 Robert Rhodes James, *Anthony Eden* (Weidenfeld and Nicolson, 1986).

40 Kenneth Young, *Sir Alec Douglas Home* (Dent, 1970).

41 Leslie Smith, *Harold Wilson* (Hodder and Stoughton, 1964).

42 George Hutchinson, *Edward Heath* (Longman, 1970); Margaret Laing, *Edward Heath: Prime Minister* (Sidgwick and Jackson, 1972).

43 The most useful, all entitled *Margaret Thatcher*, are by Patrick Cosgrave, George Gardiner and Penny Junor, published respectively by Hutchinson (1978), William Kimber (1975), and Sidgwick and Jackson (1983).

44 Hugo Young and Anne Sloman, *The Thatcher Phenomenon* (BBC, 1986).

45 Peter Kellner and Christopher Hitchens, *Callaghan: the road to Number Ten* (Cassell, 1976).

46 Paul Foot, *The Politics of Harold Wilson* (Penguin, 1968).

47 Nicholas Wapshott and George Brock, *Thatcher* (Macdonald, 1983).

48 Maurice Cowling, *The Impact of Labour* (Cambridge University Press, 1971), p. 6.

49 Only the war diaries have appeared in full but there are substantial extracts in the memoirs.

50 *The Political Diary of Hugh Dalton*, ed. Ben Pimlott (Jonathan Cape, 1986).

51 *The Diary of Hugh Gaitskell 1945–56*, ed. Philip Williams (Jonathan Cape, 1983).

52 Only extracts from the Butler and Eden diaries are available in their memoirs, but they are also quoted by their official biographers. See notes 39 and 59.

53 Richard Crossman, *The Diaries of a Cabinet Minister*, 3 vols. (Hamish Hamilton/Jonathan Cape, 1975, 1976 and 1977).

54 Lord Moran, *Churchill: the struggle for survival* (Constable, 1966).

55 Evelyn Shuckburgh, *Descent to Suez* (Weidenfeld and Nicolson, 1986); William Clark, *Three Worlds* (Sidgwick and Jackson, 1986).

56 Arthur Bryant, *Triumph in the West* (Collins, 1959); John Colville, *The Fringes of Power* (Hodder and Stoughton, 1985).

57 Charles Mowat, *Great Britain since 1914* (Macmillan, 1971).

58 Rhodes James, *Eden*, p. 567. Butler's account is in *The Art of the Possible*, p. 193.

59 Anthony Howard, *RAB: the life of R. A. Butler* (Jonathan Cape, 1987).

60 At least Butler did not follow the practice of another distinguished writer of political memoirs, Philip Snowden, who destroyed the entire body of material on which he had based his account.

61 Mowat, *Great Britain since 1914*, p. x.

62 Published by HMSO between 1970 and 1983. Margaret Gowing, *Independence and Deterrence*, 2 vols. (Macmillan, 1974).

63 Undated statement, *British Documents on the End of Empire* project.

64 Hugh Thomas, *The Suez Affair*, 2nd edn (Penguin, 1972).

65 John Mackintosh, *The British Cabinet*, 3rd edn, Stevens, 1977.

66 William Keegan and Rupert Pennant-Ren, *Who Runs the Economy? Control and Influence in British Economic Policy* (Maurice Temple Smith, 1979).

67 Henry Brandon, 'Into the red', *The Struggle for Sterling 1964–66* (André Deutsch, 1966; William Davis, *Three Years Hard Labour* (André Deutsch, 1968).

68 Peter Jenkins, *The Battle of Downing Street* (Charles Knight, 1969).

69 Stephen Fay and Hugo Young, *The Day the Pound Nearly Died* (Sunday Times Publications, 1977). Their account largely agrees with that provided by Granada Television's *State of the Nation* programme on the crisis and is further confirmed by Phillip Whitehead, *The Writing on the Wall* (Michael Joseph/Channel 4, 1985).

70 Published by Faber, 1965, 1979, 1980 and 1985.

71 David Butler and Donald Stokes, *Political Change in Britain* (Macmillan, 1968; 2nd edn 1974); Bo Sarlink and Ivor Crewe, *Decade of Dealignment* (Cambridge University Press, 1983); William Miller, *Electoral Dynamics* (Macmillan, 1977).

72 There are useful surveys of the literature in Henry Drucker *et al.* (eds), *Developments in British Politics* (Macmillan, 1986); Paul Whiteley (ed.), *The Labour Party in Crisis* (Methuen, 1984). Key studies include A. Heath, R. Jowell and J. Curtice, *How Britain Votes* (Pergamon, 1985); Hilda Himmelweit, P. Humphries and M. Jacques, *How Voters Decide*, 2nd edn (Open University Press, 1985); M. Franklin, *The Decline of Class Voting in Britain* (Oxford University Press, 1985); R. Johnston, *The Geography of English Politics* (Croom Helm, 1985); Patrick Dunleavy and Chris Husbands, *British Democracy at the Crossroads* (Allen and Unwin, 1985); Ian McAllister and Richard Rose, *The Nationwide Competition for Votes* (Pinter, 1984).

73 Max Beloff and Gillian Peele, *The Government of the United Kingdom*, 2nd edn (Weidenfeld and Nicolson, 1985).

74 See note 72 above.

75 David Donnison, *Government of Housing* (Penguin, 1963).

76 K. O. Morgan, *Labour in Power 1945–51* (Oxford University Press); Henry Pelling, *The Labour Governments 1945–51* (Macmillan, 1961).

77 Anthony Seldon, *Churchill's Indian Summer* (Hodder and Stoughton, 1981).

78 For Thomas see note 64. David Nunnerley, *President Kennedy and Britain* (Macmillan, 1972); J. Malcolm Barnett, *The Politics of Legislation: the Rent Act of 1957* (Weidenfeld and Nicolson, 1969); Martin Holmes, *Political Pressure and Economic Policy* (Butterworth, 1982), *The Labour Government 1974–79* (Macmillan, 1985) and *The First Thatcher Government* (Wheatsheaf, 1985).

79 See note 12.
80 See note 69.
81 Brian Lapping, *The End of Empire* (Granada and Channel 4, 1985).
82 First published in 1946.
83 Defensible though anonymity is in theory, since it allows a greater degree of frankness, much depends on continued excellence in the choice of reviewers and an encyclopaedic knowledge of the personal feuds and rivalries that can so easily distort the process. Given the differing schools of historical thinking, it seems safer to have the names of the reviewers out in the open, where their authority and likely bias can be weighed.

Since the chapter was written, there have been new editions of the books by Punnett and Waller; Sir James Callaghan has become Lord Callaghan; Lord (Bernard) Donoughue has published an account of his period with Wilson and Callaghan in No. 10 (*Prime Minister*, Jonathan Cape, 1987); David Owen has talked to Kenneth Harris (*David Owen Personally Speaking*, Weidenfeld and Nicholson, 1987); and Geoffrey Foote has published *A Chronology of Post-War British Politics* (Croom Helm, 1988).

4

Surveys and Opinion Polls

Tom Nossiter

Political historians too often adopt an atheistical, or at best agnostic, stance towards numerical data, allowing the political scientist (who is frequently a lapsed 'historian') to queer the pitch. It is hard to see any justification for this attitude. The primary business of the historian is to explain how the particular occurred, and to deny the use of statistics in this quest is to dismiss a useful explanatory tool. Why James Callaghan decided not to go to the country in the autumn of 1978 may be a question for his biographer; but when in June 1979 'Labour's Baldwin' lost to the less popular figure of Mrs Thatcher, the outcome was influenced by a number of factors – the 'winter of discontent', the radical-right thrust, sociological change and the campaign itself – all in part susceptible to quantitative evaluation, which is to say that the statistician can supply evidence of their relative importance. If sources exist which shed light on what may turn out – with benefit of hindsight – to be the most profound change in the direction of British history since the supplanting of the Liberals as HM Opposition by the Labour Party, what self-respecting historian would ignore the data merely because it was statistical? By their training, historians have honed one skill to a fine edge: the ability to examine the nature of a source of information. They need now to encompass statistical data in their range of evidence deemed worthy of study.

This chapter is concerned with the nature of the numerical sources relevant to the concerns of the contemporary political historian, and will draw attention to their pitfalls as well as their potential. Space does not permit a detailed explanation of statistical and computational techniques, but recourse may be had to one of the several excellent books on the subject,[1] as well as to specialist colleagues. Bear in mind that the statistician is best able to help if he or she knows what it is that one wishes to test. The more precisely specified the problem, the better. The statistician is also sure to underline that all the available techniques rest on particular assumptions which need to be understood if proper conclusions or inferences are to be drawn from analysis of the data. Statistics, it cannot be said too often, are no more able to speak for themselves than a written document is. They too need to be interpreted, and with the same caution.

Some problems with survey data

Before turning to the range of sources available, some general comments are necessary. First, the historian will ordinarily be relying on data collected by others – government, commercial agencies, fellow academics – and collected for purposes quite different from his own. The opinion pollster, for instance, is primarily interested in the temperature of bodies politic as measured by answers to the question, 'If there was a general election tomorrow, how would you vote?' The fact is that the respondent knows that there is not going to be an election tomorrow. The results can make good copy on the front page of a newspaper but it would be rash to assume that at mid-term the electors are genuinely expressing a considered view of what they would do in an impossible contingency. More likely they are sending a message to Downing Street about how well, or badly, they think the Government is doing, which may be a reason why 'electoral' volatility halfway through a parliament is not matched when it comes to making real choices on polling day. Beyond the temperature, opinion polls normally take a few other measurements – leader ratings and ranking of issues especially – but the sort of data which might permit diagnosis of the reasons for shifts in opinion is usually insufficient.

Second, data-sets fall into two distinct categories: aggregate and individual-level data. Aggregate data will typically be returns of comprehensive information for a territorial unit, possibly a constituency; individual-level data will usually be based upon some sampling procedure. The former, while complete, suffers from the problem that there are many variables but insufficient cases – for example, 650 parliamentary constituencies – to enable even powerful statistical tools to shed much light on political dynamics. Individual-level data-sets, on the other hand, suffer because the expenses involved in conducting interviews mean that rarely will there be more than 2000 respondents, and frequently they will number only 1000. If the selection of the individuals has been random in the strict statistical sense, then it is possible to calculate the margin of error for any size of sample in relation to the population universe from which they were selected. However, the largest data-sets we have – opinion polls – are usually based on quota sampling. For example, interviewers seek so many young working-class males, and the final figures are subjected to correction (weighting) on the basis of census and similar information to ensure that the sample contains the proper proportion of this category relative to others. Quota sampling is often treated as if random in character and, to the degree that any opinion-polling organization produces meaningful and consistent patterns over time, there are some common-sense grounds for this assumption if what we are concerned with is overall measures of political popularity. However, the non-random character of such surveys undermines their utility when we proceed to analyse the shifts of opinion in the light of the demographic, sociological or political variables, because the numbers in each category are small enough for distortions to matter. The phrase used to describe where electors were interviewed – 'sampling points' – may well mean supermarkets; and it is human for interviewers subconsciously to select the more congenial faces to approach for answers.

Third, the vast majority of data on individuals are cross-sectional in nature. We may interview 1000 individuals this month and 1000 next month, but they are *different* individuals. If in the 1959 general election one third of the working class interviewed voted Conservative, and the same was true in the 1964 election, it would seem to follow that there had been little change in the composition of the Conservative working class. But the fact that the net figures are the same may mask considerable gross changes. More generally, and seriously, the political stability of a class-aligned electorate has been contrasted with the recent volatility of a class-dealigned electorate. Since, prior to the early 1960s, we have almost no information on the political behaviour of individual electors over two elections or more, we cannot actually be sure that the gross figures do not hide significant real shifts in opinion. There is suggestive evidence that this may indeed be the case.[2]

Longitudinal or panel designs are preferable but are disproportionately expensive, since individuals interviewed in the first round have to be chased and cajoled into a second interview, and so on. Unsurprisingly, the dropout rate is high, and, even though it is possible to test whether there is demographic bias in the falling sample, more subtle biases may still exist. For example, in their remarkable study *How Voters Decide* (2nd edition 1985), covering fifteen years and six general elections, Hilde Himmelweit and her colleagues are open to the criticism that those patient enough to accommodate their interviews so many times *would* end up politically conscious, and so may have become untypical.

Last, it is critical to remember that all statistics are founded on the concept of covariance or correlation. However, the fact that two variables – the dependent variable of political opinion, and the independent or predictor variable of, say, class – correlate with each other positively or negatively does not establish a causal link between them. What significant correlations do is merely to alert us to the *possibilities* of causal explanation. The observation that the height of a person – controlled by sex – correlates well with voting preference in Britain does not mean that because people are taller they vote Conservative. Large correlations are in fact few and far between, and, conversely, there is some truth in the old adage that everything correlates with everything else at a level of $\pm.3$, or 9 per cent of the total variation. Such levels normally become interesting only when they persist with all other sources of variation 'controlled' out and when there is a theoretical model which suggests a meaningful connection. Reverting to our sample of tall Tories, it is obvious that nutrition in childhood will influence final height and that income, social class and education will condition nutrition. Without a plausible hypothesis the observed correlation is meaningless.

Electorally relevant data

Election data are probably the principal kind of statistical material that the contemporary political historian will wish to use. Ironically, the historian of Britain before 1872 is a great deal better placed in this regard than a colleague studying much of the twentieth century. He or she can consult records of how individuals voted and the original census returns.[3] Although the first opinion poll was conducted in Britain in 1937, it was not until the 1950s that statistics enabling us to chart the flows of opinion in the mass electorate with any degree of accuracy became available.

The 1950s, then, mark the electoral 'enlightenment': in quick succession we had the 1950, 1951 and 1955 studies of Bristol by R. S. Milne and H. C. Mackenzie,[4] Gallup and National Opinion Polls; the Labour Party controversy on the marketing of politics like a consumer product and the consequent argument about the embourgeoisement of the electorate in Richard Rose and Mark Abrams' *Must Labour Lose?* (1959). Then, with the 1959 general election, came the acceptance of (campaign) political argument as a proper function of public-service broadcasting on television and radio. The effects of television on politics were immediately tested in Joseph Trenaman and Denis McQuail's *Television and the Political Image* (1961), Jay Blumler and Denis McQuail's *TV and Politics* (1968) and the neglected but challenging article by A. H. Birch and colleagues, 'The Floating Voter and the Liberal View of Representation' (1969)[5] – challenging because it can be read with hindsight as suggesting that the class-polarized Red (Labour) and Blue (Tory) Monkey theory of post-war electoral stability may be an artefact of available research designs. By 1963 David Butler and Donald Stokes had embarked on the panel study of electors which led to the first edition of *Political Change in Britain* (1969). Likewise the opinion polls had become an established part of the electoral landscape, notwithstanding Aneurin Bevan's complaint that they took the poetry out of politics.

The electoral rolls are updated annually; constituency boundaries are revised at best decennially, owing to administrative delays in census work and sometimes to the political turpitude of governments. Returning officers responsible for the preparation of the electoral registers offer a little-known bonus to the contemporary historian. For six months after an election anyone may see (or purchase a copy of) the 'marked up' register, so affording an opportunity, in conjunction with other sources such as census data, to investigate electoral turn-out. Turn-out itself is another concept which is frequently treated as far more solid fact than it really is. The register, even when fresh (collated in October–November, published in February) is by no means a complete record of all those entitled to vote, as the head of household may not have entered all relevant names. The young and the old are under-represented, as are certain ethnic groups.

More important is the degree to which the register deteriorates in accuracy through population movement at an average of approximately 1 per cent a month. Were it not for postal votes on the one hand, and deaths on the other, the turn-out, as a percentage of all registered voters, would need to be 5 or 6 per cent higher in a spring election than in an autumn one on the same register to give the same effective percentage turn-out in terms of the number of registered voters still living in the constituency where they are registered. The 1 per cent per month formula provides a rough estimate. But how misleading it is can be illustrated by considering the 1950 and 1951 general elections, when turn-out was a democratically impressive 80 per cent plus. Indeed, it is often assumed that familiarity with, or cynicism about, politicians and political parties has contributed to a secular downward trend in turn-out in Britain since the war. However, if we consider the housing shortage of the immediate post-war period, and the attendant geographical immobility of a youthful population, and contrast this with the recent situation where, on the one hand, some 10 per cent of the population move house annually and, on the other, the proportion of the (very) elderly is growing fast, then it is far from obvious that the average citizen is less mindful of his democratic duty than Tommy Atkins who had just returned from a war fought in defence of democracy.

Population movement from the inner cities to the suburbs is the fundamental reason for the revision of constituency boundaries, only partially compensated for by immigration into some urban areas from the 1960s onwards. In the ten to fifteen years between one boundary revision and the next, not only do imbalances in the size of constituencies occur but, more interestingly, so too do changes in the make-up of the constituency. One is reminded of the character in N. F. Simpson's *One Way Pendulum* who pleaded not guilty to the crime he was accused of committing in Chester-le-Street six months previously on the philosophically ingenuous grounds that he was no longer the same person. Constituencies too may alter significantly, even profoundly, over a decade: the swift gentrification of Islington has helped the SDP just as the ageing of Bermondsey (and the old are overwhelmingly female) contributed to the success of the distasteful campaign against Peter Tatchell, the gay Labour candidate there, in 1983.

Since 1966, census information has been officially published by parliamentary constituency. Prior to that, demographic and sociological data on constituencies were a rough-and-ready approximation from census units which bore only an adventitious relationship to constituency boundaries. In 1983, which witnessed the most radical changes in parliamentary boundaries since 1885, and possibly since 1832, a different problem arose. The census has not caught up with the new boundaries, and so for data on the revised constituencies we have to rely on the psephological paratroops of the BBC and Independent Television News, Robert Waller's *Almanac of British Politics* (1983, 1987) and Ivor Crewe and Anthony Fox's *British Parliamentary Constituencies: a statistical compendium* (1986). Together these sources give insights which not only raise the issue of the 'Political Geography of Britain', as Ian McAllister and Richard Rose call it,[6] but also provoke the question of how far – if the relevant quantitative and qualitative data were available – a political geology of contemporary Britain might be discerned. The geographically inclined may find Henry Pelling's *The Social Geography of British Elections 1885–1910* (1967), Michael Kinnear's *Atlas of British Politics* (1982), Robert Waller's *Atlas of the 1983 General Election* (1987) and my own *Influence, Opinion and Political Idioms in Reformed England* (1976) stimulating. Fascination with that early tool of mass political arithmetic, Robert McKenzie's 'swingometer', has led to some exaggeration of the degree to which post-war British politics has exhibited a nationwide movement of opinion. Even in 1945 there was intriguing regional variation, which would be hard to explain away on grounds of the old psephological warhorse of class.

Opinion polls

The biggest single source of politically relevant data for the contemporary historian is the opinion poll; at the same time it is the most problematic. Regular opinion polling has been a feature of election campaigns since 1959. Between election periods, Gallup and National Opinion Polls have produced soundings of the state of political opinion and (reported) behaviour on slightly different but fairly consistent technical bases. Other pollsters – Marplan (from 1959) Harris (from 1965) and Mori (from 1969) – have broadened the field. By the late 1960s opinion polling was an established part of the political scene, publicly sometimes impugned by politicians when the results did not suit their interests but avidly consumed and privately commissioned. The 1970 general election, however, challenged the pollsters' credibility. Four out of five opinion polls incorrectly predicted a Labour victory and even the one which got the result right underestimated the Conservative lead. During the 1970s the technical problems which had led to the disaster were ironed out and opinion polls were so far rehabilitated that by 1983 Ivor Crewe could talk of 'saturation polling'. 'Polltalk' has become part of the tactics of campaigning itself: selective release of privately commissioned polls by political parties is common, and so is the less-than-impartial presentation of results by some of the newspapers that are the major patrons of opinion polling: results supportive of their partisan line make front-page leads, while less comfortable findings tend to be tucked away on one of the inner pages. By 1987 newspapers had begun to have recourse to the 'poll of polls', so many being on offer.

The integrity of the polling organizations themselves is not in doubt: at the very least it would be commercial suicide to fiddle polls when predicting election results, the most visible of all their activities. For the historian such embarrassments as the pollsters' failure to get the result right in 1970 are essentially trivial. His or her interest is not in the perverse electoral geography of Britain under a simple plurality system or the technicalities of allowing for a lower turn-out in the holiday month of June, or whatever other special factors may have thrown the pollsters off the scent, but in trends over time. Exact representativeness is marginal. What the contemporary historian is concerned with is movements of opinion and how they might be explained.

Let us consider an example. Table 4.1 charts the rise, retreat and recovery of the SDP, Liberals and SDP–Liberal Alliance in the context of Conservative and Labour fortunes from the creation of the SDP in March 1981 through to the general election of 1983. A preliminary inspection draws attention to some intriguing features: how little Labour's support varies through the series; the marked jump of Conservative support with the onset of the Falklands crisis in April 1982; the way that support for the Alliance tends to fluctuate in line with support for the SDP rather than the Liberals; the downward trend of SDP (and Liberal) support from the peaks at the end of 1981 well before the 'Falklands factor' took effect; and the awesome contrast between the 50.5 per cent of those polled in December 1981 who would have opted for the Alliance parties if the hypothetical general election had been imminent, and the 26 per cent who actually did vote Alliance in June 1983. Awareness of the political events of the period would suggest hypotheses transcending notions of the SDP as a creation of the media, and of the Falklands War as the parting of the ways between the electorate and the Alliance, to be tested against the detailed analyses of the Gallup polling.

Academic survey data

While academic surveys of political attitudes and behaviour are not as common in Britain as in the United States, they are sufficiently common to

TABLE 4.1   SDP, Liberal and Alliance support compared with Conservative and Labour support as measured by Gallup's unprompted question on voting intentions[a]

Date	SDP	Liberal	Alliance	Alliance total	Conservative	Labour
1981						
Mar.	14	18	–	32	30	34
Apr.	19	14	–	33	30	34.5
May	11	18	–	29	32	35.5
June	12.5	18	–	30.5	29.5	37.5
July	12	14.5	–	26.5	30	40.5
Aug.	19	13	–	32	28	38.5
Sep.	17.5	11.5	–	29	32	36.5
Oct.	26.5	13.5	–	40	29.5	28
Nov.	27	15	–	42	26.5	29
Dec.	36	14.5	–	50.5	23	23.5
1982						
Jan.	26.5	13.	–	39.5	27.5	29.5
Feb.	21.5	14.5	–	36	27.5	34
Mar.	19.5	11.5	2	33	31.5	33
Apr.	20.5	11	5.5	37	31.5	29
May	13.5	9.5	6	29	41.5	28
June	15	10	3.5	28.5	45	25
July	13	7.5	3.5	24	46.5	27.5
Aug.	13.5	10.5	3.5	27.5	44.5	26.5
Sep.	12	8.5	2.5	23	44	30.5
Oct.	11.5	12	3.5	27	40.5	29
Nov.	11.5	8	2	21.5	42	34.5
Dec.	10.5	9	2.5	22	41	34.5
1983						
Jan.	9	11.5	2	22.5	44	31.1
Feb.	8	10.5	3.5	22	43.5	32.5
Mar.	13.5	10.5	5	29	39.5	28.5
Apr.	7.5	10	5	22.5	40.5	35
12 May[b]	6	7.5	4	17.5	49	31.5
19 May[b]	6	9	4	19	46	33
25 May[b]	6	7	5	18	48	33
29 May[b]	6	6	6	18	49	31.5
3 June[b]	8.5	9	5.5	23	47.5	28
5 June[b]	7.5	7.5	7	22	45.5	31.5
9 June (election result, GB)				26	43.5	28

[a] The 'prompted' question naming the Alliance as a choice sometimes indicated a significantly greater amount of support for the Alliance, particularly during the SDP's first year. The total Alliance support as measured by the prompted question for each of the 10 months in 1981 was: March 46%, April 45%, May 40%, June 37.5%, July 39%, August 41.5%, September 39.5%, October 46.5%, November 43%, December 51%.

[b] Poll during election campaign; date is that of publication in the *Daily Telegraph*.

Source: Gallup Political Index.

be a major source for the contemporary political historian. In contrast to opinion polls, their objective is to offer a theoretical insight into the political process: the number of questions asked is usually larger; the background variables are more searching and numerous; and the processing is more sophisticated. However, they are by nature anything but instant and are normally geared to predictable 'events' in the political life-cycle of a democracy. Many, but not all, of the more recent studies involve a panel design, whereby the same respondents are interviewed more than once. Yet it cannot be said that such surveys achieve anything of the unanimity that opinion polls do. Although a large slice of Social Science (now Economic and Social) Research Council budgets have been spent on the study of British voting behaviour, we still do not know how or why the voter decides. It may be that smaller, more tightly controlled surveys specifically designed to test one hypothesis to destruction will be the way forward.

For the contemporary historian there are two ways to utilize the findings of such surveys: simply to cull the published work for relevant tabulations; or to engage in the time-consuming work of secondary analysis, by subjecting the data set to further processing. The Essex Data Archive has collected some of the best surveys of the last twenty years, 'cleaned' the data, and made the package available in standard form. The historian exploiting this rich resource would undoubtedly be wise to examine the nature of the sample, the quality of the questionnaire, and the logic of the argument. Survey work is littered with battered reputations.

Official statistics

The serious historian will doubtless be stimulated by the findings of pollsters and psephologists but it is very likely that he or she will soon have recourse to the less glamorous, indeed often pedestrian, outpourings of the government machine for 'hard facts' on the trends of the economy, on the state of law and order, even on how many people saw an allegedly opinion-forming current-affairs programme on television. Official and semi-official statistics – literally facts and figures for the use of the state – are our biggest source of numerical data.

Surprisingly, however, though censuses have been compiled since 1801, the British Government Statistical Service was not established until 1941. Its wartime origin and its subsequent expansion under Harold Wilson's premiership in the 1960s underline the point that governments do not collect statistics for the benefit of historians or social scientists. None the less, official figures are a mine of information as well as a minefield for the unwary. The returns are only as sound as the quality of reporting and processing. Mistakes are made. Two that did come to light were an apparent balance-of-payments crisis stemming from the accidental omission of a zero by the employee of a major firm reporting its exports, and the publication, undetected for several months, of a nonsensical set of trade figures, for the simple reason that a clerk had transposed two lines of figures on the coding sheet.[7] We may assume other errors have passed undetected into 'history' to bemuse the doctoral student.

British government statistics emanate from three main sources: the Office of Population Censuses and Surveys, the Business Statistics Office, and the statistical units of the main government departments, the whole coordinated by the Central Statistical Office. The greatest undertaking of all is the decennial census, costing roughly a pound per head of the population. By international standards it is comparatively limited in scope – for example, ethnic origin was still not directly included in 1981 – but undoubtedly highly professional. England and Wales are divided into just over 100,000 enumeration districts – some 180 households per district – and data for this level is available in machine-readable form.

The censuses are supplemented and updated by a number of official sample surveys. These include the Family Expenditure Survey, which began in the 1950s, and charts the income and spending of households; the General Household Survey, dating from 1971, which deals with population, housing, employment, education and health; the Labour Force Survey, begun in 1973; and the National Readership Survey, started in 1956. There are more specific surveys and it is fair to work on the presumption that some government department has collected the information you are interested in, even if, as happens on occasion, it was politically too sensitive to be published immediately, if at all. Catherine Hakim's *Secondary Analysis in Social Research* (1982) is an excellent overview of official government statistics; the Central Statistical Office's annual *Guide to Official Statistics* is definitive; and the Royal Statistical Society's periodical *Review of UK Statistical Sources*, edited by W. F. Maunder, is invaluable. On the census, David Rhind's *A Census User's Handbook* (1983) is well worth reading.

The most obvious and readily accessible sources for the historian are the *Annual Abstract of Statistics*, which dates from the last century, and the *Monthly Abstract*, from which it is aggregated; *Social Trends*, a 'good read', which may be the place to begin; *Economic Trends*, also accessible; the more intimidating *British Business*, on which *Economic Trends* is based; and *Regional Trends*, providing a provincial breakdown of the national information in the parent *Social Trends*. Other important sources are *Population Trends, Criminal Statistics* and the *Employment Gazette*, a monthly publication which records figures for the unemployed as well as for those in work.

This last publication provides a salutary illustration of how careful one must be in using and interpreting official (and other) statistics. As Martin Slattery has written,

By excluding or ignoring certain groups the [Conservative] government has managed to stabilise unemployment at about 3.3 million over the [1982–6] period. In 1982 Norman Tebbit, the then Minister of Employment, changed the counting rules to exclude from the official figure those who did not register for unemployment benefit. This alone cut 264,000 people from the dole queue. In 1983 men over 60 on higher long-term rates of supplementary benefit did not have to sign on at an unemployment office, thus removing a further 162,000. . . .[8]

No party has a monopoly in such administrative 'adjustments', and the moral is to look carefully at the explanatory notes, mindful of Disraeli's aphorism about 'lies, damned lies and statistics'.

Official statistics deal with facts, even if they are not necessarily the facts in which historians, sociologists or political scientists devil. What is missing from the official record is systematic data on opinion and attitudes. However, in 1983 the Department of Employment and the Department of the Environment agreed to co-sponsor a national survey of social attitudes, based on a sample survey which echoes the invaluable American General Social Survey. The *British Social Attitudes Survey*[9] has already established itself as a major source of reference and deserves to be a protected species of socio-political inquiry.

Content analysis

One other kind of quantification which the contemporary historian may occasionally find useful is content analysis of the mass media. Political information and political messages assail the democratic citizen through television, radio and the press. Only rarely is there reason to suppose that a particular headline, article or party political broadcast could have swung opinion as the Zinoviev Letter is alleged to have done in 1924. More plausible, given the volume of propaganda, and the low levels of attention of a family audience to a tabloid press or a news bulletin, is the dripping-tap effect.[10] Here a distinction should be made between the daily press, which in its mass-circulation popular form is unashamedly partisan, and the broadcasting organizations, which are bound by public service requirements to be fair, impartial and accurate in their treatment of news and current affairs. In practice, the balance between political parties on television is measured by ratio of airtime, usually known as the 'tot' (total).

The Committee on Political Broadcasting, an *ad hoc* and unofficial group composed of representatives of the political parties, the BBC and the Independent Broadcasting Authority under the chairmanship of the Leader of the House of Commons, meets at least annually to agree a ratio for party election (or, between election campaigns, for party political) broadcasts, which then, unofficially, determines the ratio for news coverage during the election period. Note, however, that out of campaign periods no such convention exists for news coverage. In 1983 the ratio for the Conservatives, Labour and the Alliance was 5:5:4, in 1987 it was 5:5:5. By contrast, without such informal regulation the popular press coverage in terms of column inches in 1983 was in a ratio of 5:5:2. Seconds or column inches, of course, tells us nothing of the direction of the coverage. Measuring the coverage of particular issues, as in Paul Hartman and Charles Husband's study of the treatment of race in the British press from 1963 to 1970 (*Racism and the Mass Media*), can offer revealing background to the development of public attitudes.[11]

As content analysis passes from basic categorization into such refinements as coding for positive and negative statements and context, the work becomes enormously time-consuming and it is unlikely that the contemporary historian will lightly undertake such investigation himself. Especially difficult is the content analysis of television, which, to be convincing, requires analysis of the visual as well as the verbal dimension, and where, as in the case of news programmes, one has to reckon with a large number of brief items. The controversy over the Glasgow University Media Group's *Bad News* (see for instance Martin Harrison's *Whose Bias?*), illustrates the problem.[12] Harrison criticizes the Glasgow group's work but did not have access to most of the videos of the material on which the group based its analysis. For those with the inclination, an increasing amount of news and current-affairs programming is available as script or videotape.[13] Party political broadcasts and election programmes of all kinds from 1974 onwards are on tape at the University of Leeds, as are the programmes made for the EEC referendum campaign of 1975.

Even when scrupulously conducted, content analysis begs as many questions as it answers. How far does 'biased' coverage reinforce attitudes as opposed to creating them? Do newspaper readers read the *Sun* because of its Conservative line or are they Conservatives because they have been exposed to the *Sun*? A Mori poll in 1979 found that only 28 per cent of its readers thought that the *Sun* was biased towards the Conservatives, while in 1983, despite such headlines as the notorious 'GOTCHA!' when the *General Belgrano* was sunk in 1982, the *Sun* reader was only 6 per cent more likely to have voted Conservative than the average voter was.[14] As for television, the consensus amongst researchers suggests that any effects it may have are complex, strongly influenced by viewers' prior dispositions, and are far less than commonly supposed by some politicians. Party political broadcasts, like commercial advertising, tend to be more defensive than proselytizing: they remind the faithful that their party is still in the field. Whatever the technical objections to the Glasgow University Media Group's work on preferred readings of industrial relations or the problems of the British economy in the 1970s, the alleged bombardment with the notion that strikes were a fundamental cause of the country's difficulties did not avert the 'winter of discontent' in 1978-9 – i.e. the alleged bias seems to have had little or no effect on events.

Preparing your own survey

Despite the mass of under-used data available, it may still be that the historian has no choice but to embark on his or her own survey. Without going into the techniques involved,[15] it is worth stating here a number of principles that should be borne in mind if the time and effort, which is always considerable, are to be well spent.

First, once your questionnaire has gone out, there is no going back because you forgot to include something. In any sample of ordinary citizens, there are likely to be a goodly number that you will never find again, let alone persuade to give more of their precious time; and a sample of, say, Lobby correspondents will be far too busy to answer further inquiries. Remember too that, unlike the unchanging archive, people change their views over time as they respond to experience.

Second, and clearly linked to this admonition, it is imperative to define your purpose clearly if the inquiry is essentially fact-finding. The carpet sweeper is no use. Where the investigation is designed to test a hypothesis then it must be rigorous and capable of falsification from the information gathered. Such an approach will impose its own discipline: do I need this question and why?

Third, a hypothesis is about the relationship between concepts, but those concepts need to be operationalized into measures and indicators which can be understood in the same way by all members of the sample. A simple example will illustrate the point. Take the question usually rendered as 'Do you think you have a duty to vote, or do you think you should vote only if you want to?' On the face of it this question, familiar enough in political-science surveys and designed to tap the citizen's internalization of democratic norms, is straightforward. Unfortunately, young voters asked the question in the early 1970s had a quite different perception of the term 'duty' from their parents. Had 'responsibility' been substituted for 'duty', the findings might have been more satisfactory.

Fourth, it is better to have fewer but more reliable data. In the world at large, attention spans are not geared to the forty-five minute lecture or the 4000-word article. The number of questions must take into account the staying power of the least attentive respondent; and, like a good lecture, the questionnaire should begin by gaining attention, raise the crucial issues a few minutes into the encounter and devote the last few minutes to bread-and-butter matters as the audience loses concentration.

Fifth, never put words into your respondent's mouth, as it is so easy to do. Questions such as 'What class would you say you belonged to?', where it has not been established that the respondent construes his or her world along class lines, are very misleading and so inadmissible.

Finally, when the questionnaires have been returned, do remember that analysis of the data is at least as demanding as its collection. The phrase 'number-crunching' is quite misleading. The possible permutations of tables of this variable against that, controlling for some other variable, are endless; and, for reasons which will be clear from even the above short list of pitfalls, the best-organized surveys rarely offer up neat, consistent and incontrovertible conclusions. The analysis of a survey is something of a military operation where a strategy is essential if one is not to become bogged down in the trenches hoping vainly for some new statistical weaponry to come to the rescue. If nothing else, conducting a survey teaches humility.

Conclusion

The attentive reader will have noticed that it appears to be the masses who are counted, not their governors. This is not far wide of the mark, even though one might instance exceptions such as studies of elite recruitment or of legislative behaviour – from W. O. Aydelotte's classic inquiry into the ideological dimensions of the House of Commons in the 1840s to Hugh Berrington's studies of backbench opinion through 'early day' motions in the 1950s and 1960s.[16] From quite another perspective, however, political marketing experts share the belief that political communications are influential. To the extent that 'sources close to the party leaders' believe things to be real to the masses, they are real in their consequences. Even the political historian who takes the high-politics view of decision-making must now take into account the statistical reports on mass politics, sound or not, which modern Tadpoles and Tapers lay before their leaders. The long-forgotten Sir William Petty, who wrote his *Political Arithmetick* as long as ago as 1691, deserves tercentenary celebrations in 1991.

Notes

1 See for example Roger Jowell, Gerald Hoinville *et al.*, *Survey Research Practice* (Gower, 1986).
2 A. H. Birch, R. Benewick, Jay G. Blumler and A. Ewbank, 'The Floating Voter and the Liberal View of the Representation', *Political Studies*, 17, no. 2 (June 1969); T. J. Nossiter, 'Working-class Tories', *Socialist Commentary*, February 1974.

3 See for example J. A. Phillips, *Electoral Behaviour in Unreformed England* (Princeton University Press, 1982); T. J. Nossiter, *Influence, Opinion and Political Idioms in Reformed England* (Harvester, 1976); R. J. Olney, *Lincolnshire Politics 1832–1885* (Oxford University Press, 1973).

4 R. S. Milne and H. C. Mackenzie, *Straight Fight* and *Marginal Seat 1955* (Hansard Society, 1954 and 1958); and M. Berney, A. P. Gray and R. H. Pear, *How People Vote* (Routledge and Kegan Paul, 1956).

5 See note 2 above.

6 See Ian McAllister and Richard Rose, *The Nationwide Competition for Votes: the 1983 general election* (Francis Pinter, 1984).

7 J. Irvine, I. Miles and J. Evans, 'Demystifying social statistics 1979', quoted in Martin Slattery, *Official Statistics* (Tavistock, 1986) p. 130.

8 Slattery, *Official Statistics*, p. 83.

9 Roger Jowell and Colin Airey, *British Social Attitudes Survey* (Gower, from 1984).

10 See Jay G. Blumler and Michael Gurevitch, 'The political effects of mass communication', in Michael Gurevitch, Tony Bennett, James Curran and Janet Woollacott (eds), *Culture, Society and the Media* (Methuen, 1982); G. J. Goodhart, A. S. C. Ehrenberg, M. A. Collins and Aske Research Ltd, *The Television Audience: an update*, 2nd edn (Gower, 1987).

11 P. Hartmann and C. Husband, *Racism and the Mass Media* (David Poynter, 1974).

12 Glasgow University Media Group, *Bad News* and *More Bad News* (Routledge and Kegan Paul, 1976 and 1980); Martin Harrison, *Whose Bias?* (Policy Journals, n.d.).

13 The British Film Institute is perhaps the largest public source. The broadcasters can assist on a modest scale.

14 M. Bilton and S. Himelfarb, 'Fleet Street', in D. E. Butler and D. Kavanagh (eds), *The British General Election of 1979* (Macmillan, 1980), table 5.16, p. 113; P. Dunleavy and C. Husbands, *British Democracy at the Crossroads*, (Allen and Unwin, 1985).

15 See Russell Langley, *Practical Statistics for Non-Mathematical People* (Pan, 1986).

16 W. O. Aydelotte, 'The House of Commons in the 1840s', *History*, October 1954, pp. 249–62; Hugh Berrington, *Backbench Opinion in the House of Commons 1945–55* (Pergamon, 1973).

5

Public Records

Nicholas Cox

The letter had been brought in at twenty minutes to nine. It was just on ten minutes to nine when I left him, the letter still unread. I hesitated with my hand on the door handle, looking back and wondering if there was anything I had left undone. I could think of nothing. (Dr Sheppard, in Agatha Christie, *The Murder of Roger Ackroyd*, ch. 6)

A fictional snippet of autobiography. Whether or not we care who killed Roger Ackroyd, readers to the end of the story discover that the village doctor's bland account had concealed the purpose of his visit, accomplished in those blank ten minutes, which was murder by stabbing.

This is an extreme example of deliberately misleading testimony. Contemporary historians have access to new techniques, such as tape-recording of oral evidence, and much more in published form, through newspapers, broadcasts, film, parliamentary debates and memoirs, than existed for earlier periods. Although they neglect these secondary sources at their peril,[1] the quotation may explain why they are likely, for the foreseeable future, to pursue investigations behind the outwardly more appealing faces of public personalities by stepping into the dry world of official archives.

Using archives, and in particular those of central government, presents historians with difficulties which do not exist for users of books, of documents published in editions, or of private manuscript collections. They arise largely from the special nature of archives as a source, from the circumstances of their creation, from the consequential way in which they are arranged and made available for research when they come to be transferred to a record office, and from the fact that there are usually restrictions on their availability. Additional difficulties are caused by the fact that the quantities of material generated by modern central governments are so vast that what is preserved can usually only be a selection from what was originally brought into being.

What are archives?

'Archives' and 'manuscripts' tend to be used interchangeably as terms to describe collections and accumulations of papers and records. But in fact they are not the same thing at all. What are archives, then? They are not like manuscripts, accumulated by libraries or private collectors, or kept by individuals, because they are not artificially gathered collections of items. They consist of the papers (or, usually, a selection from the papers) which official authorities (in the case of the archives of the state, the central government) drew up for the purposes of the conduct of their affairs, or which they used in conducting them. They are papers which themselves *formed an actual part of that conduct of affairs.* They may not even be 'papers' at all, but may consist of any objects conveying information in the administrative context in which they were created or used. They will have been preserved afterwards by those responsible for the transactions in question, or by their legitimate successors, in their own custody and for their own reference.[2] Above all it is their *official* character which defines them.[3]

Archives have particular and significant characteristics which follow from this definition. First, as what has been called 'the secretions of an organism', they form a natural accumulation in government departments or other official bodies, because documents, as objects, form a real part of the administrative actions which produce them. Indeed, they may now be the only physical residue of those actions. Secondly, their natural 'secretion' by the administrative process means that they form an organic whole, in the same way that the organization that created them formed one, and so any item among them is likely to be closely related to other items, both within and outside the series of records in which it exists. It is on these relationships that very much of the significance of archives depends. Lastly, archives, as a natural secretion, are historically impartial: that is to say that (with some very significant exceptions) they were not drawn up for the benefit of historians – or, for that matter, of anyone else outside the administrative process.

For researchers in libraries, used to author, title and subject catalogues, the move into a record office can be bewildering and exasperating. Because books are deliberately manufactured articles, they can be equipped with an identification, and with internal means of reference, such as a contents list and index, when they are published, and they nearly always are. Because they are individual, discrete items, each with its own separate significance and title, and normally with an identifiable author, they can be acquired and then catalogued individually. Because they tend to exist in multiple copies, possessed by many different owners, the librarians who care for them have long since been able to develop shared standards for describing them and providing means of reference to them – in fact they have had to do so – and researchers who have used one library will usually have no difficulty in finding their way round another library's catalogue, whether in the same country or not. Furthermore, depending on its specific acquisitions policy and the funds at its disposal, a library can decline to acquire any particular item, because the librarians know that another major library, such as one of the British copyright libraries, is bound to possess a copy, and that the item will therefore be available elsewhere. Similar considerations apply to newspapers and other publications.

Because archives are the incidental by-products of official actions, they usually have no obvious personal 'author', and very often not even a declared title. Because they consist not of discrete items, but of selections from accumulated *series* of records produced by official activities, they have to be described largely by reference to the administrative activities which created them. Because the archives in any one record office are likely by definition to be unique, archivists have been much slower than librarians in establishing principles and in developing common standards for arranging and describing what has been transferred into their custody. In countries such as the Netherlands, with a centrally organized system of record offices, national principles and standards were developed relatively early on,[4] but in countries such as Britain or the United States, without a centrally controlled archive network, each record office may have its own, slightly different, methods, and some may present the researcher with the need to learn a whole new system from scratch. This may apply too in moving from record offices in one country to those in another one.

Last, when selecting or handling archives, archivists know that what they have before them is unique, and that its destruction, or any step which makes it unavailable, will almost certainly obscure the particular information that it contains. However, they will be aware that its underlying organic interrelations with other archives may mean that the information is indirectly recoverable elsewhere, and this awareness is likely to affect their approach in deciding whether to preserve it or not. What the researcher finds is the result not of a purchasing or acquisitions policy based on the availability of funds for buying, but of archivists' selection policy based on appraisal of the informational value of the material.

This excursion into archival theory may seem a little arcane to prospective users of archives, but it is worth putting what follows into context. Setting out the underlying reasons for the peculiarities of research in archives may help to explain some of them. It is unfortunate, perhaps, that nearly all the explanatory literature on the way to use archives has been produced by the archivists, who keep them, and hardly any by the historians, who use them, even though there has always been a two-way traffic in careers between the two professions. The resulting slant in approach has often given archivists the appearance of being obsessed by the world that they inhabit and by their own problems and procedures, to the cost of their relations with researchers. Anyone who knows Michael Frayn's play *Alphabetical Order*,[5] in which an earnest newcomer is inducted into the ludicrously idiosyncratic filing system of a newspaper-cuttings library, will understand what is meant. This chapter is probably no different, and its readers ought to bear in mind (but maybe it will be only too apparent) that it has been written by an official archivist.[6] It is also written by one who works in the Public Record Office in London, and a great deal of what follows is particularly related to the history of the PRO and its records.

How are archives created and how are they arranged?

Archives were created by official activities in the past. By now they may well be the only evidence for them. But, since they are not simply a retrospective account of those activities, but the documents which played an actual role in them, they are not merely evidence for the facts. They are part of the facts.

Most researchers, other than historians of administration, are only incidentally interested in what officials were doing in the past. They are more likely to be concerned with a wider subject of investigation, on which official activities had some bearing. But, if you are working on archives, you have in front of you records which exist because they played a part in what officials were doing in the past. You are using the written transactions, the part of the facts which has come down to us in tangible form, to reconstruct the activities, or to throw light on the wider topic of research.

To say that archives are part of the facts is not to say that what is written in them is, or was, the 'truth'. It is to say that what they contain had a particular significance at the time it was written, and in the circumstances of the time. So, if you are to make a right use of the written transactions, you need to understand the reasons that the officials who created them had for being involved in the subject we are concerned with, and for writing or doing what they did. You have to know how they worked in their particular organizations, and also – this is important – how they used and created the documents we are looking at. That is why record offices' guides to their contents tend to describe them in terms of administrative background and record-keeping practices, rather than by subject matter. If you are more interested in a subject than in what clerks in an office or court were doing, or in how papers were being arranged, these guides can make for dry reading. After all, it is not so long since interest in good filing systems was seen by Anthony Crosland as going hand in hand with advocacy of total abstinence as a mark of an over-austere approach to life.[7]

All this may appear obvious: master the sources. It may seem arid advice too, until you order up a bundle or file of documents, which for all you know may never have been read by anyone in the record office before, and find a paper which you do not understand. Then it is worth recalling. Each piece of paper, however enigmatic it may appear, is there for a reason, even if you cannot at first understand what that reason is. It was not placed there as a conundrum. Someone in the past wrote it, and had a reason for writing it. Someone was intended to read it – maybe the writer, if it was written as a reminder; maybe someone else. Unless you can understand what the writer was engaged on, what part he (until the twentieth century, almost certainly *he*) was playing in the office that produced the records you are looking at, you may not be able to fathom the writer's purpose. To understand the part he was playing, you will need to understand how his office worked, and the kinds of document that its workings might have produced. Above all, to understand why he might have written what you have in front of you, and to be able to use the information it might convey, you have to put yourself in the writer's position and achieve a realization of the circumstances in which he was working. This calls for a leap of imagination, whether you are dealing with records of the thirteenth century or of the twentieth. Of course, the ability to make this leap is a matter of historical training and experience. But it is more likely to be made in the right direction if it is based on a full understanding of the nature of the records being used, and of the whole range of related records available for use.

But users of archives in a record office face a further complication. Not only do they have to understand the workings of the original creators of their sources. They have also to cope with the way in which archivists themselves have, maybe imperfectly, tried to understand those workings, and to present the resulting archives accordingly.

Although this chapter has been written with contemporary historians in mind, a little delving into the past is needed to explain the rationale behind the organization of the papers they may want to see. The archival arrangement of papers goes back to medieval times, but a brief account of what was done during the nineteenth century may show how the present system emerged, and also show how work on papers by the departments which created them affected the subsequent approach of the Public Record Office, once it had come into existence.

The British Treasury had begun to number incoming papers and to keep systematic annual registers of them in 1782, and it was not long before it employed a succession of members of its staff to investigate and sort into some sort of order its older unregistered papers. The Foreign Office has appointed a librarian in 1801, and had begun to keep registers of its despatches and papers in country series, and to index them. In 1811 the Admiralty had begun an even more elaborate scheme for sorting and indexing its correspondence, and for making a subject-arranged summary of the papers, the 'Digest', which also carried out some retrospective 'digesting' of its correspondence back to 1793. Soon after the PRO was set up in 1838,[8] officially to deal with the records of the courts of law and to provide them with a single home, its staff were being called on by departments to provide assistance in working through, reporting on and arranging their accumulations of non-current records. It began to accept deposits of these records, and from this point onwards its archivists began to become much more closely involved not only with older records, but also with arrangements for the way in which records were handled in their originating departments, a process which was accelerated by an Order in Council in 1852 which brought all departmental records under the 'charge and superintendence' of the Master of the Rolls, the senior Chancery judge who was then also Keeper of Public Records. The process was taken further in 1854 by the incorporation into the PRO of the State Paper Office, which by then held records of the Home, Foreign and Colonial Offices down to 1830, and some even later material. The Treasury, exercising its growing powers over other departments' organization and methods, and taking advantage of the existence of the PRO and the extension of its area of responsibility, set about a series of investigations into government records, and began to interest itself in departments' arrangements for handling papers, and in ways in which their records could be transferred systematically to the PRO for safe keeping.

The great change in current record-keeping which came about in this process was the development of the registered file. Instead of simply numbering papers in order as they came in, or as they were generated in the office, and keeping registers of these numbers, departments began to organize their papers by subject, keeping incoming letters, internal minutes, drafts of replies and any other related material, together from the start, in a cover with a reference and, usually, a title. Twentieth-century researchers are so used to using registered files that it is often hard for them to remember how recently they appeared on the scene. Departments which were new, or which had had only loose control over their correspondence and papers, tended to be the earliest to move over to this new system. The War Office began to keep structured subject files in 1855, and the Home Office in 1871. Departments which already had a highly developed system of keeping and registering numbered series of papers were usually the slowest to reform. The Treasury did not completely abandon the system it had set up in 1782 until 1920, although from the 1850s it began to formalize methods of bringing numbered papers on one topic together, and storing them out of their original numerical order, recording their movements and their final physical locations in a separate series of registers. This was the pattern followed by most departments. They retained annual numbered series of papers, but devised ways, which were usually cumbersome, either of keeping correspondence on the same subject together, as those working on new incoming papers called for any earlier related papers, or of cross-referencing papers on similar topics. Relatively homogeneous departments, such as the Home Office or Treasury, maintained office-wide registration systems for the whole of their correspondence. Departments broken down into distinct divisions, with markedly different areas of responsibility, decentralized their systems. The Board of Trade, for instance, initiated separate series of numbered papers for its Commercial, Marine, Railway, Finance, Harbour, Establishment, Companies and Bankruptcy Departments, as they were set up.

As archivists came into contact with other departments and had to take in orderly transfers of usually already arranged papers from them, their growing understanding of departmental registration systems rapidly led to a realization of the basic principles of the arrangement of archives, although they were realized more quickly abroad, and in a more systematic form, than in Britain. In 1841 the French Ministry of the Interior, which was responsible for the Archives Nationales, developed the principle of *respect des fonds*, according to which the records of any particular institution were to be grouped together as that institution's *fonds* (there is no adequate English translation) *and not arranged together with records from other fonds* on the basis of any similarity in subject matter or format. Archives should be classified so that the organization and functions that produced them would be clearly reflected by them. In 1881 the Prussian State Archives reformulated this principle, in the German guise of a *Provenienzprinzip*, or principle of provenance, and developed it further by establishing as well a *Registraturprinzip*, or principle of original order. According to this the records within each institution's *fonds* were to be arranged, or maintained, when transferred to the Archives, in the order in which the original institutional registry had arranged them.[9] If the records had become disordered, it was the foremost duty of the archivist to discover and restore the original order. These principles aimed, as far as humanly possible, to preserve the impartiality of the archives, and to leave the facts that they represented undisturbed. They were set out, and argued for, at length, in 1898, in the Dutch *Manual* alluded to above,[10] and have been the basis for all archivists's operations ever since.

In the British Public Record Office these principles have led to the arrangement of the records in *groups*, each of which consists of the archives resulting from the work of an administrative unit of government which was an organic whole, complete in itself, capable of dealing independently with every side of its business – i.e. what most people would recognize as a separate government department or court. Within each group are *classes*, each of which represents an original series of records (in most other English-speaking countries what the PRO calls classes are called *series*), all resulting from the same accumulation or filing or recording process, and all of similar physical nature and informational content. Within each class are the individual *pieces* (or items), which are the single files, bundles of papers, maps or volumes which made up the original series.

The record groups in the PRO were originally all given mnemonic letter codes, representing the courts or departments of government which created, or transferred, the records in them. So, records of the Treasury are in the T group, those of the Cabinet Office in CAB, those of the Court of King's Bench in KB, and so on. Within each group the classes are arbitrarily assigned numbers, simply in the order in which the decision to transfer them was taken; the numbers have no other significance. Each piece or item within the class is separately numbered, so that, in theory, every item can be referred to, or ordered up, using a simple three-part reference.

This system worked well for 'dead' archives, and for those created during a period when administrative structures were stable and relatively uncomplicated. It would still work well in an archival institution which had the ability directly to control records in other departments, and to classify them, from the point of their original creation or from very soon after it. In countries such as Canada and the Netherlands this is so. In Britain, the PRO has no direct executive control over other departments' filing systems, although it can advise on them, and does not have the opportunity to classify or arrange archives until the point at which they are due to be transferred, usually after they are twenty-five years old, and after the process of selecting them for transfer is over. During that timespan, administrative changes, and transfers of administrative functions from one department to another, usually involving the physical transfer of the related working papers as well, have often made strict adherence to traditional principles impossible.[11]

Getting the records into the record office

In the United Kingdom the general process of selecting, transferring and giving public access to the state's archives is governed by the Public Records Act of 1958. But most of the detailed processes are not statutory. They are controlled by principles laid down in the 1954 Report of the Committee on Departmental Records, usually known by the name of its chairman, Sir James Grigg.[12]

The Committee's aim was to devise arrangements which would ensure that records that had a permanent historical or administrative value would be selected for transfer to the PRO to be made available in due course; that material which was clearly identifiable as having no permanent use would be got rid of as quickly as possible, so as to simplify the job of selection from the rest; and that these two aims would be achieved without a huge increase in the numbers of the staff of the PRO, and of those who were responsible for records in government departments.

Briefly, the Committee recommended that departments should prepare schedules of standard series of routine papers, according to their own arrangements for classifying papers in use, which they would have discretion to dispose of automatically after fixed, probably short, periods of time, without going through them paper by paper. Other standard series might be marked at this stage as automatic candidates for permanent preservation. All other papers, those which could not be dealt with at the series level, should be reviewed by their departments, file by file, five years after they had passed out of active use. The departments should destroy the ones which they did not need to keep any further for their own use. At this stage the staff reviewing papers should exercise their judgement according to the criteria that they understood best, by putting the question, 'Is my department likely to require this paper any longer for its own purposes?' The Committee believed that, if this question was properly answered, taking account of papers which were still related to current business, and of the department's need to document its own activities, to keep precedents, and to provide guidance for possible future activities in similar circumstances, the papers which survived this first review would include those which had a material historical significance.

However, some of the papers which survived this first review would not be worth keeping permanently. So the Committee recommended that, when the papers which had survived were twenty-five years old, they should be reviewed again, file by file, on this occasion directly using the criterion of permanent historical value in the perspective brought about by the intervening lapse of time. In general, the Committee believed that the responsibility for these selection procedures would have to rest on the departments, with the PRO acting as coordinator and supervisor, but that decisions about what to keep or destroy after twenty-five years should be taken jointly by the department and a representative of the PRO. The records selected after this second review should be transferred to the PRO, unless they still needed to be kept in their department for administrative use.[13]

When the Grigg Committee reported, there was no legal right of public access to British government records at all. Most departments which had transferred records to the PRO had agreed dates after which researchers could see their papers. But these dates were at the departments' discretion, and the dates differed from department to department. The committee recommended that a period of fifty years should be fixed, after which departments' records would become accessible automatically, unless notice was given by a department that it did not want particular records to be made available.[14]

As a result of these recommendations the Public Records Act was passed in 1958. It did not provide for the details of the reviewing procedures outlined above, but it did provide an administrative framework in which they could be carried out. And it provided the fixed period of fifty years after which records would become accessible, as recommended. But it gave the Lord Chancellor, the minister now responsible for public records, the power to prescribe an increase or decrease in this period for particular records, if he saw fit. The Act is the basis on which the PRO operates today, and the only major amendment to it has been the reduction of the fixed period for access to records to thirty years. This change was brought about by a second Act in 1967.

These arrangements for selecting records differ from those in many other countries, in that such very large numbers of files are examined individually during the process of review.[15] In Australia, for instance, although the archives legislation is much more detailed in its provisions for the review process, selection is carried out almost entirely at the class level, and it is the whole run of files in any particular classification that will either be kept or destroyed. But in the process of review in the United Kingdom sight is not lost of the principles of archival arrangement described earlier. Files are reviewed individually within their file series. At the point at which a new series is due for its final review, arrangements are made within the PRO for a new *class*, with its own appropriate letter code and an individual class number, and a title, to be assigned to the records which will be transferred after the review has taken place. Once that has happened, the records, although they have been reviewed individually, will be kept together in their series, and will appear within the appointed period, as pieces in the assigned *class*.

The statutory provisions for access also differ from those in countries which have freedom-of-information legislation, as Australia, Canada, Sweden and the United States do, although it is possible for countries to operate simultaneously under a Freedom of Information Act, giving a right of access to categories of current government papers, and archival legislation as well, which provides for general access to records in the archives after a much longer fixed period. Australia does just that. The UK legislation is also different in that its access provisions are expressed negatively, rather than positively: 'Public records in the Public Record Office . . . shall not be available for public inspection until the expiration of the period of thirty years . . . .'[16] There is a presumption against disclosure before the prescribed period is over. But the period is calculated for each single file or item separately. The calculation is made so that an item is available at the beginning of the year following the year in which the latest paper in the item is thirty years old. Thus 1956 papers, so long as they were not included in files or volumes running on beyond 1956, were opened to the public at the beginning of 1987.

As mentioned earlier, there can be exceptions to the thirty-year access provision, and under section 5(1) of the Public Records Act the Lord Chancellor can approve a longer or shorter period. Successive Lord Chancellors have approved longer periods for exceptionally sensitive papers whose disclosure would be contrary to the public interest, on security or

other grounds; for records whose release would or might constitute a breach
of an undertaking of confidentiality; and for records whose disclosure
would cause distress or danger to living individuals or their immediate
descendants. The Act also prohibits the release of records which contain
information that government has obtained under statutes which themselves
prohibit its disclosure. For instance, returns made by farmers under the
1979 Agricultural Statistics Act and its predecessors, and by businesses
under the 1947 Statistics of Trade Act, are permanently withheld under
those Acts. There is also provision in section 3(4) for departments to retain
records with the Lord Chancellor's approval, and under this section
'blanket' approvals have been given for the retention of records concerned
with intelligence and security and with civil and home defence planning, and
of those dealing with atomic energy. Some records are retained for
continuing administrative use, and are accessible in their departments,
although most retained records are simply unavailable. The approvals for
retention are subject to reconsideration after stated periods. [17]

The fact that nearly all records transferred to the PRO are examined
individually as part of the selection process, and also as part of the process
of declassification which has to be carried out before transfer, means that
there is an opportunity at the same time for each item to be described
separately as well. Where records are handled at the series level, as in some
other countries, the means of reference provided for them on transfer is
likely to be simply a description of the series rather than a detailed list of its
contents, or, at best, to consist merely of the original departmental file
docket book. This may be rudimentary, and even misleading, since the file
titles shown in it will probably be those that were given when the files were
first brought into use – as a mark of intent, as it were, rather than as a
description of the business which was actually transacted on the files after
they began to be used. The detailed listing of files by departmental staff, in
a specified standard form, after the final selection is made, and before they
come to the PRO, has now become part of the Office's regular procedures
for transfer. The legal arrangements for access mean that each item needs
also to be dated, and appropriately marked as well if any variation from the
thirty-year 'rule' has been prescribed by the Lord Chancellor. And so the
dates of each item, and a note of any variation from the normal access
arrangements, can also be included in the descriptive list.

In most record offices, the greater part of the staff's time may be spent in
sorting and describing accumulations of records after transfer or deposit.
Individual members of staff who have worked in this way on particular
bodies of records will usually have acquired very detailed knowledge of
their contents, and so be able to advise prospective researchers about them –
if necessary, before any detailed inventory of the records has been
completed. In some archives, and the National Archives of the United

States is a particular example, the whole process of making more modern records available to researchers depends on having members of staff available to discuss with them the topic of research, and to identify for them series of records, or items from series, on which they can work, rather than on the provision of pre-prepared detailed item-by-item listings.

The arrangements for transferring records to the PRO mean than, at the point at which any class of papers arrives, there is a detailed inventory of its contents already in existence, which can be *immediately* available for use by researchers. There has to be, if the papers are to be effectively prepared for access in the fairly short time between the process of their final selection and the point at which the thirty-year period runs out. But there is a consequential disadvantage, in that the PRO's own staff have usually not worked on the papers themselves and so built up a prior knowledge of their contents. Or, at least, that knowledge will have been acquired by the twenty or so people, out of the PRO's staff of 420, who are involved in the process of selection and description, and who are therefore away working in other departments and not readily available to advise prospective users. So researchers need to acquaint themselves with the very detailed, but at first sight (and, some may think, at second and third sight as well) mystifying means of reference that are provided. Because the archives themselves are so extensive and complex, reflecting the complex administrative activities which produced them, the means of reference are bound to be complex too, but in theory the PRO's system provides the means for researchers to find their way through to the archives that will provide the material for their investigations.

Up to this point, in discussing general aspects of archival arrangements, comparisons with the situations in other countries and other record offices have been made. What follows relates entirely to what the user of the records in the Public Record Office in London will find.

Finding what you want

In a letter to *The Times* on 7 May 1977, Lord Greenhill of Harrow, former Permanent Under Secretary of State at the Foreign and Commonwealth Office, wrote,

> I think all my colleagues would agree that it will be in the future quite impossible for anyone to unravel with any accuracy from the archives the detailed history of events. The sheer volume of documents, the inevitable decline in the standards of filing, the mass of unrecorded telephone conversations, all contribute to the fact that the course of events can no longer be followed from the original documents, and individual documents of special interest may well be overlooked.

Lord Greenhill's words are discouraging, unless seen as a challenge to the contemporary historian, but they do at least point out some of the problems posed by modern archives. The complexity and extensiveness of the records have just been referred to. It has been estimated that contemporary British government produces around 100 miles of paper every year. Of this, usually, a little under one mile eventually comes to the PRO, after the reviewing procedures described earlier. That mile probably consists of around 50,000 files, volumes or bundles of papers.

The complexity of the records was just as much a problem for their creators and filers as it is for their users nowadays. Civil servants who put papers on the wrong file, or kept them in their desks because they could not find the right file, were not just making it difficult for their colleagues to trace them. They were making the task of the future historian that much more complicated.

The last problem is probably the most important to bear in mind. We can only find on a file what was put there at the time. If an official transacted a piece of business on the telephone, or by walking down the corridor to speak to a colleague, and then saw no reason, or did not take the trouble, to note what had been said, then we shall have no record of it. Parts of discussion at meetings which were deliberately not minuted will in the same way not be available to us. The missing piece of business, or the unminuted statement at the meeting, may well be implicit in what follows in the papers, but it will be left to historians to understand what really happened through their handling of the evidence. They need to remember what was said earlier about realizing the circumstances in which the writers of the papers were working.

The problem of unrecorded pieces of business is one we can now do nothing about. It is a fact about the nature of the records. It will affect the way we use the records, once we have found what we want. But the problems of the bulk and complexity of the records are ones which it is the archivist's job to help the researcher overcome, by providing guidance through the apparent maze.

Researchers planning to visit a record office usually try to find first a published description and analysis of the records that it holds, so that they can be fairly sure that they are visiting the right institution, and so that they have some notion of the area in the archives that they ought to be investigating. In 1963 the PRO published a two-volume *Guide* to the whole of its contents, which was up to date down to the middle of 1960. In 1968 a third volume was added, completing the coverage to 1966.[18] But, with almost a mile of new records, consisting of around 1000 new classes, or additions to old classes, coming into the Office every year, there is now no hope of keeping researchers who are interested in the most modern records fully up to date by means of a traditionally produced printed publication. It would always be too far in arrears to be fully of use to them.

The *Current Guide to the Contents of the Public Record Office*, which is superseding the whole of the published *Guide*, is a loose-leaf production (for ease of constant updating) which is available in 'hard copy' form in the PRO, and is also being made available for sale on microfiche. Although it contains all the information that was available in the old published *Guide*, but in a much more up-to-date form, it is arranged quite differently. It is in three parts. Part I contains detailed administrative histories of the departments, courts of law and other organizations which have transferred records to the PRO, and follows each section of the administrative history with a series of cross-references to the classes of records in the Office which contain material produced by the various departments and organizational subdivisions just described, giving the letter and number code assigned to them. Part II consists of a description of the classes of records, arranged alphabetically and then numerically, by their class codes, giving their titles, the date range of the records so far transferred into them, the number of items transferred and their general form, and, more importantly, a general description of the records that make up each class. If the class represents one original file series of a department's records, as most recently transferred classes do, or possibly a number of such series, the description will explain the purpose for which the original file series was created for use in the department. Failing such correspondence, it will explain the nature of the class. If some basis for selection of the records other than the one which has already been described has been adopted, that also will be explained. Part III is a persons, places and subject index to parts I and II.

From the descriptions of the classes in the *Current Guide*, part II, it is possible to move straight to the descriptive list of the contents of any class described there. The lists are arranged on the shelves in the same way as the descriptions of classes in part II, in alphabetical and then numerical order. Most modern lists are preceded by an introductory note, which sets out the same sort of background information provided in the *Guide*, though in greater detail; explains the arrangement of the list, if it needs explanation; points out the existence of any indexes or registers of the papers in the class and of any related series of papers in other classes; and also explains why any records which you might expect to be in the class are absent, either because they did not survive at the point at which the class was transferred, or because they exist elsewhere.

In using the *Guide* researchers will notice that many of the letter codes now used to designate classes are not obviously meaningful. Those who are used to finding Cabinet Office records in CAB classes, or War Office files in WO classes, are likely to be confused at first to find classes of records of the United Kingdom Atomic Energy Authority with AB codes, and Department of the Environment classes with AT codes. These codes are without any significance of their own – AB does not 'stand for' some descriptive title, such as 'atomic bomb'. As explained earlier, frequent transfers of functions between departments, with consequential transfers of series of files as well, mean that most modern departments' records contain quantities of files inherited from their predecessors in exercising their functions, and worked on by them. Some very short-lived departments, ŗ··ːh as the Ministry of Land and Natural Resources (1964–7) and the Department of Economic Affairs (1964–9), while they existed, held in their records a great preponderance of material taken over from other departments. The inherited files continued to be worked on in the new department, and were probably reregistered. But, when the new department ceased to exist, these inherited records together with newly created records were probably taken over and reregistered again by their successors for their own use. There may well now be hardly any records which are clearly identifiable from their file covers or their registered references as having been used in the two departments mentioned. In most cases, then, their existence would only be revealed by an investigation of the relevant files' contents. In such circumstances, the use of meaningful letter codes, although helpful in that they are easy to remember, would actually be misleading, because it would suggest something which is not actually true – i.e. that records with a particular PRO letter code are records of the department that the letters supposedly stand for, when they may in fact largely consist of papers inherited from other departments.

To take another example, the Ministry of Supply, while it existed from 1939 to 1959, incorporated into its records considerable quantities of material from the Ordnance Office, which it superseded. Its own records were in their turn later incorporated in large measure into the records of its successors, and in particular into the records of the Atomic Energy Authority and of the Ministry of Aviation, which itself took over records created within the Ministry of Aircraft Production. At first sight, a researcher who finds classes with SUPP and AVIA letter codes would expect that those codes 'meant' that the classes must contain records originally created by the departments that the codes suggest, and perhaps that they contain all such records. From what has just been said, the reader can see that this might be very far from being so, although I should add that there are many identifiable Ministry of Supply files in existence, because the Ministry existed long enough for files which it created to have passed out of active use during its own lifetime. So the use of unsuggestive letter codes for the records of new departments is a way of avoiding misleading impressions. But their use means that researchers will have to rely on the administrative analyses and on the class descriptions in the *Guide*, rather than on the suggestions offered by the letter codes themselves, to pick out the records of the department they are interested in investigating.

Once a class has been identified, and its class list found, the researcher is faced, at last, with the description of its contents. The standard form of an entry in a list provides not only a description of the contents of each item, but also its date range and its original departmental reference, together with the modern number within the class by which it can be referred to or ordered up. The date range is important, because the final date determines when the item first becomes available.

Most classes are arranged as far as is possible in the order in which the papers were arranged in their original registration system. Because of the way the access date is calculated, and because only a few departments (the Foreign Office was one) organized their files so that no file extended over more than one year (most departments' files extended without uniformity over several years, and sometimes over a very long period indeed), the individual files in any class may become available at a wide variety of dates. If research is being conducted into records of the 1950s, or even of the 1940s, it is common to find that the papers of interest are on files which extend beyond the latest date to which records are generally available, and are therefore not yet accessible. For instance, the records of the Cabinet Home Affairs Committee for 1956 (CAB 134/1250) are bound together with records of that committee for January 1957, and the Economic Policy Committee records for 1956 (CAB 134/1231) are in the same volume as those for January 1957. Thus at the time of writing (1987) neither volume was available, access being permitted from 1988. In the past, departments sometimes ran files for very long periods. 1916 Treasury papers on accommodation for the Post Office Savings Bank may be found in a file which ran on until 1952 (T 219/199) and so was unavailable until 1983.

If the original series of files being worked on was a long-lasting one, the contents of the class to which they now belong may be very extensive. For instance, the series of General Correspondence, Political, which the Foreign Office began to use in 1906 continued well beyond the date at which records are now available, and the class in which the papers are now to be found, FO 371, already contains nearly 126,000 items and is still growing. It must be admitted that, however good the means of reference are to an accumulation of papers of this size, and there are very detailed indexes to most of FO 371, it is very daunting to be faced with a list of this length. Most classes are nothing like FO 371 in size, but the advantage of an all-inclusive class of this sort is that it is at least fairly obvious in which class to look for a particular category of material (in this case, records of diplomatic activities transacted by the political departments of the Foreign Office). The more decentralized and subdivided a department's filing system was, the more difficult it may be to find the particular series in which the papers produced by any specific area of activity were originally filed.

These 'nuts and bolts' suggestions of the way to find particular series of records are probably only useful if the researcher already has a clear idea of the departments responsible for the areas of activity that are being researched. The index to the *Guide* will help in giving ideas, but, like all subject indexes, the references it gives for very broad subjects, such as economic policy, are likely to be so numerous as to be unhelpful, and the broadest subjects may, for this reason, not appear at all. In its *Handbook* series the PRO has begun publishing analytical guides to the records relating to particular major policy areas.[19] Where no published analytical guides exist, the records created in this century by the machinery for the co-ordination of government policy can satisfy the need for them.

The records of the Prime Minister's Office, and in particular PREM 3 and PREM 4 (1940–5), PREM 8 (1945–51) and PREM 11 (for the Conservative administrations from 1951), can give a particular insight into the way successive prime ministers initiated or co-ordinated policy and handled Cabinet and government business. What is there depends a great deal on the 'style' of the prime minister in question. But, because of these differences in style, the PREM records, invaluable as they are for policy studies, are not likely to give as complete a conspectus of the whole range of government activities at any time as those of the Cabinet.

From 1916, when the Cabinet Office first came into existence, the records of the Cabinet and its committees, and the working files of the Cabinet Office staff themselves, provide an invaluable guide to the ministers and departments who had responsibility, or were made responsible, for particular areas of policy or activity.[20] They 'comprise the most valuable single collection of modern material for historical purposes that can be obtained from official sources'.[21] Working through the minutes of Cabinet meetings and the memoranda prepared for them, and the parallel records of the complex structure of committees which has grown up below the full Cabinet, particularly since 1945, can provide an insight into the structure of modern British government that can hardly be obtained elsewhere.

But there are pitfalls in this approach. Memoranda put up to the Cabinet and its committees, and the recorded minutes of decisions taken on them, are highly refined documents. They are the result of meticulous processes of drafting and of interdepartmental diplomacy. So they often lack the quality of unself-consciousness that the working papers of the departments themselves possess. Precisely because the Cabinet Office records are so structured and ordered, it is very tempting to concentrate on them and to fight shy of grappling with the great mass of records produced by the workings of government in the departments, where policy was formed and executed.

No one in his right mind – and perhaps least of all the archivist, who has had to try to reduce it to usable order – would suggest that dealing with this mass of records is a simple matter. The temptation is to be, like Lord Greenhill, too discouraging to the researcher. But the very extent of the archives of the modern state means that the researcher who makes the attempt, and takes account of the complicated interrelations between the various organs of government when pursuing investigations, and is not content to pursue obvious and well-trodden paths through the records, can hardly ever fail to find undiscovered material. Perhaps it is not as inappropriate as it may have seemed at first that this chapter began with a quotation from a detective story.

Access to the Public Record Office

Most modern departmental records are held at the PRO's building at Kew. The reading rooms at Kew and in the original building in Chancery Lane are open from Monday to Friday from 9.30 a.m. to 5 p.m. No records can be ordered up for the same day after 3.30 p.m., although until 3.45 orders can be made for records to be available the following day. It usually takes about half an hour for a record to arrive after being ordered, and, to enable this 'production time' to be kept to, the number of items which can be ordered at any one time is limited to three. Like nearly all record offices, the PRO only allows pencils and typewriters to be used in the reading rooms, in order to minimise danger to the records from ink. Full details of the Office's public services can be found in its leaflet *Information for Readers*.

Notes

1 See Patrick Cosgrave, 'Can we believe these papers?', *The Times*, 2 January 1987, p. 12.

2 Cf. Hilary Jenkinson, *Guide to the Public Records: introductory* (HMSO, 1949), p. 2, and *A Manual of Archive Administration* (Lund, Humphries, 1937), pp. 11–13. Sir Hilary instanced a difficulty in dealing with objects, which he described as a *reductio ad absurdum*: 'Supposing, for example, that a Viceroy sends to the Secretary of State in England an elephant, with a suitable covering note or label; or supposing, to take a more actual example, that the Governor of a Colony presents to the First Commissioner of Works a two hundred foot spar of Douglas Pine: the question may be imagined to arise: Is the spar 'annexed' to correspondence with the Governor of British Columbia? Is the elephant attached to the label or the label to the elephant?' (*Manual*, p. 7).

3 It is often thought that the term indicates some quality of antiquity, as if it were comparable with words in English beginning with 'archaeo-', derived from the Greek *archaios*, 'ancient'. It is not: it derives from the Greek word *archeion*, 'a public office'.

4 Cf S. Muller, J. A. Feith and R. Fruin, *Handleiding voor het Ordenen en Beschrijven van Archieven* ('Manual for the arrangement and description of archives') (Society of Netherlands archivists, Groningen, 1898).

5 Michael Frayn, *Alphabetical Order* (French, 1977).

6 However, the chapter is written personally, not officially.

7 C. A. R. Crosland, *The Future of Socialism* (Jonathan Cape, 1956), p. 524.

8 By the Public Record Office Act, 1 & 2 Vic cap. 94.

9 See T. R. Schellenberg, *Modern Archives; principles and techniques* (F. W. Cheshire, Melbourne, 1956), pp. 174–5.

10 It was translated into German in 1905, into Italian in 1908, and into French in 1910, but did not appear in English until 1940, in the United States. There has never been a British edition.

11 See Michael Roper, 'Modern departmental records and the record office', *Journal of the Society of Archivists*, 4 (1972), pp. 402–3.
12 *Report of the Committee on Departmental Records*, Cmd 9163 (HMSO, 1954). The records of the Committee, which carried out its functions administratively, rather than as an inquiry hearing evidence and then reporting on it, are available among the files of the Treasury's Organization and Methods Division (T 222/606–15).
13 *Report of the Committee on Departmental Records*, paras 57–71, 78–87, 240–41.
14 Ibid., paras 153–5, 240–1.
15 In 1985 just under 172,000 feet of records were reviewed when they were five years old, and 22,100 feet of twenty-five year old records underwent the final review. That adds up to almost 38 shelf miles of records reviewed file by file in a year. 1985 was not untypical. See *The Twenty-seventh Annual Report of the Keeper of Public Records on the Work of the Public Record Office, 1985* (HMSO, 1986), appendix V, p. 46.
16 Public Records Act 1958, section 5(1), as amended by the Public Records Act 1967.
17 A leaflet, *Access to Public Records*, gives fuller details.
18 *Guide to the Contents of the Public Record Office*, 3 vols (HMSO, 1963, 1963 and 1968).
19 For example, *Records of Interest to Social Scientists, 1919 to 1939: introduction* (1971), *The Second World War: a guide to documents in the Public Record Office* (1972), *Unemployment Insurance, 1911 to 1939* (1975), *Records of Interest to Social Scientists, 1919 to 1939: employment and unemployment* (1978). A handbook on records relating to the control of economic policy after the Second World War, and one on records relating to the British colonial empire, are being worked on currently.
20 A handbook, *The Cabinet Office to 1945*, was published by HMSO in 1975.
21 *Report of the Committee on Departmental Records*, para. 147.

6

Private Papers
Angela Raspin

This chapter aims to show in outline what researchers can expect to find in the private papers of politicians and of other figures of interest to the contemporary historian, and to provide some basic advice on the use of such sources. Attention is drawn to the obstacles that the researcher may encounter, as well as to the natural limitations of the material itself. Provided such limitations are borne in mind, private papers can offer the contemporary historian remarkable advantages in the form of 'unofficial' information.

Since there is little agreement about archive terminology among archivists themselves and none between archivists and historians, it is necessary to begin with some definitions. In what follows, 'private papers' and 'personal papers' are interchangeable terms signifying 'the private documents accumulated by, belonging to, and subject to the disposition of an individual person';[1] 'repository' is the normal, neutral term for a manuscript-collecting and holding institution, and 'depositor' for the person who donates or loans a collection to a repository. For brevity, I have used 'originator' to denote the person who originated a set of personal papers of interest to historians.

What do private papers contain?

Personal papers are the physical survivals of a life. A politician's papers may contain correspondence with family and personal friends and political colleagues, minutes and notes on informal meetings, drafts of policy papers, formal correspondence, and official papers retained from periods of office. Unless the originator kept copies of his letters or asked for the originals back, his papers will contain only letters written to him.

All these kinds of record are produced as a by-product of a particular activity or as a means of carrying it out, not for their own sake. The fullness of a collection of private papers depends on a number of factors independent of the importance or interest of the originator. The major one is the degree to which he used writing as a means of clarifying his thoughts or communicating with others. Labour politicians of the old school, such as Ernest Bevin or Emanuel Shinwell,[2] clearly preferred speech as a means of doing business, so their papers tend to be very thin.

Technological change has had its effects. Much important business is now carried on by telephone and is very sparsely recorded. Letters dictated to a secretary and typed tend, whoever the recipient, to be more impersonal than those written by hand. People's paper-keeping habits vary: some keep almost everything, as did Sir Winston Churchill and Sir William Beveridge;[3] some, like R. H. Tawney,[4] keep nothing of consequence; some discard their papers when they move house or retire; and some sort and, one suspects, edit them when they come to write their memoirs, as with Hugh Dalton and the first Earl of Swinton.[5] Memoir writing is often the crucial stage in the originator's realization that a mass of old letters is in fact an archive of some general interest.

Most twentieth-century collections of private papers consist of fascinating fragments. It is very unlikely that they will give a complete picture of the originator's activities. Even in cases where papers have survived in fair abundance, there will almost certainly have been a degree of editing, conscious or unconscious. The parts of the life which were particularly unhappy, unsuccessful or just boring for the person who lived it are likely to be documented less fully. So, on the other hand, is carefree youth.

The paper-keeping habits of small organizations are very similar. Their active lives are often longer, but their officers and thus the place where the papers are kept may change at intervals of a few years. The result is that records which are felt to reflect the corporate existence of the organization – minutes especially – will survive, while material felt to be of only temporary importance will not. It frequently happens that, by the time the archivist or historian examines the records, all the correspondence and reports which actually explain the minutes have gone.

So far conventional manuscripts have been considered. There may also be Hansards, election leaflets, broadsheets, sound records, pieces of film. Sound recordings, where the originator has taped meetings or conversations, are likely to become more common and offer peculiar problems as regards both conservation and consultation. It is relatively easy to skim a written text by programming the eye to pick out certain text combinations; skimming a recording is slower and inherently less accurate, since it can only be done by listening to a series of short samples.

One special kind of record found in private papers offers particular problems of interpretation. Personal diaries are not kept as an essential part of normal business. The diarist has to decide to keep a diary and to go on keeping it. A detailed political diary represents a considerable expenditure of time and mental effort, and its character will depend on the diarist's motives for keeping it: it may be a deadpan record of events for reference, like Sir Walter Citrine's;[6] or, like James Meade's,[7] it may be confined to a particularly stimulating or unusual part of the diarist's life; or it may serve, like Sir Alexander Cadogan's,[8] as a safe vent for frustrations and for subjects which could not be discussed elsewhere.

The reader, in evaluating the information in a diary and in accounting for omissions, should always attempt to gain some idea of the diarist's intentions. This entails reading a substantial amount of the text, not just consulting an index. He should also consider the mechanical aspects of diary keeping. Was the record a set of instant shorthand notes, written up every day, or at intervals by the diarist? Was it dictated to a tape recorder, or dictated at intervals to a typist from notes or from memory? Answers to such questions will help to establish to what extent the record has been subjected to subsequent analysis or to conscious or unconscious editing. Diarists of today and tomorrow may well use word processors to keep their diaries. Such techniques are seductive but make editing, without leaving traces, alarmingly easy. The distinction between diary and memoirs, between what a person thought at the time and what that same person says in retrospect, becomes ever slighter.

Because private papers are so fragmented, and because of problems of incomplete knowledge and conscious and unconscious bias on the part of their originators, it is impossible to write more than the most limited study from one collection. The historian should be prepared to undertake a kind of mosaic work with incompatible scraps of information from a great variety of sources and to spend a good deal of time and heart-searching in evaluating their relative unreliability as well as their meaning. He may indeed find that the narrative framework comes from the public records and from printed sources and that private papers provide the occasional but essential moments of illumination.

The 'archivization' of private papers

One of the defining characteristics of private papers is that they are at the free disposition of their owners. No legislation directly applies to them (with the partial exception of some controls on export of material of national importance). They are usually held by the originators or their heirs, by manuscript-collecting institutions or by third parties, usually biographers or research institutes. As with government records, but for different reasons, private papers usually do not become available to the historian until long after the events they record. Politicians rarely allow outsiders any kind of access to their papers until their active careers are drawing to a close, and the papers rarely become available to all comers in public institutions until the originator has died or has wholly withdrawn from public life.

Where the owner still holds the papers, the user has no right of access, moral or legal. The owner may agree to show his papers, or a section of them, as an act of generosity. This is probably the only way of consulting very recent material and has the advantage that the originator may be available to give explanations. The disadvantages are that it may be very difficult to gain an accurate idea of the extent or contents of the archive, and that the time available for consultation is likely to be very short. Users under these circumstances should do their best not to annoy or inconvenience the originator in any way. They should take particular care to leave papers in the state in which they found them, to remove nothing, and to resist the temptation to rearrange them. To do so may suit their own research but destroy underlying relationships to the detriment of future researchers. The same absence of rights applies to papers held by third parties, though here the potential user's moral position is stronger if the papers are already in use for research purposes.

The position is radically different when the papers are held by an institution. In the United Kingdom these fall into three main groups: institutions funded by central government, including the Public Record Office, the national libraries and the major museums; institutions funded by local government, in this context primarily the local record offices; and educational establishments, mainly universities.

In the United Kingdom there is a marked absence of central direction, central funding and legislation controlling the administration of private papers. With the exception of the national and county record offices, manuscript departments form part of larger institutions, usually libraries or museums. This fact has important consequences for funding. Most manuscript departments are funded out of their institution's block grant. This is usually inelastic and some of the most active institutions rely on grants from private sources. These are usually earmarked for specific projects, not for general administration, acquisition and cataloguing. The system has, in the past, proved highly flexible in adapting to new research trends, but has serious deficiencies. The low level of long-term funding available to most institutions has meant that few have been able to grow sufficiently to make economies of scale in the balance between professional and non-professional staff, and that it has often been easier to set up a new repository to deal with a new branch of research than to provide extra staff and space for an existing one. There are, in consequence, a large number of small repositories and standards of provision vary considerably.

From the researcher's point of view however, the situation is less chaotic than this outline may suggest. The demands of institutional prestige, the existence of influential professional organizations and of a common curriculum for the training of archivists, and the co-ordinating role of the

Royal Commission on Historical Manuscripts (HMC) have meant that there is a fair degree of agreement about basic standards. There are, however, marked differences between institutions on matters of principle, in relation to access to material and to reprographic facilities, and in matters of practice, as in the running of search rooms.

Manuscript collections may come into the custody of archives by a number of different methods. For recent political papers of importance, purchase by auction or through a dealer is uncommon and acquisition is usually by negotiation with the originator or his heirs. These negotiations are generally confidential and may involve direct purchase or an element of indirect purchase – for example, if the collection is set against inheritance tax. Even in the case of an outright gift, the archive will probably accept certain conditions as the price for accepting the collection. The degree to which the repository agrees to accept such conditions depends on the importance of the collection, the policy of the institution and the perceptions of the negotiator. If the collection is thought to be exceptional, it is easier to accept conditions which will be expensive to operate. There may be an element of quiet competition for such papers and some depositors may shop around for the best package.[9]

The conditions of deposit which are most likely to affect users are restrictions on access to the collection and on the publication of information. Such restrictions may be imposed for one or a combination of reasons. They may be imposed to comply with the Official Secrets Act and other legislation controlling the availability of information.[10] Institutional policies differ considerably on the degree to which it is necessary and politic to co-operate with the authorities on matters of official secrecy. Some repositories prefer the evasive, some the compliant stance. Restrictions may be imposed to protect the depositor. The depositor may wish to protect his own reputation or his privacy. He may wish to prevent his friends from discovering what he said about them in his diary. He may require the repository to accept the obligations of confidentiality which he assumed towards his informants. Such obligations are frequently accepted by a member of Parliament towards his constituents in trouble, by a politician towards a civil servant who tells him about malpractice in his department, by an anthropologist towards the people he interviews, or by a university teacher towards his students. Restrictions may also be intended to protect third parties. Information which they did not know was recorded may embarrass or damage them. The final reason for restrictions is to protect the repository and its parent institution. A reputation for reckless indiscretion does not help an acquisition programme.

The purist argument is that everything which is in a manuscript collection should be open to inspection and that material which cannot be inspected should not be acquired. In the long run this is a truism. Private papers are collected for use and one of the essential points in a negotiation is to set a time after which all restrictions are lifted. In the short run the negotiator is frequently faced with the choice between acquiring the whole archive with restrictions or rejecting material of real historical value in the knowledge that it may be lost or even deliberately destroyed.

The three principal methods of restriction are as follows.

1 *Absolute closure*. The collection is placed under seal. This is the preferred method of dealing with highly confidential papers or those closed under the Official Secrets Act.
2 *Restrictions on access*. The papers are closed but a procedure is set up whereby the potential user may apply for permission to consult them, either from the original depositor or his representative, from a special committee or from the governing body of the repository. Some institutions accept this system as a matter of course, others only as a last resort. It is often useful as a means of reassuring a nervous donor. Some collections appear to be hedged around by the most obstructive conditions and yet permission to see them has never been refused.
3 *Restrictions on publication*. This method is usually combined with restrictions on access. The user undertakes, in return for permission to consult the papers, that he will not attempt to publish any information from them without permission. The user is in any case prevented from publishing actual text by the law on copyright. A few institutions impose such restrictions as a matter of course. Always take care to keep a record of your acceptance of such conditions. Infringement may prevent your use, on a later occasion, of material in the same institution.

Political historians, partly because of the nature of their subject, partly because of the importance to them of the closed periods of official records, are particularly sensitive to restrictions on access. My own experience suggests that the problems here are usually easier to surmount for private papers than for some other kinds of material. Records of interest to social historians and anthropologists' field records can cause agonizing moral dilemmas over the scientific value of the material and the rights of those who supplied that material in confidence. It is worth noting, too, that business firms tend to be far more protective of the inviolability of their records than most politicians are.

How to locate private papers

The historian who proposes to use private papers should draw up two lists of names: names of those whose private papers are known to exist and must be consulted, and names of those whose papers may not have been kept or be accessible but whose activities were relevant to the subject. Even if the papers of the second group cannot be found, useful letters by them are likely to turn up in other collections. These lists will be constantly added to in the course of research. New collections are constantly being acquired or freed for research and the historian must be flexible in revising his research plans.

The best overall guides to manuscript holdings in the United Kingdom for modern political history are the *Guide to the Papers of British Cabinet Ministers 1900–1951*, by Cameron Hazlehurst and Christine Woodland,[11] and the guides to British political archives 1900–51 by Chris Cook and others.[12] The second source updates the information in the first and its *First Consolidated Supplement* also includes post-1951 papers already in repositories.

The master indices to manuscript holdings in the British Isles (primarily the United Kingdom, but also including some information on the Republic of Ireland) are compiled by the National Registry of Archives (NRA) at the Royal Commission on Historical Manuscripts (HMC).[13] These are arranged by name, place and subject. For the present purpose, the name indices are the most useful. They also include entries for important runs of correspondence by one person in the papers of another. The indices are based on annual returns made to the HMC by collecting repositories, on the detailed lists of the contents of collections supplied by those repositories, and on information collected by the HMC itself. Inevitably there are gaps, owing to incomplete or delayed reporting, but the indices are the most up-to-date source outside the repositories themselves. They may be consulted together with the lists on which they are based at the HMC search room, and the NRA will also answer questions by post.

Apart from the general guides noted above, many repositories also publish overall guides to their holdings and there are a number of special guides to particular subject areas. The HMC and the Institute of Historical Research[14] have good coverage of these. The HMC publishes a summary list of the major repositories, *Record Repositories in Great Britain*. For a more eclectic guide with fuller information, Janet Foster and Julia Sheppard's *British Archives* should be consulted.[15]

A number of important manuscript collections, including the archives of the Conservative and Labour parties, are becoming available on microform.[16] These packages are published in very small editions and are not reliably listed in *Books in Print* or in specialized bibliographies. The best course for the interested historian is probably to ask a friendly librarian to show him the publishers' cumulated catalogues, and, if he cannot locate a copy of the package himself, to consult the publisher. The advantage of microform for this form of publication is that it is easy to make very small numbers of copies so they do not readily go out of 'print'.

How to approach the repository

This section is expressed as a series of instructions. Many of these will be obvious to most readers, but all are essential.

It is advisable to write to archivists in advance. Explain the subject of your research. Ask whether the repository holds the collection in which you are interested; whether it holds similar material which you should consult, and whether there are any special conditions attached to consultation; what the opening hours are and whether you need to make an appointment for your first and subsequent visits.

It is wise, if you want a prompt reply, to keep your questions brief and to include a stamped addressed envelope. It is useful to be able to produce a general letter of introduction from a person in a position of responsibility; if you are a research student this should be your director of studies. If you wish to consult restricted access collections, be prepared to produce a curriculum vitae, a full statement of your research project and a specific letter of recommendation. When you first arrive in the repository you will probably be asked to fill out a record card and to sign an undertaking to observe the rules of the repository as a condition for being allowed to consult the manuscript collections.

The usual sources of information about a repository's contents are the overall guides to its holdings and the detailed catalogues. Guides consist of a list of collections, arranged either alphabetically, by dates covered, by subject, or by order of acquisition. Their object is to give the user a quick overview of what is available. They usually give, for each collection, its name, a brief indication of subject and date coverage, the size of the collection and information about catalogues.

The usual practice is for repositories to prepare a separate catalogue for each collection of reasonable size, usually in the form of a bound volume. The basic rules in cataloguing manuscript collections are (1) to observe the principle of provenance – that is, to keep all material from the same source together and to introduce nothing extraneous; (2) to retain the original order of the collection as far as possible; and (3) to lay out the material in such a way that the user can see what is there, how it fits together, and, equally important, what is not there. The amount of detail given by catalogues varies. The collections most likely to be described item by item are very important collections, very small collections (where the contents are so disparate that they cannot be summarized) and collections received in a very chaotic state – i.e. collections that can only be sorted into a comprehensible state by writing a description of every separate item and playing happy families with the slips of paper on which the descriptions are written. If the collection was already divided into files, the catalogue description may be limited to a general summary of the contents of each file with perhaps a note on any particularly significant document. Very detailed listing is expensive, and may leave the reader unable to see the wood for the trees. In general, archivists prefer to expend the resources needed for one detailed catalogue in producing four summary catalogues. The repository may also have indices which cover all collections. Subject indices, which are expensive to produce and raise severe methodological problems, are uncommon. How does one predict the future subjects of research? Name indices can be produced by intelligent unskilled labour – students, for instance – from existing catalogues. They are, however, only as good as the catalogues on which they are based. For example, summary catalogues will not list the names of all correspondents and are generally well in arrears. They are worth consulting, as they may lead to quite unexpected material, but should not be relied on as the sole source. It is worth spending time and care on a repository's finding aids and drawing up a list of material for examination. It is important to note the exact call mark on every item you wish to consult so that you can order it for inspection and so that you can identify it clearly and accurately when you come to write up your research.

Archive repositories permit the consultation of manuscripts only in a closely supervised reading room. The material you wish to consult will be fetched for you and you will probably be required to use a pencil when making notes. You should take great care in handling original documents. Modern paper is of poor quality and easily damaged. Do not rearrange files, and, if you find any discrepancies, report them to the person in charge of the reading room. Find out what the arrangements are for fetching as these vary according to the layout and staffing of the repository. Documents may be fetched on demand or at fixed intervals. For example, there may be no fetching in the middle of the day or after a certain time in the afternoon. The time taken to deliver orders will depend on the distance between the reading room and the storeroom. Some material may be kept in another building. You may be able to order in advance: establish the correct method, because it will save you a considerable wait on your next visit. You will probably only be able to consult a few items at a time in order to minimize the dangers of misplacing, but you may be able to ask for additional items to be kept ready for you.

Reproduction and copyright

The Copyright Bill, at present before Parliament, is expected to simplify the law with regard to unpublished material by making it equivalent to that for printed publications. The concemporary historian should assume that any text which he wishes to quote is in copyright and that a large proportion of the copyrights in any given collection never belonged to the originator of that collection. If A writes a letter to B, the letter belongs to B, but the copyright remains with A, the author, and his heirs. Many repositories require readers to sign some kind of undertaking to clear copyright. In cases where it is intended to publish large quantitites of copyright text – an edition of a diary, for instance, or a book with an extensive documentary appendix – outline copyright permission should be sought at the start of the project. If the project is likely to make money, the copyright holder may require a special fee or a share of the royalties.[17]

The law of copyright relates only to actual quotations, not to the transmission of information. If you have not undertaken to seek permission before publication, you may freely paraphrase, while avoiding plagiarism, but should take care to identify the source you have used. Give the name or number which the repository uses to identify the collection, instead of, or as well as, any pet name in common use; the section- and item-numbering system used by the repository; and a brief summary of the contents. The *British Standard Recommendations for Citation of Unpublished Documents* is a useful guide.[18]

There is a marked divergence of opinion among British archivists about photocopying. Some take the view that nothing may be photocopied without the permission of the copyright owner if it is less than 100 years old; others that the difference between permitting someone to copy a document by hand and selling him a photocopy is not great enough to justify a ban. Those offices which do photocopy insist on the work being done by their own staff and charge a price which covers labour costs and in some cases overheads. They will also reserve the right to refuse to photocopy material which may be damaged or about which there are special problems of copyright or confidentiality. Expect long delays over photocopying, especially during the Long Vacation. Do not assume that the provision of photocopies implies the right to publish. Some repositories can also provide microfilm. However, the potential problems over copyright are here much more severe, because of the larger quantity of material involved (it is usually not worth ordering less than 200 pages to be filmed) and because it is so easy to make subsequent copies illicitly.

Principal repositories

The main repositories where valuable material on contemporary British history may be found are the British Library and the British Library of Political and Economic Science, London; the Bodleian Library, Oxford; Churchill College, Cambridge; the Cambridge University Library; the Brynmor Jones Library at the University of Hull; the Modern Records Centre at the University of Warwick; the National Library of Scotland; the National Library of Wales; and University College, London.

The papers of political parties are in various stages of availability and order. The Conservative Party's papers are housed at the Bodleian Library, Oxford, and are open up to 1964. Access to subsequent material is by prior arrangement. The Labour Party's papers are at its headquarters at 150 Walworth Road, London, and it operates a fifteen-year rule on access. In the case of both parties, files which are obviously 'personal' are closed. Some Liberal Party archives are held at Bristol University Library and the British Library of Political and Economic Science. The Social Democratic Party's papers will also be unavailable for the foreseeable future. The Trades Union Congress operates a thirty-year rule on its papers, which may be consulted by prior arrangement.

Notes

1 Definition of 'personal papers' in *Dictionary of Archival Terminology*, ed. Peter Walne, International Council on Archives, Handbook no. 3 (K. G. Saur, Munich, 1984).
2 Ernest Bevin (1881–1951), papers at Churchill College Cambridge; Emanuel Shinwell (1884–1986), papers at British Library of Political and Economic Science (BLPES), London School of Economics.
3 Sir Winston Churchill (1874–1965), papers at Churchill College; Sir William Beveridge (1879–1963), papers at BLPES.
4 R. H. Tawney (1880–1962), papers at BLPES.
5 Hugh Dalton (1887–1962), papers at BLPES; Sir Philip Cunliffe-Lister, 1st Earl of Swinton (1884–1972), papers at Churchill College.
6 Walter McLennan Citrine (1887–1985), diary at BLPES.
7 James Meade (1907–), diary at BLPES. An academic economist, Meade was Director of the Economic Section of the Cabinet Office, 1946–7.
8 Sir Alexander Cadogan (1884–1968), diary at Churchill College.
9 For a more extended summary of conditions of deposit see the forthcoming information leaflet to be published by the Publications Committee of the Society of Archivists, *The Transfer of Private Papers to Repositories*, by Angela Raspin.
10 For instance, the Rehabilitation of Offenders Act.
11 Cameron Hazlehurst and Christine Woodland, *A Guide to the Papers of British Cabinet Ministers 1900–1951*, Royal Historical Society Guides and Handbooks, Supplementary Series no. 1 (Royal Historical Society, 1974).
12 *Studies in British Political History 1900–1951*, compiled by Chris Cook *et al* (Macmillan): vol. I, *A Guide to Archives of Selected Organisations and Societies* (1975); vol. II, *A Guide to the Papers of Selected Public Servants* (1975); vols III–IV, *A Guide to the Private Papers of Members of Parliament* (1977); vol. V, *A Guide to the Private Papers of Selected Writers, Intellectuals and Publicists* (1978); vol. VI, *First Consolidated Supplement* (1985).
13 The Royal Commission on Historical Manuscripts, Quality House, Quality Court, Chancery Lane, London WC2A 1HP. The HMC also publishes an annual *Accessions to Repositories* (HMSO), a list of collections acquired during the preceding year, arranged by repositories.

14 Institute of Historical Research, Senate House, University of London.

15 *Record Repositories in Great Britain*, 7th edn, compiled by the Royal Commission on Historical Manuscripts (HMSO, 1982); and Janet Foster and Julia Sheppard, *A Guide to Archive Resources in the United Kingdom* (Macmillan, 1982). Both works are being revised and updated.

16 Both these packages (in progress) are published by Harvester Press Microforms, Brighton.

17 For British and American practice, see J. B. Post 'Copyright mentality and the archivist', *Journal of the Society of Archivists*, 8, no. 1 (April 1986), p. 17; and Michael Les Benedict, 'Continuing controversy over fair use of unpublished manuscript materials', *American Historical Review*, 19, no. 4 (October 1986), p. 859.

18 *British Standards Institution Recommendations for Citation of Unpublished Documents*, BS 6371:1983 (British Standards Institution, 1983).

7

Parliamentary Sources
Dermot Englefield

'The functions of the Parliament of the United Kingdom may be broadly
described as legislative, financial, representational and judicial.'[1] Parliament is, therefore, concerned with passing legislation, with debate in both
Houses on Government policy and administration and in the House of
Commons with consent to taxation and control of expenditure. There is
also the role of the House of Lords with regard to appellate jurisdiction,
which is not considered in this chapter.

As we enter either of the small chambers used by the Lords or the
Commons or one of the two dozen or so even smaller committee rooms, we
find ourselves listening to a series of voices: the voice of Government policy
and its administration delivered through a hundred or more ministers; the
voice of backbench members expressing constituents' views through their
own particular political filter; increasingly the voice of lobbies and special
groups seeking to show how the shoe of current policies pinches them; and
finally the voice of experienced citizens – though it might be argued that
with the advent of life peers this experience may be richer and more varied
in the House of Lords. These chambers, unlike the hemicycle opera house
of many foreign parliaments designed for *ex cathedra* speeches, are built for
argument and the clash of ideas.

Westminster then, as the media still recognize, remains very much the
sounding board of contemporary society, and it would be surprising if the
information submitted to Parliament and the information generated by it,
nearly all of which is published, were not essential for the understanding of
the society which is speaking, first for immediate commentators, and
subsequently for contemporary historians. This chapter discusses first the
main areas of Parliament's work and the documents they produce and then
the mechanics of reaching this material.

Parliament's legislative work

Before a new Parliament meets, the different political parties will have set down their policies in election manifestos for the judgement of the electors, who decide on society's contemporary priorities at the polling booth.[2] These manifestos are an essential part of the election system but they also reveal the current needs of society as well as submitting proposals to meet them. They are published by the individual political parties but are also included in *The Times Guide to the House of Commons*, published after each election, and collected in *British General Election Manifestos 1900–1974*.[3]

The Queen's Speech, delivered at the opening of Parliament before both Houses and outlining the programme of work during the coming session, derives, at least to some degree, from the Government's election manifesto.[4] Although carefully structured to reflect the different elements of the British Constitution, the Queen's Speeches, examined over a period, give an idea of the problems on the mind of the government of the day, and the general debates which follow during the first six days of the session – technically the debate on the Address – offer a chance for backbenchers to test ministers on their policies and for Parliament to indulge in a *tour d'horizon*, a luxury which seldom comes its way. But the session is only a few days old when the Government begins to introduce its programme of legislation. Parliament takes up its first role. (Private members' bills are limited to a few each session, often quite important but normally concerned with less political issues. Procedurally their history is similar to that of Government bills.)

By the time a bill is introduced and receives its first reading, and the House where it is introduced orders it to be printed for all to know the text, it is already late in the cycle of its preparation. Civil servants and ministers, often consulting lobbies and specialists, will already have spent weeks, maybe months, modifying drafts. Parliamentary counsel have clothed the resulting compromises in a legally acceptable draft bill. This bill is published with a long title defining its scope and, of increasing importance, an explanatory and financial memorandum is attached which has been written by the responsible department to help explain the background to the proposed legislation. The second reading gives the minister in charge of the bill, the Opposition shadow spokesman and an assorted number of interested and sometimes knowledgeable backbenchers the chance to discuss the principles of the bill. The vote at the end of this debate is of key importance; if there is not a majority in favour, then the bill will be withdrawn.

Very occasionally, following this second reading in the House of Commons, a new procedure introduced in 1980 is used. Before the bill is considered in Standing Committee, a special Standing Committee, moved for by a minister, takes evidence on the bill in the same manner as is done by a

Select Committee. The maximum period for which it can take evidence, which is of course published, is three two-and-a-half-hour sessions. This procedure is sparingly used and when bills are not politically controversial, but it does enable the House to secure more information on a bill at an early stage of its journey through Parliament.

The Standing Committee stage is of course a detailed examination when amendments and new clauses are proposed; as academic studies have often shown, however, the number of amendments accepted is not great. But the Government listens and may introduce amendments itself when later the bill reaches the House of Lords. Further stages of passing legislation are the report stage, when the Standing Committee reports back to the House and amendments can still be made, and the third and final reading, when amendments are accepted only in the House of Lords. The Royal Assent is given in the House of Lords.

Many Acts empower ministers to issue Statutory Instruments and the important ones are published with an explanatory note and are laid before Parliament. If they require an *affirmative* resolution of the House of Commons, this will be moved by the minister of the responsible department and debated for up to an hour and a half. If, however, they come into effect unless there is a motion to annul them within a certain time (i.e. a 'prayer'), then the initiative to table such a motion rests with members.

As law establishes the framework for society and attempts to ease the tensions within it, Parliament's legislative proceedings offer many insights into the society of the day. Above all, legislation reflects the country's changing needs, whether major, as with the European Communities Act 1972, or a matter of a specific urgent problem, as in the case of some swiftly enacted legislation on immigration. Bills may be introduced to tidy up administration, for purely political reasons or to meet a moral dilemma.

In studying Parliament's work on legislation it is necessary to consider several printed sources. The first printing of the bill is cited, if introduced into the House of Commons, as [session, bill number], or, if introduced into the House of Lords, as [session, (number)]. The explanatory memorandum may refer back to earlier statements of Government policy on the subject which have been published as Command Papers [prefix followed by running number 1–9999]. The relevant Hansards for the second reading, report stage, third reading and consideration of amendments of the other House are cited [HC Deb., volume, or HL Deb., volume]. The text of amendments and new clauses to the bill is published [HC Supplement to the Votes and Proceedings, or HL session number and letter]. The Commons Standing Committee debate is a separate part of the Official Report [HC Deb. SC]. Indexes to these papers are considered later in the chapter.

Following royal assent the bill is published as an individual Act, later in the annual volumes of *Public General Acts* and often in the loose-leaf series of volumes called *Statutes in Force*, a subject arrangement of major current legislation which has an alphabetical list of statutes included. More up-to-date than these printed sources is the computer-based database LEXIS. Statutory Instruments are published individually and later by serial number in a series of volumes each year. They number 2000 or more a year, while statutes normally number 100 to 150 a year. The *Index to the Statutes* (a subject index) appears every two years, and so does the *Chronological Table of the Statutes*, which includes Acts which have been repealed. The equivalents for Statutory Instruments are the *Index to Government Orders* and the *Table of Government Orders*.

Parliament's financial work

The second main area of House of Commons work concerns taxation and control of expenditure. The financial procedures of the House of Commons are often regarded as recondite, but if the student of history sets out to look at the broad structure of parliamentary responsibility regarding financial matters it is possible to see a clear pattern of information.[5]

The House is always interested in the country's economic situation. At the beginning of the session, if it starts at the usual time of early November, the Chancellor of the Exchequer makes an Autumn Statement concerned with economic proposals for the following year and providing a review of his medium-term financial strategy. The Statement and strategy are examined by the Treasury and Civil Service Select Committee almost immediately, with Treasury officials and the Chancellor himself giving evidence; the Committee then reports to the House, which debates the matter before Christmas. The Government's expenditure plans follows in January, and are examined by the same committee, which takes evidence and reports to the House, where there is a subsequent debate. Finally, there are the Financial Statement and Budget proposals, followed by four or five days of wide-ranging debate, much of it on the general economic situation.

The Budget will have included any proposals for changing taxation to raise revenue and these will be included in the Finance Bill introduced in about April, which has to receive the Royal Assent by 6 August. The Treasury and Civil Service Select Committee will have supplied a further report as background information for the second reading. The committee stage is taken partly in a committee of the whole House and partly in a Standing Committee. Many of these procedures, especially with regard to securing information, have evolved since the late 1970s.

A second feature of this House of Commons financial work is that various Estimates, Supplementary Estimates and Votes on Account are laid before Parliament during the year. They give a great deal of information under about twenty main classes, subdivided into nearly 200 votes, which cover the whole range of government expenditure. This service to

Parliament is of great importance in understanding the allocation of central government funds. The expenditure is authorized by Consolidated Fund Bills, which are taken formally.

Finally, at the end of the financial year lines need to be ruled, columns totalled and the accounts audited by the National Audit Office. They are then laid before the House as the Appropriate Accounts. It is the Public Accounts Committee which examines them, takes evidence from accounting officers (civil servants) and reports to the House. It is not policy that concerns the Committee but the administration of policy – 'efficiently, effectively and economically'.

A small library results from this House of Commons interest in economic affairs and its work concerning taxation and control of expenditure. The debates in the House include a day on the Autumn Statement, a day on the Government's expenditure plans, and the four or five days on the Budget. There is a day's debate on the second reading of the Finance Bill and then the debates during subsequent stages. There are three days of debate on the Estimates, with the subjects chosen by the Liaison Committee (a Select Committee including all the chairmen of the departmental Select Committee) after it has examined the work of the Public Accounts Committee and the departmental Select Committees. There is also a day spent debating the reports of the Public Accounts Committee itself. All these are to be found in Hansard [HC Deb., volume]. The Autumn Statement, the Financial Statement and Budget Report, the reports of the Treasury Committee, the Estimates and related material, and the reports of the Public Accounts Committee, together with the Government replies to those reports called Treasury Minutes, are published as House of Commons Papers [session, HC number]. Finally, the Government's expenditure plans are published as Command Papers.

Parliament's oversight work

The third main area of parliamentary work consists mostly of debate on Government policy and scrutiny of Government administration. Debates on policy may be based on a Government motion seeking approval, or, if conducted on one of the twenty days available to the Opposition each session, will normally be a motion of criticism. Debates may also be a backbench short adjournment debate before a holiday, a private member's motion on one of about nine Fridays each session, or a short, half-hour adjournment debate at the end of the day's proceedings. Whichever type of debate is used, some aspect of proposed policy is probed, new ideas are floated or the administration of agreed policy is challenged. In the last case the debates may be concerned with problems at constituency level. All this work is to be found published in Hansard [HC Deb. volume]. The House of

Lords, which does not need to spend its time either on constituency matters or on financial ones, has more time for considering wide-ranging subjects such as 'the arts' or 'conservation' and contributions to such debates are often very well prepared by a range of speakers with impressive credentials. The House of Lords also devotes more time to European Communities matters than the House of Commons is able to do. Their work is to be found in Hansard [HL Deb., volume].

The consideration of Government policy and the scrutiny of its administration is also the focus of Select Committee work. Select Committee inquiries on behalf of each House of Parliament have for centuries been the traditional means whereby Parliament gathers information. In the nineteenth century a highly developed Select Committee system not only provided an archive of published information superior to that found in any other country at the time, but, Whitehall being then only a small dot on the political–administrative landscape, was often the seed-bed of legislation, initiated by committee members on the basis of their findings in committee. Today, as we have seen, most bills are introduced by the Government. During much of the first half of the twentieth century, in the face of growing government powers stimulated by wartime conditions, regular Select Committee work was on a very modest scale, but in recent decades and especially since 1979 a much more co-ordinated approach to committee work has been adopted.[6] The fourteen House of Commons departmental Select Committees and the House of Lords European Communities' Committee with its seven sub-committees do set out to examine more systematically than hitherto the Government's policy concerning, and administration of, domestic matters, foreign affairs and some aspects of British membership of the European Communities.

The traditional method of work is to take written and oral evidence from the relevant government department (both the minister and his civil servants), to invite written evidence more generally and then maybe to select a number of specialist witnesses to give oral evidence. The oral evidence is normally published, sometimes on a sitting-by-sitting basis. The written evidence is also published but sometimes selectively. Written evidence from government departments would always be printed, and, with the committee's permission, witnesses may publish their own evidence. Written evidence reported by the committee but not ordered to be printed may be consulted in the House of Lords Record Office, which is mentioned later in this chapter. People take great pains in preparing evidence for Select Committees – they are a very good public platform – and for this reason all types of researchers find the evidence of interest. But these days it is very rare for reports and certainly for evidence to be indexed, which means both have to be examined very systematically. They are published as House of Commons Papers or House of Lords Papers.

If evidence is published on a sitting-by-sitting basis then it will have a roman sub-number for each sitting – for example, 1982–3 HC 285 i–v, indicating the publication of oral evidence taken on five occasions. For the most part, these House of Commons departmental committees are concerned with the domestic scene, though the Foreign Affairs Committee is one of the most active and prolific. The House of Lords European Communities Committee publishes the most far-ranging reports on EC matters, and they are more widely read in Europe than the reports of any other member parliament. In conclusion, it should not be forgotten that the committees may order evidence submitted to them to be printed even if they do not choose to make a report.

There are two further methods whereby Parliament can scrutinize the Government's performance and draw out information. One is the use of Parliamentary Questions tabled by individual members. In recent sessions the number of these probes has exploded. Oral questions for answer by ministers in the House remain at 6000–7000 a session, because the time devoted to them has not increased, but questions for written answer have more than doubled from less than 20,000 to more than 40,000 a session. All are indexed in the computer-based index POLIS (see below). From the viewpoint of researchers, the written answers to questions which are concerned far more with facts than with politics are especially important. Indeed, sometimes information is set down in such convenient form that one wonders whether it has been presented in this way specifically to help researchers. Ministers will, however, be told by their civil servants if the cost of answering a question is more than £200 and may sometimes decline to answer on the grounds of cost. Equally, ministers sometimes use written answers to release quite important information. Oral questions and answers are in the main text of Hansard. Written questions and answers are in a separately numbered sequence at the back of Hansard, and sometimes in their own issue called 'Part II' of a particular date.

The Government is also subject to scrutiny through the work of the Parliamentary Commissioner. Since 1967, members have been able to pass on to him complaints which they have received concerning maladministration by government. About 800 cases a year are examined. About a quarter of this number are pursued and the complainant has been upheld on about half of these occasions. The Commissioner works directly to a Select Committee of the House of Commons. He issues annual reports, a quarterly selection (about one third) of his case reports, and occasionally a report on a specially important case. With his high-level access to files, his probing can often be highly effective, his reports sometimes entertaining. Civil servants and ministers may be called to give evidence to the Select Committee, and this can be quite revealing of how policy decisions are arrived at and especially of how they are carried out.

How to find material

The published record of Parliament's work fills five to ten yards of shelving every session and is not the most straightforward of research material. It can be divided into three main groups. The first consists of the working papers – future programmes together with a record of what has taken place. Some of the latter material ends up in the Journal of each House, which is the permanent and legal record. The second group is the record of what was said. The third group consists of the papers laid before or created by Parliament. The following tabulation summarizes the material in each group.

1 *The record of what takes place*

HOUSE OF COMMONS

'Vote Bundle'

(a) Votes and Proceedings: minutes of the previous sitting; a list of papers laid before the House
(b) Order Paper: agenda for the day's sitting
(c) Notice Paper: motions to be moved, Parliamentary Questions to be asked in the future
(d) Division List: detailed results of votes
(e) Public Bill List: indicates the stage reached by Public Bills
(f) Supplement to the Vote: list of amendments to Public Bills

HOUSE OF LORDS

Minutes

(a) Minutes of the previous sitting; a list of papers laid before the House
(b) Notice of business for the next sitting day
(c) Notice of business for the next month
(d) Parliamentary Questions for written answer
(e) List of Public Bills
(f) List of future committee meetings

2 *The record of what is said*

	Frequency	*Indexes*
HOUSE OF COMMONS		
Official Report	Daily; weekly; fortnightly (volume)	Fortnightly; volume; session
Official Report, Standing Committees	Each sitting	None
HOUSE OF LORDS		
Official Report	Daily; volume	Cumulating by volume; session

3 *Papers*

	No. each session	Indexes
HOUSE OF COMMONS		
Public Bills	About 150	Sessional
House of Commons Papers	400–600	Sessional
Command Papers	About 350	Sessional
HOUSE OF LORDS		
Public Bills and Papers	200–300	None

(From 1987/8 these have been published as two series: (1) Bills, (2) House of Lords Papers)

These papers are all published by HMSO. Group 1 can only be purchased or part-purchased by subscription. In group 2, House of Commons debates are also available on microform from Pergamon Press. In Group 3, House of Commons papers can also be bought on microform from Chadwyck-Healey, Cambridge. Although groups 2 and 3 mostly have published indexes, the ability to retrieve information from these documents has recently been transformed by the introduction by the House of Commons Library of POLIS (Parliamentary On-Line Information System). Started in 1980, this computer-based index, compiled in the House of Commons Library, adds some 60,000 to 70,000 parliamentary references a session to the main database. From the general election of 1987 it has been run by Inspectorate UCC with Battelle BASIS software. It is available through a number of larger public and university libraries and is a very comprehensive index to all of Parliament's proceedings and papers. In addition, POLIS is used by the Library to prepare the indexes to the House of Commons Hansard and the sessional indexes to House of Commons Bills, Papers and Command Papers. This means that the subject terms used in the reports of the spoken word and in the parliamentary papers are being aligned, to the benefit of those seeking information. The full implications of this powerful information-retrieval system have yet to be realized by commentators, researchers and historians.

The following tabulation summarizes the coverage of parliamentary material by POLIS.

Parliamentary material	*Abbreviation*	*Starting date*
Proceedings		
Commons Hansard	CH	4 Nov. 1981
Commons Hansard (Legis)	CH	3 Nov. 1982
Lords Hansard	LH	4 Nov. 1981
Lords Hansard (Legis)	LH	3 Nov. 1982
Commons Standing Committee	SC	3 Nov. 1982
Early Day Motions	EDM	3 Nov. 1982

Questions
| Commons Questions | PQ | 27 Nov. 1980 |
| Lords Questions | LPQ | 4 Nov. 1981 |

Legislation
Public and General Acts	PGA	9 May 1979
Local and Personal Acts	LPA	3 Nov. 1982
Laid Statutory Instruments	SI	3 Nov. 1982

Papers
Commons Public Bills	Bill	9 May 1979
Command Papers	Cmnd, Cm	9 May 1979
Commons Papers	HC	9 May 1979
Lords Papers and Bills	HL	4 Nov. 1981

(From 1987/8 House of Lords Bills are abbreviated as HL Bill. House of Lords Papers continue as HL)

Collections of these papers are available in a number of places throughout the country. The HMSO catalogue *Government Publications* includes a list of those libraries, in addition to copyright libraries, that subscribe to official publications, and most of them hold a collection of parliamentary material. The catalogue advises a telephone call to ensure availability and gives the telephone numbers. The Public Information Office of the House of Commons Library, which is always ready to respond to letters and telephone calls, has prepared *Access to Parliamentary Resources and Information in London Libraries* (APRIL), a detailed union list of those public libraries in London and the South East which hold collections of parliamentary papers. A third edition was produced by the Library in 1987.

Finally, Parliament has its own record office for the public, the House of Lords Record Office, situated in the Victoria Tower in the Palace of Westminster. Apart from manuscripts dating back to 1497, it holds comprehensive collections of the printed sources mentioned in this chapter and has a public reading room open Monday to Friday, from 9.30 a.m. to 5 p.m. The staff have specialist knowledge not only of the bibliographical background but also, most importantly, of the historical and procedural background of Parliament's work. There is a *Guide to the Records of Parliament*[7] which lists and explains the various collections, and the Record Office publishes an annual list of new accessions as well as a number of memoranda on special aspects of the collection, which numbers some 3 million items.

Newly added to the Record Office are the sound archives, from the beginning of parliamentary broadcasting on 3 April 1978. At the moment these are available only to members and staff at Westminster, the broadcasting authorities and a number of academic and training organizations. The reason is lack of staff and space. It is likely, however, that the material over seven years old will be transferred to the National Sound Archive, where it would be readily available for consultation. There are also recordings of Select Committee evidence-taking sessions. Actually to hear the debates which have taken place at times of crisis might help to sharpen the flavour of historical writing. A selection of TV coverage of the House of Lords, started in January 1985, is also being added to the archive. Finally, the trial TV coverge of the House of Commons expected to start in late 1988 is likely to be added to the archive.

Conclusion

This chapter in some respects complements chapter 5, on public records. Parliament and government have been entwined for centuries, although their cultures are rather different. Government, like law, is sharply concerned with precedent and is conceived in privacy – hence the twenty-five years before the final selection of documents and the thirty-year rule governing access. Parliament, on the other hand, has changed from being a privileged, rather private club (it was only in this century that it offered the vote to all and took responsibility for reporting its own debates) to being an advocate of openness.[8] Democracy today means access to your constituency member, to the Palace of Westminster, to information. Though its means are procedures leaning on precedents, Parliament's end is public debate and a search for greater accountability. In the background the communications revolution of telephone, air travel, television, computers, and so forth, has virtually eliminated time and space and has transformed the scale and tempo of Parliament's work. The resulting accumulation of first-hand evidence offered by minister, civil servant, backbencher, specialist and citizen and made available in Parliament's published records is, not surprisingly, a vital resource for the contemporary historian.

The workings of Parliament have been transformed during the last generation. Consider a random list. The House of Commons has, by statute, separated itself completely from executive control. It has greatly increased its staff, by about 500 per cent in the information field. It has introduced significant allowances for members to pay for secretaries and personal research assistants. It has established a Public Information Office to help anyone who wishes to know of its work. By telephone, by letter, by publications such as the *Weekly Information Bulletin* and the *Sessional Information Digest*[9] it is, today, very easy for everyone to learn about its past and present proceedings. It has modernized and set in order its Record Office and added to this archive its broadcast and televised proceedings. It has gathered together its work in a computer-based indexing system, POLIS. It has introduced a positive and comprehensive Select Committee system and given members the opportunity to probe administration through the services of the Parliamentary Commissioner. The catalogue of change could be lengthened but suggests that those shelves of parliamentary debates, annual reports, accounts, committee reports, evidence, and so forth, which attempt to lay bare the way we are, are part of today's democratic accountability and as such are important contemporary evidence for the writing of history.

The words 'democratic accountability' have a fine ring; what do they really mean? One straw in the wind: a generation ago it would have been unthinkable for a minister to come and explain his conduct to a Select Committee. Today it is commonplace and is often broadcast too!

Appendix: official publications

While Parliament's papers are all published by Her Majesty's Stationery Office, the situation is less clear-cut with regard to other official publications. In recent years, although more material has been issued by government, its bibliographical control has become far less assured. Some of this material is closely related to the role of Parliament. The result is a grey area in official publishing which is a matter of concern to librarians, researchers and academic writers. Government departments are encouraged to apply their initiative in getting material published, with the result that today HMSO is publishing only a proportion of papers coming from the departments. Where HMSO is the publisher, details of the material will be found in the HMSO *Daily List*, the *Monthly Catalogue of Government Publications*, and *Government Publications*, the annual catalogue. If HMSO is not used, then details will probably be found in the *Catalogue of British Official Publications not Published by HMSO* (Chadwyck-Healey, Cambridge, 1980–), which appears six times a year, followed by an annual catalogue.

Below are some alphabetically arranged notes aimed at elucidating some of these areas.

Annual reports and accounts

A number of annual reports and annual accounts produced by government departments and agencies are laid before Parliament. But these do not provide any comprehensive survey of the work of particular departments. The Department of Education and Science's reports, published annually until 1985, did, however, provide at least a summary of developments in the education world in the year under review. Some of these departmental reports are ordered to be printed and are published as House of Commons Papers by HMSO. A small number of annual reports are Command Papers and are published by HMSO. A large number of annual reports are laid before Parliament but are published by the organization itself. If the organization uses HMSO, they will appear listed in *Government Publications*. If they publish through another method, and this happens in over 200 cases, they will probably appear in the *Catalogue of British Official Publications not Published by HMSO*.

Command Papers

Command Papers are presented to Parliament by a minister. They cover either a statement of policy (a White Paper or Blue Book) or information generally – for example, an annual report which has been made to a minister and then laid before Parliament. Command Papers have a prefix followed by a serial number between 1 and 9999. They were first numbered in 1836, and appear in the following series.

Nos	Dates
[1–4222]	1836–68/9
C 1 – C 9550	1870–99
Cd 1 – Cd 9239	1900–18
Cmd 1 – Cmd 9889	1919–55/6
Cmnd 1 – Cmnd 9927	1956/7–85/6
Cm 1 –	1986/7–

Departmental inquiries

Internal departmental inquiries are set up by civil servants or ministers. To what extent they 'go public' is a matter for the minister. Sometimes a report may be laid before Parliament. The evidence is not published. Researchers should approach the department direct. In time most of the papers should be found in the Public Record Office (see chapter 5). Chairmen may be traced in *British Government Publications: an index of chairmen and authors 1800–1982* (Library Association, 1974–84, 4 vols). The House of Commons Library compiles a Chairmen's Index which covers some of these inquiries and is available through POLIS. Unlike other compilations, it is based not on published reports but on earlier information in Parliamentary Questions, press notices, and so forth.

Green Papers

These consultation documents are Government proposals for policy inviting comment from anyone interested. The early ones, which first appeared from April 1967, were published in green covers as Command Papers. Today there appears to be no consistency in the way they are published. They are occasionally Command Papers but also appear as HMSO departmental publications, non-HMSO departmental publications or even restricted-circulation publications. The *House of Commons Weekly Information Bulletin* lists all those sent to Parliament together with the department issuing it and the closing date for comment. This is bibliographically a very untidy area.

Parliamentary papers

The usual definition covers Public Bills, House of Commons Papers and Command Papers and House of Lords Public Bills and Papers. The House of Commons Papers were arranged from 1800 to 1968/9 as Public Bills, Reports of Committees, Reports of Commissioners, and Accounts and Papers; from 1969/70 to 1979/80 as Public Bills, and Reports, Accounts and Papers; and from 1980/81 as Public Bills, House of Commons Papers and Command Papers, in these three sequences arranged numerically. House of Lords Public Bills and Papers were in one sequence until the end of 1986/7. From 1987/8 they are in two sequences, Public Bills and House of Lords Papers. There are no Command Papers in the House of Lords set. Published indexes to these papers exist for each session (it is a House of Commons Paper) and cumulated 1800–50, 1851–99, 1900–48/9, 1950–58/9, 1959/60–68/9. There is no cumulated index after 1968/9. House of Lords Papers have cumulated indexes 1801–59, 1859–70, 1871–84/5 but none during the twentieth century.

Royal Commissions

These are set up by the Government by Royal Warrant. There are a number of Standing Royal Commissions – for example, Ancient and Historical Monuments. Other Royal Commissions are set up to examine a specific topic, although the Conservative Government of 1979–87 did not make use of them. To date, thirty-two have been appointed since 1945 – the last, on Criminal Procedures, being set up in December 1977 and reporting in January 1981. Royal Commission reports are published as Command Papers, but their evidence is not a parliamentary paper, though published by HMSO. The Stationery Office Sectional List no. 59 lists Royal Commissions from 1937 to 1981. *British Government Publications: an index of chairmen and authors 1900–1940* (Library Association, 1974), pp. 168–74, includes a list of Royal Commissions from 1900 to 1940.

Treaty Series

Agreements with foreign countries or concerning commodities, and the like, are ratified by the Government after the text has been published for twenty-one days. After ratification they are published in the Treaty Series, in different languages if appropriate, as Command Papers. Lists of ratifications, accessions, and so on, are published every few months as Command Papers and an annual index is produced. A general index to the Treaty Series used to be published every three years or so, but this ceased after 1979.

White Papers

These are statements of Government policy published as Command Papers. The term 'Blue Book' was used when they were big enough to merit a blue cover. It is used less frequently today. See the section above on Command Papers.

Notes

1 Erskine May, *Treatise on the Law, Privileges, Proceedings and Usage of Parliament*, 20th edn, ed. Charles Gordon (Butterworth, 1983), p. 3.
2 *Conservative and Labour Party Conference Decisions 1945–1981*, compiled and ed. F. W. S. Craig (Parliamentary Research Services, 1982).
3 *British General Election Manifestos 1900–1974*, compiled and ed. F. W. S. Craig (Parliamentary Research Services, 1975).
4 *The Most Gracious Speeches to Parliament 1900–1974: statements of Government policy and achievements*, compiled and ed. F. W. S. Craig (Parliamentary Research Services, 1975).
5 See Dermot Englefield, *Whitehall and Westminster: Government informs Parliament: the changing scene* (Longman, 1985), pp. 80–91.

6 See Dermot Englefield (ed.), *Commons Select Committees: catalysts for progress?* (Longman, 1984). This includes (pp. 136–278) a comprehensive list of the work of the committees from 1979 to 1983, prepared with the aid of POLIS. A supplement listing the membership and reports of departmental Select Committees 1983–7 is available gratis from the publisher. See also Gavin Drewry, *The New Select Committees: a study of the 1979 reforms* (Clarendon Press, 1985; paperback edn with updating chapter, 1988).

7 Maurice F. bond, *Guide to the Records of Parliament*, (HMSO, 1971).

8 See the Croham Directive (1977) on Disclosures of Official Information, and the Memorandum of Guidance for Government Officials Appearing before Parliamentary Select Committees (1980). These are published as appendix 3 and appendix 2 of *Whitehall and Westminster* (see note 5 above). The Memorandum was reissued in late 1987.

9 The House of Commons *Weekly Information Bulletin* is published each Saturday during the session. The *Sessional Information Digest* is published a few weeks after the end of the session. Both are published by HMSO.

Part II

The Theatre of Contemporary History

This part of the book considers the study and writing of contemporary history in the modern and in the Classical world. The focus of this book is naturally on the most recent period, and chapters 8 and 9 survey the development of academic study of the period in Britain, in three other European countries and in the United States. But the writing of contemporary history is nothing new: Herodotus and Thucydides, among others, practised it; and so, to give the contemporary historian a better sense of perspective, chapter 10 looks at the writing of contemporary history in the Classical world. The chapter considers how the historians active in this period worked, why they wrote, what value that contemporaries attached to their work, and what value we today can place on it. Finally, chapter 11 returns to the modern world and, specifically, to the writing of biography, considering the extent to which an understanding of the role of individuals is essential to a grasp of history more generally.

The survey of attitudes towards contemporary history in different countries today reveals very different approaches. Britain and to an extent the United States lag behind the continental European countries considered. Almost every West German university, for example, has a chair in *Zeitgeschichte*; in British universities there are only two chairs of contemporary history, at Salford and Birkbeck College, London, and both embrace politics too. In France, since 1982, every schoolchild studying for the *baccalauréat* (400,000 every year) has had to prepare for an examination covering French history from 1939 to the present day. In Britain, barely a handful of A-level history students answer questions on post-1945 British history, and not all boards include questions on the period. In Italy, there is considerable academic writing and study of post-war history in universities. In Britain, by contrast, many university departments still do not run courses on British history since 1945, abandoning the subject altogether to politics departments, whose own courses are often not historically based.

In Britain there are signs that that sluggish beast, the history establishment, is waking up to the fact that Britain has lived through over four decades (to date) of the most compressed and fast-moving history of its existence. But the realization is painfully slow in coming. So too is it in the United States, where, as chapter 9 illustrates, the study of post-war American history still has to be established as a discrete area of study worthy of concentrated scholarly attention. The period is still left largely to journalistic histories and to political science departments. It would appear that these two English-speaking nations have much to learn from continental Europe and, indeed, from our forefathers in the Classical world.

8

Contemporary History in the Modern World: Europe

Britain

Anthony Seldon

A deep cloud of inertia hangs over the history establishment in Britain. We live in an era of the most exciting and rapid change in the country's history, yet few of our schoolchildren, history undergraduates, or, dare one say it, university historians, know much about the period, which has witnessed the end of Empire, the birth of the welfare state, the emergence of Britain as a nuclear power, and British accession to the European Economic Community, against a background of a generally declining economy and the attempts of successive Labour and Conservative administrations to find a role for Britain in a changing world. The inattention to such momentous developments indeed appears puzzling.

In practice it is not, because the British have never regarded the study of contemporary history very highly. When history became established as a firm subject in schools and universities at the end of the nineteenth century, periods beyond the Napoleonic Wars were seldom studied.[1] Llewellyn Woodward reminds us that the *English Historical Review* from its first number in 1886 until after 1918 did not print a single article on English domestic history after 1852.[2] He notes further that the syllabus of the Modern History School at Oxford in 1914 excluded English political history after 1837.

The First World War provided a major boost, spawning an unprecedented burst of literature, and flooding the library of the Imperial War Museum in London within ten years of the armistice with over 13,000 books and pamphlets on the war. The war also precipitated a novel release of government papers by the Soviet Union from 1917, and by Germany from 1918.[3] In Britain, the Government decided that it too should be releasing documents on the war, and from 1930 started to publish a massive series.[4] The Royal Institute of International Affairs was founded in 1920 in the wake of the war, providing a further stimulus. But were these developments enough to ensure that students in the 1930s would learn about the origins and course of the war that had so affected their lives? 'I deplore', wrote Sir Charles Oman angrily in 1939, 'the present trend away from the preliminary centuries towards the very last periods that are permissible. . . . Someone lately called the curriculum "the School of *Very* Modern History".'[5] One might be forgiven for assuming that the history frontier had at last indeed crept forward on the verge of the new war. Not so. Even in 1946 the Oxford modern history degree terminated in 1878.[6]

The post-war period has seen conservatism again triumph, at least as regards syllabuses. The predictable flood of literature followed the Second World War, outstanding early examples being Lewis Namier's *Diplomatic Prelude 1938–39*, Chester Wilmot's *The Struggle for Europe*, and Hugh Trevor-Roper's *The Last Days of Hitler*.[7] Looking back on his work nearly forty years after the events described, Trevor-Roper (Lord Dacre of Glanton) wrote, 'My evidence was largely "contemporary oral evidence"; even my documents were, in large part, contemporary oral evidence written down. What makes them more accurate, in some respects, than later reconstructions is this contemporaneity: the evidence was given when it was fresh.'[8] Not even the imprimatur of such a distinguished historian flexing his muscles on recent history, however, nor the legions of good and great historians who came to work on the massive official history of the war and its origins,[9] were sufficient to convince others that the diplomatic history of the 1930s and the events leading up to the war were subjects worthy of study, not at least until a number of years after 1945.

-Major events were meanwhile occurring in the history world which should have made the study of contemporary history more attractive. The most notable of these was the Public Records Act of 1958. In the 1940s, the latest documents available for consultation at the Public Record Office were dated 1885, and for most of the 1950s the terminal date was 1902. The new Act ensured that year by year, without the need to lobby, most documents fifty years old would become available for inspection. The procedures for selecting documents for preservation were also standardized and improved.[10] In 1967, after a prolonged campaign, the Labour Government of Harold Wilson was persuaded to pass a new Public Records Act reducing the period after which documents became available from fifty years to thirty, issuing forth a rich harvest of documents on the inter-war years. Historians were not slow to capitalize on the cornucopia, one of the first fruits being Keith Middlemas and John Barnes's *Baldwin* (1969).[11] Other events, such as the transmutation of the Wiener Library into the Institute of Contemporary History in 1965, and the establishment of the Social Science Research Council in 1966, served to boost the cause of contemporary history, though in later years the SSRC, some felt, failed to give adequate support.

Yet again, developments proved insufficient to swing the study of history towards the contemporary period. Even the take-up by sixth-form A-level history students of questions on the inter-war years is negligible.[12] In 1987 there are still several universities that do not offer courses on post-war history. Insignificant numbers answer questions on post-1945 history at A-level, and pre-A-level students barely study the period, although the new GCSE exam will provide a boost.

The Institute of Contemporary British History, established in 1986 in London, is merely the latest body to enter into the long debate about the proper 'end point' for the study of history. It would be pleasant to conclude this report on Britain on an optimistic note, but the signs are still not very encouraging.

Notes

1 See E. A. Fulton's paper presented to the London Branch of the Historical Association in 1913, reprinted as 'The teaching of contemporary history', *History*, July 1928, pp. 118–25.

2 Llewellyn Woodward, 'The study of contemporary history', *Journal of Contemporary History*, 1, no. 1 (1966).

3 F. W. Pick, 'Contemporary history: method and man', *History*, March 1946, pp. 32–3.

4 Gavin Henderson, 'A plea for the study of contemporary history', *History*, June 1941.

5 Sir Charles Oman, *On the Writing of History* (1939) p. 255, quoted by Pick in *History*, March 1946, p. 29.

6 Pick, ibid.

7 L. A. Namier, *Diplomatic Prelude 1938–39* (Macmillan, 1948); Charles Wilmot, *The Struggle for Europe* (Collins, 1952); H. R. Trevor-Roper, *The Last Days of Hitler* (Macmillan, 1947).

8 Letter, Lord Dacre of Glanton to authors, 8 April 1982, quoted in Anthony Seldon and Joanna Pappworth, *By Word of Mouth* (Methuen, 1983), p. 171.

9 The Foreign Office authorized the publication in the 1950s of the eleven-volume series *British Documents on the Origins of the War*, ed. G. P. Gooch and Harold Temperley.

10 The message of the 1958 and 1967 Acts is discussed in Donald C. Watt's article 'Contemporary history: problems and perspectives', *Bulletin of the Society of Archivists*, 1968.

11 Keith Middlemas and John Barnes, *Baldwin* (Heinemann, 1969).

12 Anthony Seldon and Stephen Howarth 'Plugging the gap', *The Times Education Supplement*, 29 May 1987.

The Federal Republic of Germany

Norbert Frei

The term *Zeitgeschichte* (contemporary history) combines two separate words, *Zeit* and *Geschichte* ('time' and 'history'). The German language is infamous for this habit, but *Zeitgeschichte* makes sense as a rare example of terminological clarification. Even good words and clear terms go unused, however, and for a long time this was the case with *Zeitgeschichte*. According to the Grimm brothers' German dictionary, the word *Zeitgeschichte* dates back to the seventeenth century,[1] but historians took it up only after 1945.

Zeitgeschichte arose as a scholarly term in Germany after the Second World War. Contemporary history was by no means a new academic field, but until 1945 examination of the recent past had no significant tradition in the writing and teaching of history in Germany. That its probably one reason why many historians after the Second World War saw the idea of *Zeitgeschichte* as something totally new.[2] This view neglected the fact that during the Weimar Republic scholarly historians were heavily involved in the discussion of German war guilt in 1914 – a highly political topic. Furthermore, it failed to take into account classic studies in contemporary history such as Arthur Rosenberg's books on the foundation of the Wilhelmine Reich and the Weimar Republic.[3]

Despite this, in the late 1940s and the 1950s the academic study of *Zeitgeschichte* was primarily perceived as a consequence of Germany's Nazi experience. In historical research as in many other academic fields, the Third Reich disrupted lines of continuity.[4] A consensus arose among historians that they should assist any attempts to investigate and interpret National Socialist rule. Both politically and morally this was an appropriate reaction, since the community of scholars was under suspicion of 'spiritual' collaboration with the Nazi regime.

Thus it was no surprise that prominent historians welcomed the foundation in 1947, by the *Länder* (states) of the US Zone of Occupation, of the Institut zur Erforschung der nationalsozialistischen Politik (Institute for Research on National Socialist Politics). The independent Munich-based Institute was set up as the central organization for the scholarly evaluation of National Socialist records. In 1952 its name was changed to the Institut für Zeitgeschichte (Institute of Contemporary History),[5] and shortly afterwards it began publishing a new quarterly journal, the *Vierteljahrshefte für Zeitgeschichte*. Hans Rothfels, who in 1934 had been removed from his professorship in Königsberg by the National Socialists and had lived in exile in the United States until 1950, became its editor. The first issue included Rothfels' article 'Zeitgeschichte als Aufgabe' ('Contemporary history as a challenge'), with its often-quoted definition of *Zeitgeschichte* as the *'Epoche der Mitlebenden und ihre wissenschaftliche Behandlung'* ('epoch of the contemporary and its scholarly analysis').[6]

According to Rothfels, *Zeitgeschichte* originated in 1917–18, when a 'new epoch in world history began to make its appearance'.[7] At first, nobody seemed to notice the rigidity of Rothfels' periodization. During the 1950s and 1960s *Zeitgeschichte* was commonly understood as the history of the Third Reich and the Weimar Republic; but over time historians have recognized that *Zeitgeschichte* cannot be so restricted. Since the early 1970s, most historians have considered the period of Allied occupation and the founding years of the Federal Republic and the German Democratic Republic as a genuine part of *Zeitgeschichte*. This does not mean, however, that the Weimar period is now classified as a subject of modern history instead of *Zeitgeschichte*. As the direct predecessor of the Third Reich, the Weimar Republic is still a crucial theme of any historical research into National Socialism. Nevertheless, German history after the Second World War is of growing importance for the scholars in the field of *Zeitgeschichte*.

German historians first began writing on National Socialism, the 'adverse subject', hesitantly. After twelve years of Hitler's rule, prominent historians such as Friedrich Meinecke had been reduced to a state of shocked resignation. Meinecke's famous *Die deutsche Katastrophe* ('The German Catastrophe', 1946)[8] not only reflected the helplessness of a generation of historians who shared the traditional values of conservatism and nationalism that the National Socialists had brutally abused; it also indicated that the prerequisites of thorough historical research were lacking: documents and source materials.

The fact that the Allies confiscated all state and party documents which had not been destroyed by the National Socialists made it even more difficult to uncover the political reality of the Third Reich. During the immediate post-war years German historians had to rely almost exclusively on copies of documents prepared for the Nuremberg Trial (the so-called Nuremberg documents). The situation did not change significantly until the late 1950s, when the United States became the first of the Allies to return captured documents.[9] Only then did precise investigation of the history of the Third Reich become possible. The historians who accepted the burden of empirical research into the Third Reich belonged to the Hitler Youth generation, and many of them had been young soldiers when the war ended.[10] With great devotion they started to piece together, like detectives, 'what had really happened'.

In contrast to their teachers, who were mainly engaged in a search for general explanations of the 'unexplainable', the younger generation was interested in facts. A fresh, pragmatic approach was typical of their research in institutions such as the Institut für Zeitgeschichte in Munich, the Hamburger Forschungsstelle für den Nationalsozialismus (Hamburg Agency for Research into National Socialism) and in some universities (Berlin, Cologne). Their historical writing, based on examination of the relevant facts and documents, was remarkably little influenced by an approach which at that time began to dominate the social sciences: the theory of totalitarianism. Impressively applied in Hannah Arendt's study of the National Socialist regime,[11] the concept of totalitarianism underwent – particularly in the United States – a transformation into an almost ahistorical theory of great importance during the Cold War, because it suggested clear parallels between the Hitler and the Stalin regimes.[12]

When the Auschwitz Trial opened in Frankfurt in 1963, a new phase of historical research into National Socialism began. With large sections of German society apparently favouring a settling of accounts with the past, the judicial system of the Federal Republic now took a tough line in its investigations. Not only public morale but also historical research benefited from the efforts to bring Nazi war criminals to justice.[13]

The emphasis on German barbarities committed in Poland and Russia twenty years earlier suddenly turned the spotlight on a generation of accessaries implicated in the wartime atrocities. The young recognized among them their own parents, who had fallen into shamed silence. The conflict between the two generations, coupled with a new scholarly interest in the 'era of fascism',[14] prompted a renaissance of leftist theories of fascism. What followed were agonizing and sometimes absurd discussions about the general structure and actual forms of fascism. For many young people it seemed to be the only way to protest against what they viewed as a terrible lack of moral awareness on the part of West Germany's self-satisfied and prosperous society. The discussion was a political one, and overlooked the need for a fresh scholarly approach to contemporary history. The production of literature on fascism was impressive; but its contribution to historical knowledge of Nazi Germany was slight.

German *Zeitgeschichte* in the 1970s experienced a controversy between the advocates of a traditional history of policy and politics, and (mostly younger) scholars engaged in social history. The usefulness of the concepts of totalitarianism and fascism for historical analysis was at stake. The main question was whether the Third Reich should be described as a monocratic or a polycratic system.[15] The discussion, which after a few years declined into fruitless polemics, sprang up within the context of a highly specialized interest in National Socialism. It started with a new focus on regional studies. Some of the historians engaged in such work also tried to make use of sociological quantification methods, which were particularly popular at the time. Most recentiy, these trends seem to have been absorbed into the fashionable concept of *Alltagsgeschichte*, discussed in the next section.

The controversy over the structure of the Third Reich helped stimulate new historical research on National Socialism. As a result, the interpretation of the Third Reich as a monolithic *Führer* state has been discarded. British and American historians played an important part in this highly specialized research, and still do. [16]

Recognition of National Socialism as a crucial area of research in the history of the twentieth century had come much earlier, however. German immigrants to the United States, followed by British and American writers and scholars, were the first to analyse the Third Reich, [17] and the topic remains one of the most widely studied in international historical research. In particular, the question of the reactionary or revolutionary nature of the regime provokes persistent debate. Ralf Dahrendorf's thesis put forward in 1965, [18] that National Socialist rule unwittingly completed the modernization of German society, is still being discussed. Another reason for the extraordinary attention devoted to the subject derives from the apprehension of National Socialism as a paradigm for the forces of destruction inherent in modern mass societies. This viewpoint amply justifies the moral interpretation of the Holocaust as a terrible lesson that the world must not be allowed to forget.

That is why scholarly history should oppose an abridged, 'pedagogical' interpretation of National Socialism and the Holocaust. Cut off from attention to the complicated historical realities, history becomes lifeless and the moral lessons to be drawn from it are turned into empty platitudes. With respect to future historical research, it will become even more important to explain National Socialism and its impact within the context of Germany's political and social structure, both before and after Hitler. Without new efforts at precise historical interpretation and evaluation, as Martin Broszat pointed out, [19] we risk reverting to simplistic readings such as the old one which characterizes National Socialism as an 'accident' in Germany's history.

The dangers of compartmentalization are evident also for German history after the Second World War, which by now can be regarded as the main area of research for the majority of contemporary historians in West Germany.

Until the late 1960s, research on the foundation and political development of the two Germany states was conducted almost exclusively by political scientists. The absence of historians from this field was in part owing to the lack of original source material. While all party and government records of the Third Reich had been made available for historical research without any restriction, nothing similar could be expected for the post-war period. Contemporary historians in Germany had to accept the usual archival procedures of declassification and limited access found in other countries.

Historical research on post-war Germany in its beginnings focused mainly on the foundation and development of new political institutions, the reorganization of the *Länder*, and other crucial political problems, such as Allied post-war planning and the 'German Question'. Comparative studies became more and more important, and the need for collective self-assessment arose. It was not surprising that the title of a 1956 book by Fritz René Allemann, a Swiss journalist, came to serve as winged words: *Bonn ist nicht Weimar* ('Bonn is not Weimar'). More sceptical individuals, however, added a question-mark.

During the 1968 student rebellion, discomfort over the prevailing political self-righteousness turned into sharp protest against glorification of the German post-war achievements. The writing of contemporary history, it was argued, would decline into mere apology if former political alternatives were ignored by concentrating only on actual developments. Interest grew in socialist ideas of a 'third way', which had been overtaken by economic reconstruction, the foundation of the West German state and rearmament. Owing in part to the lack of source material, the wave of new and 'critical' post-war studies tended to produce ideological legends as well. The term *Restauration* ('restoration'), current in the 1950s as an accusation of the 'old' Left, became the slogan for the attempt to unmask as nothing but conservative propaganda the notion that the years 1945–9 had marked a profound new start (*Neuaufbau*) in democracy.[20]

Historical research has since moved beyond such black-and-white contrasts as *Neuaufbau* versus *Restauration*; the scholarly debate has become more factual and differentiated.[21] This development has been greatly assisted by the *de facto* rule allowing the release of archive material after thirty years, which means that, from the mid-1970s on, official German documents of the post-war period have become gradually available.[22] In addition, a considerable improvement took place when the Allies opened the files of their former military governments in Germany; the most generous were the Americans, who allowed an almost complete duplication of their records.[23] As a result of this access of information, a growing number of studies focusing on the immediate post-war period, the years of Allied rule and the early years of the Federal Republic have been produced.[24] Most recently, historians have tried to overcome, with ambitious overviews, the caesura marked by the end of Allied rule in 1955.[25] The gradual and sometimes delayed release of documents is not the only reason for this development. Perhaps more important, it has to do with general methodological problems German contemporary history is facing for the first time: while the Nazi period, and even more the period of military government in Germany from 1945 to 1949, can be characterized to some extent as distinct eras (though this is not to say that they can be separated from their historical context), the history of the Federal Republic can be compartmentalized only provisionally. As a result, it is much more difficult to make profound historical judgements about it. Now, contemporary historians in Germany have to deal with the same kind of problems and questions as their colleagues in Western Europe and the United States.

This is certainly a challenge, but it is also an opportunity for the integration of new perspectives and methodological flexibility. In this regard, it is encouraging to note an improvement in intellectual openness. For example, there is a strong interest among German historians in 'history from below' (*Alltagsgeschichte*), and a considerable number of contemporary historians are using the oral-history method.[26] The strong interest of both the public and the media in anything to do with 'history' has undoubtedly had a positive impact on the output of contemporary historians.

In the Federal Republic today, the study of contemporary history demands high standards and enjoys a solid academic standing. Almost every university has a chair of *Zeitgeschichte*, many commissions and working groups exist, and several public and private foundations are sponsoring research projects in contemporary history. In addition to the research institutions specializing in contemporary history, the political parties, trade unions and churches have valuable archives and also commission research work.[27] All this clearly helps strengthen *Zeitgeschichte* as a genuine part of historiography, though it is important to make sure that it does not simply lead to a proliferation of competing partisan perspectives.

One way of avoiding such dangers is through the establishment of a range of interdisciplinary and international contacts. This might very well result in a German contemporary history interested more in questions of social change and changes in attitudes, and less confined to the field of political history, compartmentalized along traditional lines. The added depth and breadth this would bring to the study of contemporary history would be to the benefit of our overall historical understanding.

Notes

1 Jacob and Wilhelm Grimm, *Deutsches Wörterbuch*, vol. XV (Deutscher Taschenbüch Verlag, Munich, reprinted 1984), col. 559f.
2 See Eberhard Jäckel, 'Begriff und Funktion der Zeitgeschichte', in Eberhard Jäckel and Ernst Weymar (eds), *Die Funktion der Geschichte in unserer Zeit* (Ernst Klett, Stuttgart, 1975), pp. 162–76. Jäckel's article corrects some rather tenacious errors and misunderstandings. For the development of German historiography in general see Georg G. Iggers, *The German Conception of History: the national tradition of historical thought from Herder to the present* (Wesleyan University Press, Middletown, Conn., 1968).
3 Arthur Rosenberg, *Entstehung und Geschichte der Weimarer Republik* (Europäische Verlags-Anstalt, Frankfurt-am-Main, 1955).
4 See Helmut Heiber, *Walter Frank und sein Reichsinstitut für Geschichte des neuen Deutschlands* (Deutsche Verlags-Anstalt, Stuttgart, 1966).

128   *The Theatre of Contemporary History*

5 For details see Hellmuth Auerbach, 'Die Gründung des Instituts für Zeitgeschichte', in *Vierteljahrshefte für Zeitgeschichte* (hereafter *VfZ*), 18 (1970), pp. 529–54. Upon request, a brochure on projects and collections is available from the Institut für Zeitgeschichte, Leonrodstrasse 46b, D-8000 München 19.

6 Hans Rothfels, 'Zeitgeschichte als Aufgabe', *VfZ*, 1 (1953), p. 2; for further literature see Martin Broszat, 'Aufgaben und Probleme zeitgeschichtlichen Unterrichts', *Geschichte in Wissenschaft und Unterricht*, 8 (1957), pp. 529–50, n. 1.

7 Rothfels, in *VfZ*, 1, p. 6 (italicized in the original).

8 Friedrich Meinecke, *Die deutsche Katastrophe: Betrachtungen und Erinnerungen* (Brockhaus, Wiesbaden, 1946).

9 See Josef Henke, 'Das Schicksal deutscher zeitgeschichtlicher Quellen in Kriegs- und Nachkriegszeit. Beschlagnahme, Rückführung, Verbleib', *VfZ*, 30 (1982), pp. 557–620.

10 See, as an example, the (auto-)biographical remarks of Ernst Nolte, 'Zeitgeschichtsforschung und Zeitgeschichte', *VfZ*, 18 (1970), pp. 1–11.

11 Hannah Arendt, *The Origins of Totalitarianism* (Harcourt, Brace, New York, 1951).

12 See (also as an excellent general introduction) Ian Kershaw, *The Nazi Dictatorship: problems and perspectives of interpretation* (Edward Arnold, London, 1985); and, for a re-examination of the debate by some of the participants, *Totalitarismus und Faschismus: eine wissenschaftliche und politische Begriffskontroverse* (R. Oldenbourg, Munich and Vienna, 1980).

13 This is the place to mention the excellent work of the Zentrale Stelle der Landesjustizverwaltungen in Ludwigsburg; see the publications of its former chief, Adalbert Rückerl – in particular *NS-Verbrechen vor Gericht: Versuch einer Vergangenheitsbewältigung*, 2nd edn (C. F. Müller, Heidelberg, 1984).

14 Ernst Nolte, *Der Faschismus in seiner Epoche. Die Action française – Der italienische Faschismus – Der Nationalsozialismus* (Piper, Munich, 1963); tr. into English as *The Three Faces of Fascism* (London, 1965).

15 The controversy found its most significant expression in a conference volume edited by Gerhard Hirschfeld and Lothar Kettenacker: *Der Führerstaat: Mythos und Realität* (Ernst Klett, Stuttgart, 1981). See Karl Dietrich Bracher, *Zeitgeschichtliche Kontroversen: um Faschismus, Totalitarismus, Demokratie* (Piper, Munich, 1976), for position of the author of pioneering books on Weimar and National Socialism.

16 One of the first local case studies was William Sheridan Allen's *The Nazi Seizure of Power: the experience of a single German town 1930–1935* (Quadrangle Books, Chicago, 1965); it is still worth consulting. Among the most important British and American contributors to research on the Third Reich, mention should be made of David Schoenbaum, Dietrich Orlow, Edward N. Peterson, Tim Mason, Ian Kershaw, Jeremy Noakes, Geoffrey Pridham and Richard Bessel.

17 It seems to me impossible to justify any selection which could be published here as a note; for bibliographical details see Peter Hüttenberger, *Bibliographie zum Nationalsozialismus* (Vandenhoeck und Ruprecht, Göttingen, 1980), and the quarterly bibliography of the *VfZ*, which is also available in three volumes as *Bibliographie zur Zeitgeschichte 1953–1980* (K. G. Saur, Munich, 1982).

18 The English version appeared three years later: Ralf Dahrendorf, *Society and Democracy in Germany* (London, 1968). For an interesting discussion of Dahrendorf's argument and the concept of modernization in general, see Kershaw, *The Nazi Dictatorship*, pp. 130–48.

19 Martin Broszat, *Nach Hitler: Der schwierige Umgang mit unserer Geschichte* (R. Oldenbourg, Munich, 1986), p. 109ff.

20 See for example Rolf Badstübner and Sigrid Thomas, *Restauration und Spaltung: Enstehung und Entwicklung der BRD* (Pahl-Rugenstein, Cologne, 1975).

21 See Christoph Klessmann, *Die doppelte Staatsgründung: Deutsche Geschichte 1945–55* (Vandenhoeck und Ruprecht, Göttingen, 1982), pp. 12 and 296–303 (with a comprehensive bibliography).

22 *Akten zur Vorgeschichte der Bundesrepublik-Deutschland 1945–1949*, 5 vols (R. Oldenbourg, Munich, 1976–83); *Wörtliche Berichte und Drucksachen des Wirtschaftsrates des Vereinten Wirtschaftsgebietes 1947–1949*, 5 vols (R. Oldenbourg, Munich and Vienna, 1977); *Die Kabinettsprotokolle der Bundesregierung* (Boldt, Boppard), vol. I: *1949* (1982), vol. II: *1950* (1984), continuing.

23 For details see Hermann Weiss, 'Abschlussbericht über das OMGUS-Projekt 1976–1983', *VfZ*, 32 (1984), pp. 318–26.

24 See in particular Ludolf Herbst (ed.), *Westdeutschland 1945–1955: Unterwerfung, Kontrolle, Integration* (R. Oldenbourg, Munich, 1986).

25 See Karl Dietrich Bracher, Theodor Eschenburg, Joachim C. Fest and Eberhard Jäckel (eds), *Geschichte der Bundesrepublik Deutschland,* 5 vols (Deutsche Verlags-Anstalt, Stuttgart, and Brockhaus, Wiesbaden, 1981–).

26 The most inspiring example of what can be achieved by this method is provided by the results of Lutz Niethammer's project in the Ruhr: *Lebensgeschichte und Sozialkultur im Ruhrgebiet 1930 bis 1960,* 3 vols (J. H. W. Dietz Nachf., 1983–). For general information and a bibliography see *Alltagsgeschichte der NS-Zeit: neue Perspektive oder Trivialisierung?* (R. Oldenbourg, Munich, 1984).

27 See *Jahrbuch der historischen Forschung in der Bundesrepublik* (Ernst Klett, Stuttgart, 1974–81; K. G. Saur, Munich, from 1982). For information on archives, Wolfgang Benz, *Deutsche Geschichte seit dem Ersten Weltkrieg,* vol. III: *Quellen zur Zeitgeschichte* (Deutsche Verlags Anstalt, Stuttgart, 1973), is still worth consulting.

France

François Bédarida

The term *histoire contemporaine* ('contemporary history') is used in France in a fashion that is both ambiguous and misleading. Traditionally it has been applied to the period from 1789 to the present day, which represents a complete break with its original meaning. Behind this apparent illogicality, however, lies a profound logic, based on the view that the French Revolution, with its associated notions of the rights of man and the principles of liberty, equality and fraternity, was a seminal event in history, the point of departure for our modern society. According to this interpretation (viewed as self-evident by liberal-democratic ideology), all the events of human history since, and therefore arising out of, the French Revolution form a whole that is close to us and constitutes our political world, our society and our culture. This is why the whole period merits the term 'contemporary'.

But this definition has come to seem increasingly unsatisfactory and inadequate. On the one hand, from a purely practical point of view, the passage of time has made this 'period' disproportionately large and unwieldy, stretching the meaning of 'contemporary' to breaking point. On the other hand, as the French Revolution has become progressively more distant and has lost its sacred character (a process paralleled by the demise of the philosophy of progress stemming from the Enlightenment), it has seemed less and less justifiable to see 1789 as the origin and point of departure of the contemporary era. None the less, this point of view had been so entrenched in the universities, in secondary schools and even among the general public that it is only very recently that it has become normal to distinguish a period of more truly contemporary history.

This has been achieved by coining a new term, *temps présent*, to escape from the ambiguity of traditional terms and to restore the original meaning of 'contemporary' – that is to say, the idea that the historian has himself lived through the events he is studying. The introduction and the subsequent popularization of this expression, within the space of just a few years, are directly linked, as we shall see later on, to the creation by the Centre National de la Recherche Scientifique of a new institution, the Institut d'Histoire du Temps Présent. The rival term *histoire immédiate* enjoyed a brief vogue in the 1970s, but has now largely passed out of use.

The study of *temps présent* history (under whatever name) has an impressive pedigree in France. Its practitioners include Froissart and Commines, Thiers and Michelet, Elie Halévy and André Siegfried, Marc Bloch and Lucien Febvre (one has further only to think of the first volumes of *Annales* in the 1930s or the work *L'Etrange défaite*). So many distinguished academics and historians have written contemporary history with distinction that the historians of today may follow them and hold their heads high.

However, the long period of dominance of the positivist school, with its narrow conception of objectivity and concomitant insistence on verifiable sources, was prejudicial to the study of 'very contemporary' history. This explains why, during the greater part of the twentieth century, notably the period from the start of the First World War to the beginning of the 1970s, the field of recent history was largely abandoned by French historians to specialists of other social sciences – to political scientists, sociologists, geographers or economists – or else to scholars abroad, principally from North America. One of the very few French historians to venture into this field, René Rémond, made a vain appeal to academics in 1957 in an outstanding article in the *Revue Française de Science Politique*, entitled 'Plaidoyer pour une histoire délaissée' (in translation, 'An apology for an abandoned period of history'). His appeal fell on stony ground.

However, certain major events – in particular, the convulsions produced by the two world wars – have had an impact on the theory and practice of contemporary history in France. After the First World War, Pierre Renouvin was immediately given the task of founding a centre for documentation of the years 1914–18. This centre, both library and museum, was to be the germ of the Bibliothèque de Documentation Internationale Contemporaine, an important institution of research into contemporary French and foreign history. Renouvin made himself famous at a stroke with the publication of a work that has become a classic on a subject that was at that time a burning controversy: the origins of the declaration of war in 1914. Equally, after the Second World War, the Commission d'Histoire de l'Occupation et de la Libération de la France was established by Edouard Perroy (a medievalist) and Georges Bourgin (an archivist). This commission was eventually transformed into the Comité d'Histoire de la Deuxième Guerre Mondiale, under the direction of Henri Michel. Like the centre set up after the First World War, the Commission was given the task of collecting evidence and initiating research on a dramatic period that was still fresh in people's memories. It must also be pointed out that the Algerian war and the 'events' of May 1968 produced a spate of studies and other publications issued hot on the heels of the events they recorded and interpreted.

But it was in the late 1970s that a real turning point was reached, producing a renaissance in the study of recent history. (The methodological advances of French historians over the preceding twenty-five years had been principally centred on the sixteenth to eighteenth centuries.) This turning point can be defined in terms of three main areas: research, sources and mass education.

In the field of research, the turning point came in 1978, with the foundation of the Institut d'Histoire du Temps Présent, a 'laboratory' for research into national and international history since 1939. During the earlier 1970s there had been a growing awareness of the need for historians to bring to bear their own methods and expertise in a field where other social sciences had already done pioneering work. The Centre National de la Recherche Scientifique responded by setting up the Institut, which absorbed the Comité d'Histoire de la Deuxième Guerre Mondiale and took up the challenging task of structuring research in the strategically vital area where past, present and future meet. The description of the Institut as a 'laboratory' is appropriate: the post-war world has witnessed rapid change, and the attempt to explore and understand it necessarily involves experimentation and risk, as well as presenting tremendous opportunities for the intrepid researcher. The Institut is thus not only an expression of new trends in historiography, but also an expression of the will of a society in crisis to understand its own present and master its future – a society in search, above all, of roots and identity.

The turning point as regards sources came in 1979, when a new law governing archives was passed, profoundly altering the legal position and conditions of access. Under the new law, official documents became available for inspection by scholars thirty years after their creation, but the situation was still further improved by the very liberal fashion in which most archivists interpreted the law, and the law's provision for *dérogations* granting access to closed material on application. All this provided researchers with facilities quite unknown before 1979, and helped them forge a new, closer relationship with the past. Moreover, the whole concept of 'archives' has broadened significantly. Oral evidence, cinema and television, and, most recently, computerized data have all proved valuable sources for the contemporary historian and are playing an increasingly important role in research. Symbolic of this change is the fact that in 1986 the congress of French archivists, concerned to prepare for the future, took as the theme of their deliberations the 'new archives'.

Finally, at the level of mass education, a highly important event took place in 1982 which affected the whole relationship between history and contemporary society and culture: this was the introduction of the study of modern history from 1939 to the present day into the syllabuses of the top classes in French *lycées*. If one bears in mind the importance of the *baccalauréat* in forming the minds of Frenchmen and the fact that history is a compulsory subject, then the fact that each year 400,000 young Frenchmen are having to study the great events and movements of the most recent era appears in its proper perspective. From the beginning the experiment proved a success, owing to the keen interest shown by pupils in developments intimately related to their present lives.

All this has contributed to the current vitality of the study of contemporary history in France. It is encouraging too to note the role played by the traditional centres of learning, such as the Fondation Nationale des Sciences Politiques, where contemporary history has always enjoyed serious attention, and the universities, where there is increasing research into the *temps présent* (as, for example, in the universities of Paris I, Paris IV, Paris VII, Paris VIII, Paris X, Paris XII, Lille, Strasbourg, Lyons, Bordeaux, Toulouse, Montpellier, Aix-en-Provence and Rennes). All in all, France is witnessing a vigorous renaissance of attention to contemporary history, with exploration of new methodologies, rich and varied source material, and fresh and challenging lines of inquiry.

Italy
Gaetano Grassi

In Italy in the last decade there has been a considerable growth of interest in contemporary history, mirrored in the increased demand for books on the subject on the part of the general public and university students.[1] This change has taken place in a climate increasingly favourable to the idea of contemporary history; the thesis that the views of those who have experienced the recent past (or even the present) are of no 'historical' value is now no longer accepted. Indeed, it is now generally held that examination of the present *must* be based on a proper understanding of the recent past, 'which is best revealed to us by those who have lived through those very recent times'.[2]

So the gap between the present and the past is in the post-war generation a good deal narrower. The fall of the twenty-year dictatorship in 1945 and the new perspectives of the more recent era have opened up a quite new kind of debate in relation to the political ideas, social progress and economic reforms that have marked Italy under democratic republican government. Nor are these new horizons restricted to the post-war era. They facilitate also a reassessment of all those issues that have filtered through to us from the years of Fascist rule, the Second World War and the period of the resistance. 'Italian historical thought', writes Pavone, 'began to pose itself new questions, and at the same time to redefine problems from a conceptual and emotional standpoint which was quite different from that adopted by the men of the previous decades.'[3]

Initially, historical writing about the period 1923–45 was somewhat restricted. It would perhaps have been asking too much of those historians who experienced those terrible times to demand from them anything other than their own 'version' of events. Many were concerned to record their impressions faithfully, without taking later events into account. The more recent historiographical works, however, display a clear tendency to view the recent history of Italy in a more truly 'global' context, by widening the field of their researches.

The political and cultural climate of the post-war years constituted the turning-point in perceptions about the history of the recent past. It was during this period that a kind of 'contemporary self-awareness' came into being in Italy, which meant of course that the historian saw his task in *political* rather than purely academic terms.

Historiography did not, however, at least in Italy, progress so smoothly that its findings were uncritically and immediately accepted by the wider intelligentsia. It is significant, for example, that in 1967, at the first conference of the Società degli Storici (the Italian Society of Historians) the period 1915–45 received nothing like the profound and detailed consideration that was accorded earlier periods of Italian history. And yet this was at a time when it was freely conceded that 'university students and the informed sections of public opinion are showing an ever greater interest in the historical events of our century'.[4]

Five years later the position was beginning to change, if slowly. In an editorial to the first edition of the *Rivista di storia contemporanea*, edited by Guido Quazza, attention was drawn to the fact that contemporary history in Italy came across, on the one hand, 'as a new academic discipline that had already produced a superabundance of results, but on the other, as an academic discipline lacking the kind of "tools" that would allow it to gain the universal support of informed critical opinion'.[5]

In this contrast between a 'young' academic discipline and a 'superabundance of results', and in the incompatability between new problems and traditional methodology, we can perceive some of the most significant aspects of the development of contemporary historiography in Italy. On the one hand, new theories and new theoretical approaches were making their appearance; on the other (as Stuart J. Woolf has pointed out), there was a return to 'those areas of study which have traditionally been of interest to Italian historians', i.e. to the study of political history and the history of ideas. 'This approach', Woolf wrote, 'has little time for the social forces that give rise to political parties or the long-term economic movements which, more often than not, form the basis of political development.'[6]

It is none the less true that, by the 1960s, when analyses of the immediate post-war years were first appearing, certain areas of research were already showing signs of a 'strongly ideological cultural mood'.[7] These included studies of socialism and the labour movement, of the Catholic political movement and of economic development. All these studies seemed to form a kind of rebellion against the more traditional mould of historical interpretation in Italy. These works also seemed to represent the first steps on the part of Italian historians 'to embrace the methodology and theoretical approaches of other academic disciplines'.[8]

It is the latter rather than the former aspect of the new trends that needs to be emphasized in discussing them: their application of theories and methods learnt from other disciplines, with the potential this afforded for new lines of development, rather than their tendency to divide historians into opposing camps. In the case of, for example, the Marxist or, more precisely, the Gramscian tradition, it is above all important to retrace the tendency towards dialogue with other historiographical models and the transcendence of the old opposition between 'Marxist historiography and the idealist heritage'[9] through the greater and lesser efforts made to enlarge the field of research proper to political history.

Certainly Italy was witnessing a kind of revolt against some of the traditional methods. This was manifested in a greater awareness, on the part of
those writing contemporary history, of the need for rigorous scientific
investigation of documentary evidence. This was of course necessary as a
counterweight to ideological and political polemic, but it was all the more
important in the face of the great mass of documentation generated in the
modern world. In these circumstances the researcher needs not merely to
scrutinize his sources carefully, but also to have a sound methodology for
selecting and evaluating them. From the 1950s onward, a large body of
studies have drawn extensively on the treasure trove of available material,
both public and private, Italian and non-Italian; [10] but the results achieved
have depended on the researcher's awareness of her problems presented by
his sources and his critical method in tackling them. Side by side with useful
research that furthers understanding there is much research which obscures
the real difficulties involved, transforming the whole exercise into a game of
retrospective 'revelations' and the historical document itself into a kind of
'artificial support for some legal controversy or political affair'. [11] Again,
while some studies are meticulously thorough in examining the available
sources, other are selective in a way that casts doubt on their findings.
Renzo De Felice's *Mussolini* is a case in point. It is based on a wealth of
documentary evidence and represents a major step forward in the field of
archive research on Fascist Italy, yet its conclusions are undermined by its
dubious selectivity in the citation and quotation of documents. [12]

The main departure from traditional methods has, however, come
through the perception that the concerns of the historian are intimately
related to those of the social scientist. As Nicola Tranfaglia has written, this
has led to a move away from an approach 'based essentially on the instruments and themes proper to traditional historical disciplines' towards one
incorporating methods and concepts learnt from the social sciences. The
contribution of economics, sociology, law, psychology and anthropology to
the analysis of historical sources has been considerable. This integration of
various disciplines has helped identify 'long neglected historical problems'
and made it possible to study them 'utilizing richer and more fruitful
methods', thus laying the foundations on which 'to confront, concretely
and not abstractly, the results obtained by the two disciplines'. [13]

This historiographical approach is still at a fairly early stage in its
development, but it has already singled out some important areas of
research. Sometimes the stimulus has come from outside academic circles
– for example, from the great political ferment which Italy experienced in
the late 1960s, which proved as significant for the development of historical
study in Italy as did foreign methodological influences such as the work
stimulated by *Annales* in France, and certain British and American
journals, notably *Past and Present* and the *Economic History Review*. [14]
Within Italy, the leaders in the field have been Guido Quazza, the Istituto di

Storia della Facoltà di Magistero of the University of Turin, and the group of scholars whose work bore fruit in *Il mondo contemporaneo*, a compendium of the efforts of some 200 collaborators, surveying the theatre of contemporary history and the methodologies employed in studying it.[15]

While one might expect the immediate post-war years to have provided the point of departure for the new historiographical approach, the turning point in fact came in the 1960s, when the demand for methods of research appropriate to new objects of study first began to bear fruit. The post-war years were certainly characterized by a new enthusiasm and productive momentum, but the ideological shift that might have set the scene for 'a codification within the historicist tradition of research methods and frameworks' did not materialize.[16] The change, when it came, was not determined by the political sympathies of historians, but rather was the consequence of the meeting between historiography and the social sciences brought about through the initiative of the so-called 'social movements'.[17]

The overhaul of historical research which was being realized in France by Braudel and by means of the various polemics against *l'histoire bataille, l'histoire événementielle*, and so on, corresponded in Italy with the definitive decline of the traditional historicist approach and the opening-up of a range of potential new approaches towards subjects proposed by the *Annales* school. At the same time, the general tendency to put less emphasis upon the 'national characteristics' of contemporary Italian history gave rise to a series of approaches offering new points of reference for the comparison of Italian history and 'world history'.[18]

The multitude of problems and controversies originating from the application of the interdisciplinary approach to the study of contemporary life, and beyond this the whole question of the relationship between interdisciplinary history and the concept of 'total history', inevitably issued in a series of debates and polemics concerning both concrete, practical issues and questions of principle. Specifically, the scientific standing of the 'new' discipline and of the whole historiographical endeavour was much debated – for example, in terms of the problem of the historian's 'professional status'. The years 1970–2 witnessed the birth of two reviews representing diametrically opposed points of view: *Storia contemporanea*, edited by Renzo De Felice, and *Rivista di storia contemporanea*, which brought together Quazza, Valerio Castronovo, Enzo Collotti and Giorgio Rochat, amongst others. Put synthetically, the debate between these two tendencies revolved above all around the question of the political conditioning of the historian and the historian's 'subordination' to the politico-cultural imperatives of the society in which he operates. On the one hand, there was a desire to protect the integrity of history, as an academic discipline, by claiming for it a kind of *positio super partes* with the objective of 'restoring the historian's professional status'. On the other hand, there was a desire to recall the intellectual 'to his political responsibilities, to his duty to produce work which openly offers the possibility of judging the choice of instruments made and the manner of their employment, thus founding its scientific validity . . . not upon an abstract objectivity but rather upon the comparative evaluation of results and the fruitfulness of the methods adopted'.[19]

In point of fact, it must be admitted that 'the comparative evaluation of results and . . . methods' has not been carried out but has simply been proposed. But the perceived need and the expressed hopes for such critical standards have not been the sole stimuli for historiographical activity in the 1970s and 1980s. Rather, the debate has opened up and broadened out, moving on from the presumptive self-defence of the historians' professionalism to address the insufficient structuring of contemporary history as a new disciplinary field. The diversity of opinion ranges from the reservations of Alberto Caracciolo and Pasquale Villani concerning 'annalistic tendencies' and 'the accentuated insistence upon the political moment', through the 'defensive' positions of Marxist historiography, balancing affirmation of the enduring validity of this tradition with recognition of the merits of a number of paths of development suggested by other traditions, to the no less critical and problematic positions of Franco Andreucci and Gabriele Turi, who, however, also invite dialogue on ideological questions and particularly on 'the line of historiographical culture to be defended'. In line with this last, constructive position are the old-established reviews *Studi storici* and *Rivista storica italiana*, which have become better disposed towards contemporary-history themes, and newer journals such as *Società e storia* and *Movimento operaio e socialista* (both founded in 1978), whose emphasis is on social history, and particularly foreign experience in the field. A similar position is taken by *Italia contemporanea* (previously entitled *Il movimento de liberazione in Italia*, edited by Massimo Legnani), whose contributors have re-examined the transition from Fascism to the Italian Republic and have entered on the complete range of controversies regarding the inter-war period.[20]

In conclusion, I must emphasize the extremely fractured character of the Italian scene, which is, moreover, in a constant state of flux. We Italians suffer, I feel, from an obsession with 'autonomy', both within our own country and in the context of our relations with others, and that is inimical to the free exchange of ideas and experiences. It is to be hoped that this will change, since only through open debate and a willingness to learn from the experiences of others can the study of contemporary history be effectively advanced.

Notes

1 For information on developments in the study of contemporary history in Italy, with particular reference to contemporary history reviews and journals, see

138 The Theatre of Contemporary History

Massimo Legnani, 'Italia contemporanea fra interno ed esterno', paper presented to the Giulianova Seminar, 26–8 February 1986, published in Italia contemporanea no. 163 (July 1986), pp. 107–16.

2 Claudio Pavone, 'La storiografia sull'Italia postunitaria e gli archivi nel secondo dopoguerra', in Rassegna degli Archivi di Stato, no. 2–3 (May–December 1967), p. 355.

3 Ibid.

4 The observation is drawn from 'La storia contemporanea in Italia: nota in margine al congresso della Società degli Storici', undersigned by the Comitato Direttivo dell'Istituto Nazionale per la Storia del Movimento de Liberazione in Italia, in Il movimento di liberazione in Italia, no. 89 (October–December 1967), pp. 108–10.

5 Rivista di storia contemporanea, 1 (January 1972), p. 1.

6 Stuart J. Woolf, 'Osservazioni sulle ricerche di storia contemporanea in Italia', Il movimento de liberazione in Italia, no. 86 (January–March 1967), pp. 56–62, with introduction by Bianca Ceva.

7 Pavone, in Rassegna degli Archivi del Stato, no. 2–3.

8 Lucio Villari, cited in Giuseppe Galasso, 'L'Italia unita nella storiografia del secondo dopoguerra', in Romain Rainero (ed.), L'Italia unita: problemi ed interpretazioni storiografiche (Marzorati, Milan, 1981), p. 133. This work comprises papers presented at the congress 'La storia dell'Italia unita nella storia del secondo dopoguerra', Palermo, 30 November to 3 December 1978.

9 See Pietro Rossi (ed.), introduction to La storiografia contemporanea: indirizzi e problemi (Il Saggiatore, Milan, 1987), p. x.

10 The proliferation of such publications is discussed and relevant statistical data are supplied in S. Carocci, L. Pavone, N. Santarelli and M. Tosti Croce (eds), Bibliografia dell'Archivio Centrale de Stato (1953–1978), coordination by Maura Piccialuti Caprioli, Pubblicazioni degli Archivi de Stato, Strumenti I (Istituto Poligrafico dello Stato, Rome, 1986).

11 Delio Cantimori, 'Avventure d'un devoto di Clio', in Conversando di storia (Laterza, Bari, 1967), pp. 185–6.

12 Renzo De Felice, Mussolini, 6 vols, in progress (Einaudi, Turin, 1965–). On the theme of the sources see Giorgio Rochat, 'Il quarto volume della biografia de Mussolini di Renzo De Felice', Italia contemporanea, no. 122 (January–March, 1976), pp. 89–102.

13 Nicola Tranfaglia, 'Presentazione', in Fabio Levi, Umberto Levra and Nicola Tranfaglia (eds), Il mondo contemporaneo, vol. I: Storia d'Italia (La Nuova Italia, Florence, 1978), pp. xiii–xvii.

14 Guido Quazza, 'Storia delle storiografie, storia del potere, storia sociale', in L'Italia unita, pp. 165–86 (in particular, see p. 174).

15 This work is in 10 volumes (La Nuova Italia, Florence, 1978–83), of which six are devoted to particular regions (Italy [see note 13], Europe, Asia, Africa and the Near East, North America, Latin America) and four to particular subject areas (international politics, economics and history, politics and society, the instruments of research).

16 Rossi, introduction to La storiografia contemporanea, p. x.

17 Quazza, in L'Italia unita, p. 175.

18 See Rossi, introduction to La storiografia contemporanea, pp. xi–xviii.

19 For information on the different positions see Legnani, in *Italia contemporanea*, no. 163.
20 Besides the article by Legnani cited in notes 1 and 19, see also 'La storia contemporanea attraverso le riviste: contributi a un'indagine', *Italia contemporanea*, no. 165 (December 1986), pp. 85–96.

9

Contemporary History in the Modern World: the United States

Gillian Peele

The historian of the contemporary United States faces enormous and daunting difficulties which may be traced to the elusive character of the country itself. In contrast to the United Kingdom, which is marked by its homogeneity and the centralization of government, America is distinguished by its pluralism, its governmental decentralization and fragmentation, and the sheer mobility of its population. And there are also difficulties arising not so much from the subject matter of American history as from its observers. Contemporary history is everywhere terrain which may be fought over by warring tribes of historians, political scientists and journalists. In the United States this competition is further complicated by the special characteristics of each of these groups and the ubiquity of a fourth tribe – the public-policy specialists – whose intellectual perspectives are quite different again from those of the other groups. Although a short chapter of this kind can scarcely hope to do justice to all the facets of American contemporary history, it is nevertheless important to look at both the professional concerns of each of these groups of American scholars as well as at the structural difficulties associated with the study of modern America.

Contemporary history and the academic specialisms

Writing in a 1984 issue of *Daedalus* Alan Brinkley drew attention to the paucity of writing by American historians on twentieth-century events in their own country.[1] 'Except for discussions of the Progressive era (which generated a serious and extensive literature) and of diplomatic history (which has tended to remain isolated within its own discrete realm) the historiography of modern America and particularly of the period since the end of World War I', Brinkley wrote, 'has attracted little attention from, and generated little excitement among, the historical profession at large.'[2]

Brinkley's discussion is worth reading in its own right as a comment on recent trends in American historiography. What is striking about his examination of the discipline, however, is the extent to which twentieth-century history – let alone contemporary history in the sense in which that term is generally used in this book (i.e. the history of the period beginning in 1945) – has been neglected in American history departments because of the history establishment's concern with other issues, substantive and methodological. What is also interesting is the extent to which, in addition to the neglect of certain areas (which may of course be the result of the excitement generated by other topics), contemporary history has been affected by the American historian's search for unifying themes, order and meaning in the flux of historical events. By drawing attention to this I do not want to suggest that history should or could be written as simple narrative, for any account of wars, revolutions or more stable periods of government must be selective and will be constructed around questions which reflect the historians' own interests and intellectual orientation. Rather, I think that American historiography is pervaded (to a greater extent than British historiography) by a demand for interpretation and synthesis which in turn reflects a search for the meaning of the nation itself.[3]

Examples of unifying themes in American historical analysis are not hard to come by. Frederick Jackson Turner's identification of the frontier as the source of a number of American characteristics offered a provocative theme to the historians of the late nineteenth and early twentieth century as they sought a key to the rapid change which was overtaking the United States.[4] The idea of conflict that was inherent in much of the writing of the Progressive historians was, of course, rebutted by the 'consensus school' of American history, which in the aftermath of the Second World War focused on the shared values and assumptions which permeate American life.[5] More recently there has been extensive interest in what might be called the 'organizational' or 'bureaucratic' school of American history as exemplified by such writers as Louis Galambos, Robert Wiebe and A. D. Chandler.[6] Here the theme is that America's economic and political development can best be understood in terms of the rise of the large corporation with its impersonal ethos, specialized roles and implicit challenge to liberal democratic assumptions.

To what extent does this desire to find some unifying theme or purpose affect the enterprise of the contemporary historian? The answer is perhaps that by itself it is not an impediment but that it tends to channel activity among historians into a limited number of areas, reducing for each generation the effort that might have gone into examining equally important topics. The tides of historical fashion are strong and they sweep not merely the scholars but also the university recruiters, the grant-giving bodies and the publishers along. This militates against production both of the specialist studies needed in American contemporary history and, ironically, of the more comprehensive and interpretative overviews so favoured by American historians. For what the contemporary historian needs above all else is both the systematic preservation of the raw data across the board and a sense of balance. It is difficult enough to apply the techniques of detached scholarship to the very recent past; it is made far more difficult by sudden rushes of enthusiasm for a particular topic – enthusiasms which in their way may almost be as debilitating and distorting as neglect.

One subject which has experienced a recent concentration of intellectual interest is religious history. Contemporary religious history was until recently something of an arcane subject, practised largely by those with a confessional axe to grind or as a part of the history of ethnic and national minorities.[7] Political scientists studied its influence hardly at all. Yet, with the attempt to mobilize the Christian fundamentalists in the late 1970s, American historians, political scientists and even the public-policy specialists awoke to the pervasiveness of this theme in America's national life.[8] The American Political Science Association acquired panels on the topic and a host of research projects, books and articles reviewed the various aspects of religious behaviour. The sceptical historian in twenty years time may well wonder whether the intense attention devoted to religion in the 1980s did not result in distortion rather than illumination of a once-neglected topic.

The professional historian cannot be held solely responsible for the condition of American contemporary history, however. The political scientist has also had an impact on the field. Political scientists are, of course, as likely as historians to produce important work in contemporary history. However, if political science emphasizes certain sorts of studies rather than others, important gaps will be left and imbalance of a kind already alluded to will occur. This is not the place to attempt an analysis of the discipline of political science in the United States. Although the scene is far from uniform – and certainly not dominated by the naïve behaviouralism which British critics have frequently attacked – there is still concern for model-building and typology to an extent which is rarely found in Britain.[9] The problem with according such priority to 'theory' is that it leaves little room for the rich and subtle information which can inform understanding about how a political institution actually works. The approach sometimes seems to be dictated not by the desire to illuminate political reality but by the concern to practise and point the value of a particular methodology. That said, the political scientist can frequently make an important contribution to the study of contemporary history, although often it will be as a student of decision-making, or of an institution such as a pressure group or a political party, or of a series of changes within a party (as in the case of Byron Shafer's detailed examination of the changes in the Democratic Party's presidential selection procedures[10]). Studies of the presidency are perhaps the most obvious example of this genre, allowing as they do the marriage of historical techniques, rich – if sometimes preselected – data in the presidential archives and the intellectual agenda of the political scientists. Fred Greenstein's book on the Eisenhower presidency is a good example of this kind of writing.[11] Equally important, however, are the narrower specialist studies of aspects of presidential government – for example, the handling of legislative liaison.[12]

If political science can make constructive contributions to contemporary history, it can also have effects which are less than desirable. The methodological sophistication of the social sciences has led many historians to adapt these techniques to their own work, with varying results. Social history and electoral history have been prime targets for the application of methodologies familiar to the social sciences. Yet it would be a pity if this meant that historians and political scientists neglected areas where the data was less precise and a tragedy if the fuzziness of some of the raw material of contemporary history led it to be discarded simply because it could not easily be fed into a computer.

Those who write on contemporary themes in any country will know the extent to which the public media can be a useful resource. In the United States the press is as important as elsewhere, though the geographic diversity of the country means that the newspapers are almost entirely local in character and, with the exception of the *New York Times* and perhaps the *Washington Post*, come nowhere near being journals of record. Journalists in the United States have made a major contribution to the study of contemporary history. Some, such as David Broder, are perceptive and well-informed students of American politics whose works could as easily have been written from within the groves of academe as in Grub Street.[13] Others, such as Strobe Talbot, have provided us with highly detailed accounts of specific areas of policy-making – in Talbot's case, arms-control negotiations.[14] Unfortunately, the decentralized character of the United States administration makes authoritative validation or rebuttal of such accounts difficult. In the absence of a centralized community of civil servants, politicians and journalists, many of these accounts escape detailed criticism. Nor is this problem confined to such dramatic incidents in American contemporary history as Vietnam.[15] Bob Woodward, a journalist who contributed much to the public knowledge of Watergate, co-authored a book on the Supreme Court which used unorthodox sources for its inside information and which is accordingly hard to verify.[16] 'Insider' campaign histories, like the Nuffield Election Studies, have the merit of recording much that would otherwise be lost; they are, however, usually written by partisans. Much of the journalistic writing is polemical in nature, though sometimes, as with Elizabeth Drew's writings on campaign finance, it accords neatly with a school of thought among academics.[17]

Journalistic writings on political personalities are in a class of their own, for in the United States journalists are often the only ones who can come close enough to politicians on a regular basis to be able to gain the insight needed for a biography. Hedley Donovan's vignettes of presidents from F. D. Roosevelt to Ronald Reagan offers an example of how the 'feel' of different presidencies can be conveyed. And the study of Reagan by Lou Cannon provides a useful contribution to understanding of the President himself and his presidency. Such studies are valuable both for the selection of issues which are felt to be important at the time and because they can convey the language and style of the period. More detached academic studies often lose this dimension, even if they compensate for it by an ability to put issues in perspective.[18]

Finally, mention should be made of the policy specialists.[19] These are the individuals who are employed by or have spent time in the various think-tanks and policy centres which can be found in Washington DC and other large cities, as well as attached to the various universities. The quality of work varies; the preoccupations and interests of the policy centres range across the gamut of foreign and domestic policy. But for the student of contemporary history these centres are a valuable resource in two ways.

First, they bring together material which is often not found elsewhere, so that, in addition to their own publications, they often provide good sources of research data. So long as the purpose of a publication or project is borne in mind, these centres can thus prove invaluable to the researcher. For example, the Brookings studies of the impact of federal aid to American cities provide an interesting series of case studies which are a contribution to contemporary history because they are the result of a systematic monitoring programme.[20] In a slightly different manner, the American Enterprise Institute has produced useful analyses of public opinion, of Congressional and electoral data and of bureaucratic activity.

Secondly, the staff of these institutes often have first-hand knowledge of policy-making and the policy-makers in a given area, as well as an ability to understand the concerns of both the academic and the practitioner. Resident scholars of these centres therefore often provide an excellent starting point for the researcher into contemporary history, since they know whom to contact and themselves have personal insights into the policy process.

Some remaining problems

Apart from the nuances of the different intellectual specialisms outlined above, there are some practical problems which arise in the study of American contemporary history. The federal organization of the United States means that the full story of an episode can rarely be told simply from the archives in Washington DC. Politicians have a double life – their life in the capital and their home state activities. There are excellent guides to state and local archives; the problem is that the mere size of the United States can make research expensive.[21] When interviews are planned, the mobility of those in government employment is also a handicap. Today's policy-makers may not be there tomorrow and tracking down their whereabouts can be time-consuming. The people who are most often helpful in relation to a public policy issue – pressure-group employees, Congressional aides and journalists – are by nature highly peripatetic, both in career and in geographical terms. In the case of the United States, the more recent the episode or the policy area to be researched, the easier it will be to find sources of information quickly. The most difficult period for researchers is probably the period of the previous two administrations. This is not because of any kind of secrecy surrounding the decisions or issues associated with them but because the papers are probably still in the process of being deposited in libraries; the actors are widely dispersed; and some documentation – especially that in the hands of private sources such as pressure groups – will not have been sorted into a form convenient for researchers to use.

It would, however, be wrong to end on a pessimistic note about the future of research into American contemporary history. The source material is abundant and where it is kept in libraries and special collections – such as the presidential libraries – it is well organized. There are fewer restrictions on access than in the United Kingdom, although any scholar trying to use the Freedom of Information Act to obtain particular documents should be aware that this can be a time-consuming task.[22] Finally, there is a great willingness on the part of key decision-makers to help scholars and interviews will usually be granted. It is, however, worth noting that attitudes to arranging interviews in the United States are not those found in Britain. The British scholar would be unwise to approach anyone without first setting out who he is and why he seeks a personal interview. Letters to American officials will, though, frequently be ignored, while a personal approach by telephone will often work even at quite short notice.

This chapter has argued that in order to understand the condition of contemporary history in the United States one must understand the situation of the various groups who have an interest in it and that some of the problems of studying contemporary America stem from the nature of the polity itself. Yet, if America's federalism, separation of powers and pluralism mean that there is a multiplicity of policy sources – even in an area such as foreign policy – they also offer a special challenge to the scholar.[23] In the absence of institutional and administrative continuity, there is a special premium on energy, flexibility and resourcefulness. With those qualities one may experience what one authority on American contemporary history has called 'the uniqueness and relevance of the American experience'.[24]

Notes

1 Alan Brinkley, 'Writing the history of contemporary America: dilemmas and challenges', *Daedalus*, Summer 1984 (*Proceedings of the American Academy of Arts and Sciences*, 113, no. 3).
2 Ibid.
3 An interesting example of this tendency in the writing of presidential election history is Theodore H. White's study of the 1980 election and its significance in terms of the decline of American purpose. See T. H. White, *America in Search of Itself: the making of the President 1956–1980* (Jonathan Cape, 1983).
4 Frederick Jackson Turner's 'frontier thesis' was originally outlined in a paper to the American Historical Association in 1893. He restated his ideas on the subject in *The Frontier in American History* (1920; Praeger, New York, 1976).
5 A good example of writing in this vein is D. Boorstin, *The Americans: the democratic experience* (Random House, New York, 1974), and the same author's *The Genius of American Politics* (University of Chicago Press, 1958).
6 These approaches can be explored further in L. Galambos, 'The emerging organizational synthesis in modern American history', *Business History Review*, XLIV (Autumn 1970); and Robert F. Berkhofer, 'The organizational interpretation of American history', *Prospects*, IV (1979). See also A. D. Chandler, *The Visible Hand: the managerial revolution in American business* (Harvard University Press, Cambridge, Mass., 1977); and R. Weibe *The Search for Order 1877–1920* (Greenwood Press, Westport, Conn., 1977), and *The Segmented Society: an introduction to the meaning of America* (Oxford University Press, New York, 1975).
7 For an excellent religious history of the United States see S. Ahlstrom, *A Religious History of the American People*, 2 vols (Image Books, New York, 1975). For recent writing in the area see Dewy D. Wallace Jr, 'Recent publications on American religious history', in Jefferson Kellogg and Robert Walker (eds), *Sources for American Studies* (Greenwood Press, Westport, Conn., 1983). See also Henry F. May, 'The recovery of American religious history', *American Historical Review*, LXX (October, 1964).
8 The Brookings Institution has, for example, published an excellent study of the role of religion in American politics. See A. James Reichley, *Religion in American Public life* (Brookings Institution, Washington, DC, 1985).
9 Those who wish to study the debate about behavioural science and the study of society could do worse than to start with Edmund Ions, *Against Behaviouralism: a critique of behavioural science* (Basil Blackwell, 1977). For a thoughtful and positive essay on the relationship between history and social science see Gordon

Wood, 'Intellectual history and the social sciences', in J. Higham and P. Conkin (eds), *New Directions in American Intellectual History* (Johns Hopkins University Press, Baltimore, 1979).

10 Byron E. Shafer, *The Quiet Revolution: the struggle for the Democratic Party and the shaping of post-reform politics* (Russell Sage, New York, 1983).

11 Fred Greenstein, *The Hidden-Hand Presidency: Eisenhower as leader* (Basic Books, New York, 1982).

12 See for example the study by Nigel Bowles, *The White House and Capitol Hill: the politics of the presidential persuasion* (Oxford University Press, 1987).

13 See for example David Broder, *The Party's Over: the failure of politics in America* (Simon and Schuster, New York, 1972), and *Changing of the Guard: power and leadership in America* (Simon and Schuster, New York, 1980).

14 Strobe Talbot, *Deadly Gambits: the Reagan Administration and the stalemate in arms control* (Picador, 1985).

15 There is now a huge literature on Vietnam but of special interest are L. Gelb and R. Betts, *The Irony of Vietnam: the system worked* (Brookings Institution, Washington, DC, 1979); D. Halberstam, *The Best and the Brightest* (Random House, New York, 1972); and Stanley Karnow, *Vietnam* (Viking, New York, 1983).

16 See Bob Woodward and Carl Bernstein, *The Final Days* (Simon and Schuster, New York, 1976). Also Myron J. Smith Jr, *Watergate: an annotated bibliography of sources in English 1972-1982* (Scarecrow Press, 1983). On the Supreme Court see Bob Woodward and Scott Armstrong, *The Brethren: inside the Supreme Court* (Simon and Schuster, New York, 1979).

17 See Elizabeth Drew, *Portrait of an Election: the 1980 presidential campaign* (Simon and Schuster, New York, 1981), and *Politics and Money: the new road to corruption* (Macmillan, New York, 1983). For a bibliography in the area see Lynda Lee Kaich and Anne Johnston Wadsworth, *Political Campaign Communication: a bibliography and guide to the literature 1973-1982* (Scarecrow Press, 1985).

18 See Lou Cannon, *Reagan* (Putnam, New York, 1982). For an example of the detachment which can be achieved after even a short period of time, compare Stephen Ambrose, *Nixon: the education of a politician 1913-1962* (Simon and Schuster, New York, 1987), with earlier biographical studies. Biography is of course particularly vulnerable to the blend of historical and psychological method known as 'psycho-history'. See for example Fawn Brodie, *Richard Nixon: the shaping of his character* (Harvard University Press, Cambridge, Mass., 1983). For holdings on presidents generally see K. E. Davison, *The American Presidency: a guide to information sources* (Gale Research, Detroit, 1983).

19 The background of those who work as policy specialists is varied. Many will be political scientists or economists; and these policy specialists will be likely to move frequently between specialist institutes, universities and government.

20 See James W. Fossett, *Federal Aid to Big Cities: the politics of dependence* (Brookings Institution, Washington, DC, 1983), as well as the individual case studies. On the role of the Brookings Institution and policy advice see D. T. Critchlow, *The Brookings Institution 1916-1952: expertise and the public interest* (Illinois University Press, Evanston, 1985).

21 Information about state and local holdings is not readily available in one single volume. However the addresses of state archives are given in Frank Freidel, *Harvard Guide to American History* (Belknap Press, Cambridge, Mass., 1973), which is an essential tool for anyone studying American history.

22 There are a number of self-help guides to using the Freedom of Information Act. See for example *Citizen's Guide to Use of the Freedom of Information Act in Requesting Government Documents* (Revisionist Press, Brooklyn, New York, 1984); and Christine Marwick, *Your Right to Government Information* (American Civil Liberties Union/Bantam Books, New York, 1985).

23 On foreign policy generally see Alexander deConde 'Themes in the history of American foreign policy', in Kellogg and Walker, *Sources for American Studies*. For a recent discussion of the state contribution to foreign policy see Michael H. Shulman, 'Dateline Main Street: local foreign policies', *Foreign Policy*, Winter 1986–7.

24 Herbert Nicholas, 'The education of an Americanist', *Journal of American Studies*, XIV, no. 1 (April 1980).

10

Contemporary History in the Classical World

A. J. Woodman

The 'father of history' was Herodotus, who flourished during the middle decades of the fifth century BC and whose work consists of an interrelated series of *logoi* or 'accounts': the earliest are a curious and personalized blend of myth, legend and travellers' tales; the last deals with the Persian Wars up to the year 479 BC. Though he is an engaging stylist and narrator, his reputation has suffered in comparison with that of his successor Thucydides (c. 460–400 BC), whose account of the Peloponnesian War (431–404 BC) is widely accepted as being the best work of history to have been written in antiquity. The views of many readers have been well summarized by the distinguished historian of historiography Momigliano:

> It is only too obvious that Thucydides ultimately determined the verdict of antiquity on his predecessor. He carefully read (or listened to) his Herodotus and decided that the Herodotean approach to history was unsafe. To write serious history, one had to be a contemporary of the events under discussion and one had to be able to understand what people were saying. Serious history – according to Thucydides – was not concerned with the past, but with the present. . . . Thucydides dictated the paramountcy of contemporary history.[1]

On this view Thucydides was responsible for seeing a distinction between ancient and contemporary history which Herodotus had failed to appreciate, for deciding that the latter was superior to the former, and for basing his whole work on that premise. But is this really the case?

In the first place, there is a passage in Homer's *Odyssey* where Odysseus says to the oral poet Demodocus 'It is remarkable how well you sing the story of the Achaeans' fate and of all their achievements, sufferings and toils; it is almost as though you had been present yourself or listened to someone else' (8.489–91). From this it is clear that as early as the eighth century BC a distinction was drawn between events described on the basis of personal witness or autopsy (whether at first- or, apparently, second-hand)

and, we must presume, mere hear-say. Herodotus himself, like the sixth-century philosopher Heraclitus (see below, p. 154), was certainly aware of the proverbial expression 'eyes are more reliable than ears' (1.8.2); yet neither this awareness nor his well-known familiarity with Homer prevented him from devoting the bulk of his work to matters for which autopsy was out of the question.

In the second place, Thucydides described the Peloponnesian War not because he was contemporary with it but, as he says himself, because it was the greatest war of all time (1.1.1–2). Indeed he devotes the whole of his long preface to demonstrating both that earlier wars were relatively insignificant (1.2.1–21.1) and that the Peloponnesian War is the greatest of all (1.21.2–23.3).[2] In this way he hopes that he and his account of the Peloponnesian War will rival and surpass both Herodotus and his account of the Persian Wars and Homer and his account of the Trojan War. Such rivalry with one's literary predecessors, and the corresponding magnification of one's own subject, were crucial features of classical historiography and help to give some indication of its highly rhetorical nature.

Why, then, is so much made of Thucydides as a contemporary historian? The answer is to be found in his famous 'chapter on method' (1.22), where he explains how he has tackled the problems posed by two types of material: the speeches made during the war, and the events of the war. Yet his remarks at least on speeches are disconcerting for the modern reader:

> The speeches have been rendered in accordance with what I thought each person would have said (namely, that which was generally necessary given their circumstances at the time), keeping as closely as possible to the general gist of what was actually said. (1.22.1)

Now, there are roughly 140 speeches in Thucydides' work, and this statement seems to suggest that each of them, while preserving the main thesis of what an original speaker said, is otherwise entirely invented by the historian himself.[3] It follows that if one of Thucydides' readers had happened to get hold of a transcript of a speech which appears in the history, he would have had (as it were) two versions of the 'same' speech: the original and Thucydides'. Thus Thucydides' representation of speeches is (to our modern way of thinking) *mis*representation. Given this gulf between the ancient concept of historiography and our own, at least as far as speeches are concerned, we should not rush to attribute to Thucydides a view of contemporary history which is based on modern preconceptions.

What of Thucydides' treatment of the events of the war? Here is his statement of method on this topic:

> As for the events which took place during the war, I did not consider it right to describe them either on the basis of what I learned from just anybody or in accordance with what I thought, but from personal experience and after

investigating with as much accuracy as possible each event reported by others. It was a fairly troublesome process because those who were present at the various events did not make the same reports about the same things: it depended upon an individual's prejudice for either side or his memory. (1.22.2–3)

This statement undoubtedly seems impressive, especially since Thucydides has earlier remarked on the difficulties of writing ancient history (1.1.2, 1.20.1–21.1); but it is essential to see the statement in its context. The passage is part of Thucydides' larger argument that the Peloponnesian War is the greatest war of all time, an argument which he has introduced in the immediately preceding paragraph (1.21.2) as follows:

To return to the present war: although men always reckon that their own war is the greatest while they are fighting it, but after demobilisation tend to magnify the past, nevertheless to those who judge the present war simply on the basis of its events, it will be seen to have been greater than any predecessor.

In other words, Thucydides' remarks on autopsy and the questioning of eyewitnesses, while undoubtedly enhancing the credibility of his narrative, do not spring *primarily* from any conviction of his about 'the paramountcy of contemporary history'. On the contrary, they are apologetic in nature, designed to forestall the objection that he has unduly magnified a war in which he took part himself.

It may of course be argued that, whatever the motivation of his remarks, Thucydides' method will have had the inevitable effect of producing superior historiography to that of Herodotus. It is, however, difficult to know which sections are based on autopsy since he refers to himself on no more than a very few occasions. At 2.48.3 he says that he caught the plague which broke out in 430 BC, and at 5.26.5 he tells us that lived to see the end of the war. At 4.104–7 he describes a naval encounter in which he as general was beaten by the enemy and for which he was later banished from his native city, Athens, for twenty years. Throughout the episode he refers to himself in the third person ('Thucydides, son of Olorus, the author of this history'), a device which some other ancient historians also adopted, thereby helping to create an impression of impartial reserve. Indeed it has been alleged that he 'makes no attempt at self-defence' and that 'in no other part of the *History* is his passion for the truth, as he saw it, so clearly displayed'.[4] Yet a more subtle examination of his account reveals, as might have been expected, that it is in fact 'a very skilful self-justification against the charges which led to his banishment'.[5]

We must also remember that Thucydides' narrative is 600 pages long and that he cannot therefore have had the benefit of autopsy for all or even most of it. Most of his material is likely to have been based on the statements of informants, although in the narrative he almost never gives us any hint of the conflicts of evidence which he mentioned in the preface; on the contrary, as Sir Kenneth Dover (co-author of the standard commentary on Thucydides) has remarked, he presents us with 'a narrative which sustains an almost unvarying level of magisterial assurance'.[6] Yet that assurance can rarely be tested because we lack any independent evidence for most of the events which Thucydides relates. Most scholars are prepared to give him the benefit of any doubt that may be going; but Dover has warned that 'it is disturbing to find that in those few cases where we can actually consider what Thucydides says in the light of demonstrably independent evidence . . . , the usual outcome is not renewed confidence but doubt'.[7] Is it simply coincidence that doubt arises on precisely the few occasions where the narrative can be checked? Or is it possible that in his chapter on method Thucydides appealed to a convention which was as old as Homer but which had only a limited effect on his subsequent narrative? At the very least, the evidence of that narrative, on the occasions it can be checked, hardly permits us to say that Thucydides' alleged superiority to Herodotus rests upon his having been a contemporary historian.

The fact is that the starting point of Thucydides' history was determined for him not by any conviction that contemporary history was superior to ancient, but by the work of Herodotus. Though Thucydides begins his history of the Peloponnesian War with the events of 435 BC, he includes in book 1 a retrospective section (89–118) in which he surveys events of the preceding fifty years up to 479. In other words, Thucydides effectively starts where Herodotus had left off, thus tacitly acknowledging the excellence of his predecessor's treatment of the Persian Wars. It was because of this acknowledgement that Thucydides treated his own subject of the Peloponnesian War to the rhetorical magnification which has already been mentioned (see above, p. 150) and which his chapter on method was designed to support. It may therefore be said that the difference between Herodotus and Thucydides is not as great as has been supposed, something which Momigliano himself later accepted when he tacitly corrected the remarks with which this discussion began.[8]

Thucydides' decision to follow on directly from Herodotus set a fashion. The next 'great' Greek historian, Xenophon (c. 428–354 BC), not only began his *Hellenika* with the year 411, at the point where Thucydides' work in its turn had left off ('Some days later . . .'), but also ended by inviting someone else to continue after him ('Let this, then, be the end of my narrative; someone else, perhaps, will deal with what happened later' – 7.5.27). Xenophon thus explicitly issues the kind of challenge which he himself and Thucydides at the beginnings of their works had implicitly accepted. Some other historians followed suit: Polybius is the continuator of Aratus (see below, p. 154), for example, and on the Roman side Pliny the Elder (AD 23–79) is the continuator of Aufidius Bassus. But if this convention meant that historians wrote contemporary history, it is important to be clear that this was due to their consciousness of the tradition of which they were members rather than to any distinctive features which contemporary history was thought to possess.

Other representatives of contemporary history in the fourth century BC are Philistus, Callisthenes, Theopompus and Ephorus. The last of these referred to the autopsy of events (see below, p. 154), as did Dionysius of Halicarnassus and Diodorus in the late first century BC, Josephus in the first century AD, and Herodian and Dio Cassius in the third.[9] Yet it is uncertain how much importance is to be attached to such references, which are neatly parodied in the second century AD by Lucian (otherwise known as the author of *How to Write History*) in his satirical and fantasist novella *True Histories*, where he professes to write 'about things which I have neither seen nor experienced nor heard about from others' (1.4).

The most systematic approach to contemporary history appears to have been adopted by Thucydides' greatest Greek successor, Polybius (c. 200–118 BC), whose original intention was to describe in thirty volumes how Rome illustrated the potency of Fortune by becoming a world super-power between the years 220 and 168 BC (the latter being the date of the battle of Pydna, after which Polybius was taken to Rome as a hostage). His first two books are largely concerned with the historical developments which led up to this period, and it is not until book 3 that he embarks on his main theme. However, he incorporates into book 3 a preface in which he explains that he has already decided to change his original plan. He now intends, he says, to extend his work in order to consider whether Rome wielded her supremacy fairly in the subsequent period down to 146 BC:

> The final achievement of this work will be to ascertain what the situation of each people was after they had all been subdued and brought under the authority of Rome. . . . Because of the importance and the unexpected character of these later events, and above all because I not only witnessed the greater number of them but also took part in some and directed the course of others, I was persuaded to write about them and to make them the starting-point of what amounts almost to a new work. (3.4.12–13, tr. I. Scott-Kilvert)

Now the acknowledged expert on Polybius, F. W. Walbank, has observed that in the last ten additional books Polybius makes no systematic attempt to answer the new question which he has set himself: 'one is led to wonder if the purpose which Polybius alleges for adding two decades to his *Histories* is really the true one'.[10] This phenomenon therefore focuses attention on the alternative reason advanced by Polybius for extending his work – namely, his own personal involvement in events, which now seems to assume decisive importance.

Now it is indeed true that Polybius recurs to the subjects of autopsy and eyewitnesses, and the related topic of contemporary history, on several occasions. At 4.2.1–4 he says this:

I considered this [220 BC] to be the best starting-point because, in the first place, Aratus' book stops at just this period and I had decided to resume and continue the narrative of Greek history from the date at which he leaves off; second, because the subsequent period, included as it is in my history, coincides with my own and the preceding generation, so that I have been present at some of the events and have the testimony of eyewitnesses for others . . . ; but my chief reason for beginning at this date was that Fortune had then (so to speak) rebuilt the world. (Tr. W. R. Paton)

Of the three reasons here advanced, the first is by now familiar: Polybius makes explicit the point which even Xenophon at the beginning of his work had left implicit (see above, p. 152). Yet both this and his second reason, his own and others' autopsy, are expressly said to be less important than the reason advanced at the start of book 1 – namely, the potency of Fortune. At the start of book 9 he gives yet another reason for writing contemporary history: 'new occurrences constantly present themselves for novel treatment', whereas if the historian decides to write ancient history, he 'must clearly be wasting his labour, since there is no denying the fact that the material which is the object of his research and composition has already been adequately recorded and handed down to posterity by his predecessors' (9.2.2–4, tr. I. Scott-Kilvert). We shall meet this point again later (p. 158), but for the moment note only that the question of autopsy is omitted altogether. Finally, at 12.23–28a Polybius delivers an extended denunciation of his *bête noire*, the historian Timaeus (flourished around 300 BC), during the course of which he says this:

Nature has given us two instruments, as it were, by the aid of which we inform ourselves and inquire about everything. These are hearing and sight and of the two sight is much more veracious according to Heraclitus. 'The eyes are more accurate witnesses than the ears', he says. Now, Timaeus enters on his inquiries by the pleasanter of the two roads, but the inferior one. For he entirely avoids employing his eyes and prefers to employ his ears. Now the knowledge derived from hearing being of two sorts, Timaeus diligently pursued the one, the reading of books, as I have above pointed out, but was very remiss in his use of the other, the interrogation of living witnesses. It is easy enough to perceive what caused him to make this choice. Inquiries from books may be made without any danger or hardship, provided only that one takes care to have access to a town rich in documents or to have a library near at hand. After that one has only to pursue one's researches in perfect repose and compare the accounts of different writers without exposing oneself to my hardship. Personal inquiry, on the contrary, requires severe labour and great expense, but is exceedingly valuable and is the most important part of history. This is evident from expressions used by historians themselves. Ephorus, for example, says that if we could be personally present at all transactions, such knowledge would be far superior to any other. (12.27.1–8, tr. W. R. Paton)

By implication, this is an impressive defence of contemporary history; yet Polybius directly contradicts himself within a few pages at 12.28a.7: 'But he

[Timaeus] naturally considers as being most important and most difficult that which is in fact of least importance and no difficulty, namely the collecting of documents and questioning those with knowledge of each event.' 'The inconsistency will be apparent', remarks Walbank: 'the questioning of eyewitnesses cannot be both the most important part of history, albeit one involving great labour and experience – and at the same time the least important and the easiest.'[11]

It will be seen, therefore, that in none of these passages is the contemporaneity of events vindicated as the primary reason why Polybius wrote history,[12] and in the introduction to the very first book any suggestion that his own experience of events may be significant for their narration is entirely missing (see 1.1.4–5). Thus we are left with the preface to book 3, in which he explains his change of plan (see above, p. 153) and which Walbank has interpreted persuasively as follows: 'Polybius wrote his main *Histories* under the stimulus of an idea, but . . . he wrote the last ten books mainly because he had material to hand and a personal story to tell. . . . The *Histories* begin by being focused on Rome, they end by being focused on Polybius, perhaps an anti-climax, but one which throws some light on the man who wrote them.'[13]

Polybius had a precedent for his additional books in Ennius, the father of Roman literature, whose history of Rome in fifteen books of epic verse (entitled *Annals*) was begun in the late 180s BC but subsequently acquired three additional books as Ennius recorded the warlike fortunes of various important contemporaries. But, if Polybius' additional books were primarily a more personalized narrative, as Walbank argued, that may be due to developments in the writing of memoirs (*hypomnēmata* in Greek, *commentarii* in Latin). Memoirs had begun to be written in the fourth century BC, became more common in the next two centuries, and enjoyed a long and popular life at Rome.[14] The Greek tradition is well illustrated by the numerous volumes (no longer extant) of the third-century-BC memoirist Aratus, of whom Polybius regarded himself as the continuator (see above, p. 154), but the classic examples are Julius Caesar's *commentarii* on the Gallic and civil wars. Though written in the 'dispassionate' third person favoured by Thucydides (see above, p. 151) and other memoirists, Caesar's *commentarii* were attacked by at least one contemporary as being a tendentious representation of his own involvement in events.[15] Another contemporary, Cicero, observed in 46 BC that Caesar, in writing them, 'wished intending historians to have material available from which they could select' (*Brutus*, 262). This observation indicates that *commentarii* were regarded as a separate genre from history proper: they provided a basic hard core of information which historians were expected to elaborate in the conventional rhetorical manner by inventing plausible circumstantial detail, speeches, topographical background and the like.[16] Such rhetorical elaboration, especially when based on material which was itself liable to tendentiousness, inevitably meant that a full-scale work of contemporary history was unlikely to accord with the recollections which contemporaries had of events. This (to us) curious phenomenon is worth considering further in its social and intellectual context.

In a society which generally paid little attention to documentary evidence, as is generally agreed, the narrator of pre-contemporary history was in a privileged position: his narrative could not be gainsaid unless it was clearly implausible. But was the narrator of contemporary history in so very different a position? His narrative was open to authoritative contradiction only if it was challenged by the report of an eyewitness, and the ancients knew as well as we do that such reports are themselves open to objection.

We must remember that law and the processes of law permeated Greek and Roman society to a far greater degree than anything with which we are familiar today. The standard procedures of prosecution and defence required, in their turn, an expertise in persuasive oratory or rhetoric, which therefore formed the basis of higher education and hence also the background to much literary activity. Now it is axiomatic that in a litigious society a higher priority is given to winning the case than to establishing the truth, and that in rhetorical performances plausibility is more important than telling the truth. Since it is generally accepted that both law and rhetoric greatly influenced classical historiography both in theory and in practice, it would not be altogether surprising if the criteria of law and rhetoric were carried over into the writing of history. A historian of contemporary events could be regarded analogously to an advocate pleading his case: his opponent, in the person of an eyewitness, might have the grounds and opportunity to contradict him; but the judicial and rhetorical aspects of historiography guaranteed that the contradiction would not necessarily prevail over the historian's narrative simply by virtue of autopsy. When the fourth-century-BC orator Isocrates maintained the superior reliability of ears over eyes,[17] he was not merely inverting the adage of Herodotus and Heraclitus in a perverse manner (see above, pp. 150 and 154), but also illustrating a fundamental characteristic of ancient society as a whole.

We may demonstrate these general remarks by means of a 'test case', the conspiracy of Catiline at Rome in 63 BC. When the historian Sallust came to write his account of the affair twenty years later, he began by saying,

Historiography seems to me to be particularly difficult, first because events require to be adapted to words, and second because most people think that when you criticize crimes you are speaking from malevolence or envy; and conversely, when you record the excellence and fame of good men, no one raises any objection to what he is capable of doing easily himself, but anything beyond that is considered to be false in the way legends are false. (*War with Catiline*, 3.2)

These reasonable comments give no hint that in his narrative of the conspiracy Sallust puts into the mouths of speakers words which they did not utter, and that in general he manipulates events to make the structure of his narrative resemble that of Thucydides. Thus, while his narrative may be impartial, it is not 'true'; but truth in that sense, unlike impartiality, is something which Sallust does not mention here.

In this respect he appears to differ from Cicero, who had taken a prominent part in the prosecution of Catiline and who in 55 BC urged a historian friend called Lucceius to write a monograph on the subject:

> Elaborate my activities even against your better judgement, and in the process disregard the laws of historiography: that prejudice which you discussed quite beautifully in one or other of your prefaces, . . . well, please don't suppress it if it nudges you strongly in my favour, but simply let your affection for me take precedence over the truth. (*Letters to Friends*, 5.12.3)

This passage in its turn needs to be seen in the context of two others, both of a much later date. In AD 107 the younger Pliny wrote to the historian Tacitus with some information which he hoped that the latter might include in his *Histories*, then in progress:

> This sequence of events, such as it is, you will be able to make more notable, more distinguished, and more important, though I'm not asking you to go beyond the norm for an incident of this type: history oughtn't to exceed the truth, and truth is quite adequate for honourable deeds. (*Letters*, 7.33.10)

About sixty years later still, the emperor Verus wrote to his friend and historian Fronto, 'My achievements are of course as great as, and no greater than, they are (whatever that is); but they will appear as great as you want them to appear.' Verus' unspoken exhortation seems to resemble that to which Cicero gave voice – namely, that the historian should disregard the truth – but the comment of Pliny is more interesting still. How could he expect Tacitus both to make the sequence of events '*more* notable, *more* distinguished, and *more* important' and at the same time not to '*exceed* the truth'? There seems to be a contradiction here which requires explanation.

Yet the contradiction exists only if truth is taken to mean 'a truthful account of what actually took place', whereas the ancient historians saw truth primarily in terms of impartiality.[18] It is clear from their various prefaces that there was a theoretical expectation that they should deal with the characters of history impartially; but it is equally clear from their various narratives that they abandoned this principle in practice. Such an ambiguity is entirely natural in an honour-based society which was more than usually sensitive to envy but in which historiography, with its basis in rhetoric, was regarded as a vehicle for either encomium or censure. Thus, when there is a debate whether Cicero should write ancient or contemporary history, the latter attracts support because it means he will be able to glorify himself and his friends (Cicero, *Laws*, 1.8). A similar debate occurs in one of Pliny's letters, written in AD 106 to a friend who had been urging him to write history:

> Meanwhile you can be giving some thought to the period on which I might best embark. Ancient and covered by others? The evidence has all been collected, but it would be a real burden to read through and compare the historians in question. Contemporary and original? There would be a risk of giving serious offence in return for scant reward. For one thing, the fallible nature of society is more likely to provoke criticism than praise; and, for another, if you praise you are accused of being grudging, and if you criticize you are accused of being excessive – despite having been fulsome with your praise and sparing with your criticism. (*Letters*, 5.8.12–13)

Within a decade Tacitus was writing as follows in his *Annals*:

> Hardly anyone objects to ancient historians, and no one now cares if your treatment of the Carthaginians or Romans is too encomiastic. But many who suffered punishment or disgrace during Tiberius' reign [AD 14–37] have descendants alive today; and in cases where the families themselves have died out, you will find people whose own analogous behaviour leads them to assume that another's crimes are being imputed to themselves. Even distinction and excellence invite hostility since they constitute too harsh an indictment of their opposites merely by coexisting with them. (4.33.4)

These passages, as will be seen, confirm the emphasis on impartiality which distinguished the extracts from Sallust, Cicero and Pliny quoted earlier (pp. 156–7).

Pliny had suggested to Tacitus that the historian should magnify Pliny's own role in events, as might be expected, but that he should not exceed the accepted limits of magnification: such excess not only risks incredulity, as Sallust made clear, but is also quite unnecessary, since Pliny evidently takes it for granted that Tacitus will share his own estimation of his role (namely, that it was 'honourable'). Cicero, on the other hand, knew from bitter experience that others did not necessarily share his own heroic view of his behaviour during the Catilinarian conspiracy: he therefore wanted Lucceius to restore the balance by exceeding the accepted limits of magnification in this particular case, whatever the risks to credibility. Thus, despite these differences of emphasis, both Cicero and Pliny leave no doubt that when they speak of 'truth' they mean 'impartiality'; the likelihood that their friends' rhetorical narratives would scarcely accord with the recollections of other contemporaries does not seem to have been an issue. This is some measure of how different classical historiography is from its modern counterpart, and how different the expectations of its readers.

The potential of historiography for praise and censure, and the reception of these two modes by readers, help to explain an otherwise curious statement in the preface of Livy (c. 64 BC–AD 17). His original intention was to write a history of Rome from the founding of the city to (probably) 43 BC in 120 volumes. Now it was normally accepted that readers would enjoy the narrative of early legendary 'history', while both Polybius and Pliny put forward arguments why authors might prefer to write contemporary history (see above, pp. 154 and 158). Yet Livy reverses these two positions:

> I am confident that the majority of my readers, in their haste to reach the present period when the forces of a long-standing super-power are bent on self-destruction, will derive less pleasure from the origins of Rome and the immediately succeeding period. But I personally regard it as a bonus, at least while the archaic age has my undivided attention, to avert my gaze from the misfortunes which for so many years our age has witnessed. (Preface 4–5)

What is the explanation for Livy's reversal?

We must remember that Livy almost certainly began writing in the mid-thirties BC, when the civil wars of 49–31 BC were at their height; and, while it was natural that he should regard ancient history as a welcome distraction from the horrors of civil strife, it was equally natural that his readers would be fascinated to see how he coped with describing the individual politicians whose power-struggles had caused that strife. Such fascination is entirely to be expected in a society such as had been outlined (above, p. 157). Horace memorably said that another contemporary historian of the civil wars, Asinius Pollio, was handling a theme in which the dice were 'loaded for danger' and that he was 'treading through fires overlaid by treacherous ash' (*Odes*, 2.1). The future emperor Claudius decided to omit the civil-war period from his histories altogether (Suetonius, *Claudius*, 41.2).

Yet Livy's understandable aversion to contemporary history seems to have abated in the course of time. When at last the historian reached the intended conclusion of his work, the emperor Augustus had long since ended the civil wars and brought peace and stability to the Roman world. In the new atmosphere of optimism, Livy decided, as both Ennius and Polybius had done before him (see above, pp. 153 and 155), to extend his work by a further twenty-two volumes, bringing his history down to 9 BC. Yet this change of plan is to be explained not by any perceived superiority of contemporary history as such, but by the changed nature of the events which were there to be recorded. Livy's extension of his history is a tribute to the emperor under whom he lived and worked.

In his enthusiasm (however belated) for contemporary history, Livy was followed in the first century AD by Velleius Paterculus, Servilius Nonianus, Aufidius Bassus, Cluvius Rufus, Fabius Rusticus and the elder Pliny – though only Velleius' work has survived to the present day. Tacitus (AD 56/7 – after 120) described the years AD 69–96 in his *Histories*; we get the impression from Lucian's *How to Write History* that contemporary military history thrived in the second century AD; and in the early third century Dio Cassius wrote a history of Rome (in Greek) down to AD 229 in eighty volumes, of which the latest deal with contemporary events, while at roughly the same time Herodian was writing an account (also in Greek) of the years AD 180–238. Yet, though contemporary history clearly flourished during the Empire, that is not the whole story.

Having explained why he has chosen to describe the years AD 69–96 in his *Histories*, Tacitus adds this promise: 'If I live long enough, I have reserved for my later years the more fertile and less hazardous material provided by the reigns of the Deified Nerva and Trajan [AD 96 onwards], a period of rare delight, when you can think what you want and say what you think' (1.1.4). Yet, even if this promise was seriously intended (which may be doubted), it remained unfulfilled: Tacitus later went on to write his account of a still earlier period (AD 14–68) in the *Annals*, explaining that previous treatments of the subject were variously unsatisfactory: 'The activities of Tiberius, Gaius, Claudius and Nero were falsified through fear during their lifetimes, and were recorded after their deaths while hatred was still fresh' (1.1.2). Thus in each of his major works Tacitus sub-divides contemporary history into more and less recent periods, and, despite his promise in the *Histories*, himself refuses to write about any living emperor. Such refusals become increasingly common amongst other imperial historians and are usually expressed in one of two forms: either the historian himself promises to deal with the period in a more elaborate style at a future date, or he says that other historians will do so.[19] Such expressions have the advantage of appearing to pay tribute to the emperor of the day while at the same time avoiding the (perhaps dangerous) necessity of having to say anything at all.

This convention, and others with which we are by now familiar, are illustrated by the history of Ammianus Marcellinus (c. AD 330–95). Ammianus wrote a history of the Roman Empire from AD 96, the point at which Tacitus' *Histories* had left off, down to the death of the emperor Valens in 378. Of the original thirty-one volumes, the first thirteen are now lost; and it seems from the opening of book 26 that at one point Ammianus considered proceeding no further than AD 363/4:

> Having spared no pains in relating the course of events up to the beginning of the present epoch, I had thought it best to steer clear of more familiar matters, partly to escape the dangers which often attend on truth. . . . Fears of this kind led some older writers not to publish in their lifetime eloquent accounts they had composed of various events within their knowledge. For this we have the unimpeachable testimony of Cicero in a letter to Cornelius Nepos. Now, however, I will proceed with the rest of my story. . . . (Tr. W. Hamilton)

Whether Ammianus was serious in what he said, or whether he was simply drawing attention to his subsequent narrative by means of the now-conventional 'change of plan' motif, is unclear: there seems no obvious reason why events before 363 should be less dangerous than those afterwards. At any rate, his narrative of AD 364–78 eventually concludes with the statement, 'The rest I leave to be written by better men whose abilities are in their prime. But if they choose to undertake the task, I advise them to cast what they have to say in the grand style' (tr. W. Hamilton). Here again it is not immediately clear why Ammianus could not have proceeded beyond 378 if he had wanted to, and it is possible that he is simply effecting closure by means of another well-established literary motif. Whatever the truth may be, the fact that we cannot be certain how seriously to take these passages provides a further indication of the rhetorical nature of classical historiography and the problems associated with it.

When imperial historians invite others to continue the narrative after them, their invitations are clearly different in kind from that issued in the fourth century BC by Xenophon (see above, p. 152) since they constitute a coded refusal to write contemporary history. As this is the first occasion on which contemporary history appears to have been distinguished on any significant grounds at all, it is worth asking whether this practical distinction was accompanied by any theoretical expression.

In this connection we should note that it is a second-century-AD antiquarian writer, Aulus Gellius, who first refers to any theoretical distinction between contemporary and other history:

> Some people think 'history' differs from 'annals' in that while each is an historical narrative, history proper deals with events in the conduct of which the narrator took part. That that is the view of some people is stated by Verrius Flaccus in book 4 of *The Meaning of Words*: he says that he himself has doubts on the matter, but thinks there may be something in it since the Greek word *historia* means knowledge of contemporary events. (*Attic Nights*, 5.18.1–2)

In any discussion of contemporary history in the Classical world, Gellius' words acquire importance simply because of their rarity; but we should note that the author himself is not primarily concerned with any alleged difference between contemporary and other history at all. Gellius is interested in the difference between 'history' and 'annals', of which in the rest of his discussion he proceeds to offer two further explanations: neither of them has anything to do with contemporary history, and he seems to regard either of them as preferable to that entertained by Verrius Flaccus. It is true that Flaccus is supported by Servius, the fourth-century-AD commentator on Virgil, who in his note on *Aeneid* 1.373 gives a similar explanation of the difference between 'history' and 'annals'; but he is contradicted implicitly by the sixth-century-AD writer Ammonius in *On the Difference between Related Words* (250, p. 66 Nickau): 'a *historiographos* narrates events which took place before his own time, like Herodotus, but a *syngrapheus* those of his own time, like Thucydides'.

It is of course natural for scholars to classify and argue, and it is perhaps not surprising that it is in grammatical works that Verrius Flaccus and Ammonius are first attested as differentiating, albeit in a contradictory fashion, between contemporary and other history. Yet, while Ammonius' definitions may rest on nothing more substantial than a misguided extrapolation from the opening words of Herodotus and Thucydides respectively,[20] it may be significant that he is thought to have derived them from sources in the first or second centuries AD and that Flaccus himself flourished during the reign of Rome's first emperor, Augustus (31 BC–AD 14).[21] That is to say: the theoretical distinction between contemporary and other history can perhaps be traced back at least to the days when historians first began to distinguish contemporary history in practical terms by simply not writing it (see above, p. 160). When this moment was is uncertain, but it is likely to have been earlier rather than later. The Augustan poets were adopting an analogous convention (of refusing to write contemporary epic) by the twenties BC, and we know from Ammianus that contemporary historians were reserving their works for posthumous publication even in the late Republic (see above pp. 160–1). It is therefore possible (but no more) that the distinction between contemporary and other history is to be associated with the movement towards autocracy at Rome in the second half of the first century BC.

From the evidence presented here it might be concluded that contemporary history was seen by the Greeks in terms of autopsy and eyewitnesses and by the Romans in terms of bias and prejudice; but such a conclusion is less likely to reflect a genuine cultural difference than to be the accidental result of the selection of texts which happen to have survived. We must remember that the Greeks were notoriously sensitive to envy and that the *locus classicus* on bias and prejudice, which served as a model for Roman historians, was the speech which Thucydides puts into the mouth of the Athenian statesman Pericles;[22] conversely, it is a Roman historian, Velleius Paterculus, who in AD 30 published a contemporary account of the emperor Tiberius which is all the more valuable for its expressly autoptic narrative of events.[23] More important than any such apparent difference between Greek and Roman is the question whether either tradition recognized contemporary history as a distinctive form of writing.

In the modern world communication is easier than ever before. We have the advantages of various news media, and there is a worldwide network of reporters and journalists whose sole purpose in life is the production of instant history for the benefit of their consumers. Yet, despite the potential checks on misinformation which these advantages imply, we know, if we stop to reflect, that contemporary history regularly fails to meet the ideals of accuracy and truth which have been associated with historiography since the early nineteenth century. In the Classical world, on the other hand, communication was exceptionally difficult and sometimes impossible, even over very short distances. Journalism as such was unknown, and the basis of historiography in rhetoric meant that it lacked its modern association with accuracy and truth. It is perhaps hardly surprising that in these very different circumstances we have found that few distinctions were made between contemporary and other history – except by grammarians and those writers who refused to indulge in it.

Notes

1 A. D. Momigliano, *Studies in Historiography* (Weidenfeld and Nicolson, 1966), pp. 130, 135.
2 H. D. F. Kitto, *Poiesis* (University of California Press, Berkeley and Los Angeles, 1966), pp. 274–5.
3 So G. E. M. De Ste Croix, *The Origins of the Peloponnesian War* (Duckworth, 1972), pp. 7–12, though by no means everyone agrees with him.
4 A. W. Gomme, *A Historical Commentary on Thucydides* (Oxford University Press, 1956), vol. III, p. 584.
5 H. D. Westlake, *Essays on the Greek Historians and Greek History* (Manchester University Press, 1969), p. 123.
6 K. J. Dover, *Thucydides* (Oxford University Press, 1973), p. 29.
7 Ibid., p. 4.
8 *History and Theory*, 17 (1978), pp. 4–5.
9 See G. Avenarius, *Lukians Schrift zur Geschichtsschreibung* (Anton Hain, Meisenheim-am-Glan, 1956), pp. 78–9.
10 F. W. Walbank, *Polybius*, (University of California Press, Berkeley and Los Angeles, 1972), p. 182.
11 Ibid., p. 73.
12 There is another reference to autopsy at 20.12.8, but since the passage is fragmentary we have no context in which to place it.
13 Walbank, *Polybius*, p. 183.
14 See A. D. Momigliano, *The Development of Greek Biography* (Harvard University Press, Cambridge, Mass., 1971).
15 See Suetonius, *Julius Caesar*, 56.4.
16 These and other invented elements of the rhetorical elaboration of history are set out by Cicero in *On the Orator*, 2.63. See A. J. Woodman, *Rhetoric in Classical Historiography* (Croom Helm, 1988), chapter 2.
17 In *Panathenaicus*, 150; see also *Panegyric*, 30.
18 This is not the place to argue so large an issue in detail, but see T. P. Wiseman, 'Practice and Theory in Roman Historiography', *History*, 66 (1981), pp. 387–8.
19 See *Classical Quarterly*, 25 (1975), pp. 287–8.
20 Herodotus had used the noun *historia*; Thucydides the verb *syngraphein*. See P. Scheller, *De Hellenistica Historiae Conscribendae Arte* (R. Noska, Leipzig, 1911), p. 13.

21 For Ammonius' sources see Scheller, *De Hellenistica Historiae Conscribendae Arte.*
22 Thucydides, 2.35.2: see P. Walcot, 'The Funeral Speech: a Study of Values', *Greece and Rome*, 20 (1973), pp. 111–21.
23 See A. J. Woodman, *Velleius Paterculus: the Tiberian narrative* (Cambridge University Press, 1977), p. 287.

11

The Role of Biography

Nigel Hamilton

In recent years biography, which enjoyed its heyday in Victorian times, has experienced something of a renaissance. Indeed, one might say that readers today are less interested in the rise and fall of empires than in those of actual people.

But how real is or was a life? The biographer operates under much the same terms and conditions as the historian – namely, the acceptance that there is no such thing as history, only what historians write. Truth, therefore, depends in large measure on the truthfulness of the historian, and this is no less true of the biographer.

The biographer, however, carries an extra burden. Whereas art is an extra in history, it is an integral part of biography. Biography is, in fact, portraiture in words, and, just as the discerning public desires of a portrait painter more than a good likeness, so the reading public expects of a biographer more than a true-to-life chronicle. In composition, colour, brushwork and human perception the biographer must be an artist as much as he must be a historian – and the two aims do not always coincide. Composition which highlights the personality of the subject may actually distort the historical context in which the subject lived. Similarly, colouring may give richness to the narrative but by implication *discolour* or even black out other historical individuals. Some historians consider these factors to be so threatening that they would like to see all individuals removed from 'history'. I am thinking in particular of Professor F. H. Hinsley's recent attempt to chronicle the influence of British Intelligence on the conduct of the Second World War, exorcizing all names: 'We have cast our account in impersonal terms and refrained from naming individuals, . . . We must admit to a feeling for the appropriateness of Flaubert's recipe for the perfect realistic novel: *pas de monstres et pas de héros.*'[1]

History without people. It certainly promises theoretical purity. It also reflects the search for egalitarian justice, as Professor Hinsley explained:

'To have given prominence to only a few [individuals] would have been unjust to the many more who were equally deserving of mention.'[2] No biographer, however, will accept such an embargo – indeed he may well feel that it is absurd! Nevertheless, most biographers will understand Flaubert's point and sympathize with Professor Hinsley's predicament. Why *must* history be tyrannized by certain individuals who get all the attention, while others 'equally deserving' are ignored? How often does the biographer receive from a prospective publisher the response 'the subject wouldn't sell' – an attitude which, when writ large, leads to a biographical market saturated with vogue or cult figures.

One way out is to extend the biography of an individual into a window looking onto a yet larger historical world – as Ben Pimlott has done with his masterful chronicle of the life of Hugh Dalton, the forgotten Labour Chancellor.[3] Years ago I made an attempt to escape this tyranny of monolithic biography by deliberately painting a *dual* portrait: that of the two German novelists Heinrich and Thomas Mann. By recording the psychological and creative tension between the two brothers I hoped to avoid the suffocating narrowness of perspective that is inherent in single biography – though it took many years to get it published, once written![4]

Embarking on the official life of Field Marshal Montgomery in 1977 I was forced to abandon unorthodox methodology. Even so I made two decisions by which I hoped to avoid the tyrannous limitations of the single-subject lens.

First, I decided to let Monty's life tell itself not to a preordained length – the so-many-thousands-of-words beloved by publishers – but at the length appropriate to the quality of the material. The result, in the end, was three volumes of almost a thousand pages each – a nightmare for the publisher, but a canvas that allowed me the space and depth I needed to 'argue' Monty's case and to paint in the different themes and contrasts of colour. This worked unexpectedly well, with each volume outselling its predecessor. (Normally, multi-volume works sell progressively fewer copies per volume.) Serial publication suited the 'epic' quality of Montgomery's life: first, the long years of self-preparation as an unknown soldier before his 'call' to the desert in 1942; then his 'historic years' as a battlefield commander from El Alamein to Normandy; and finally his elbowing off the military pinnacle by the American commanders in the final year of the war, his post-war career, retirement and death. In the same manner that TV drama serials simulate the passage of time, so, by spacing out the chronicle of Monty's life over three volumes, I was able to simulate something of the life itself.

The second decision related to content. In the shoes of many other biographers I wanted to let Monty 'speak' in the biography as much as possible, by quoting his own letters and private papers, to which I had sole access. But I felt this would give a distorted picture unless I found a foil to Monty's own self-perception. I therefore decided to delve as deeply as I could in the archives relating to Monty's contemporaries – from Churchill to Eisenhower, Alanbrooke to Patton – so that, as with Heinrich and Thomas Mann, I could use the tension *between* performers to give a fresh and dramatic historical focus.

Even this was insufficient. I therefore adopted a journalistic technique, by using a tape-recorder to interview Monty's family and contemporaries, thus amassing my own archive of personal impressions of Monty and his times, told by his contemporaries in their own words.

This is a dangerous technique – particularly when the interviewee is recording events and personalities purely from memory, often forty or fifty years later. It went against the grain of everything I had been taught as a student historian at Cambridge; yet it was responsible, I think, for much of the success of what is actually a very serious, often very detailed military historical narrative. These witnesses, by being allowed to speak in their own conversational style, give a multitude of differing perspectives on Montgomery, as well as colour of their own. Often inexact, even mistaken, their testimonies are poor history if history is restricted to the utmost verisimilitude of detail. Nevertheless, by 'fleshing out' the somewhat desiccated fruit of my archive research around the world, and contrasted against Monty's own self-righteous writings, they complement the picture and perspective of Montgomery as no other historical technique could have done. The sum of the three parts of my investigation – archive research, Monty's own papers, and the testimony of many hundreds of witnesses – resulted in a sort of biography which is both 'popular' and, I hope, a contribution to contemporary history.

But can biography influence history? Certainly the Hinsleys of this world are fighting a brave rearguard action to stop this happening. Though I admire the idealism behind Professor Hinsley's crusade, I feel that in searching for 'perfect realism' he is being very unrealistic! Life *is* full of monsters and heroes, as Flaubert well knew, and was forced to concede. In attempting to avoid giving unfair prominence to some, we cannot blind ourselves to human nature. History depends on impersonal forces; but it is the interaction of *individuals* which produces the decisions on which events hinge. By excising all mention of individuals we run the risk of writing non-history: history in which, for doctrinaire reasons, the unsightly innards have been removed. Worse still, such puritanism – which nobly seeks to avoid prejudice and injustice – may in fact conceal the historian's *own* prejudices and injustices. Hiding himself behind a veil of purdah, the impersonal historian may in fact be seething with personal likes and dislikes; moreover, by refusing to interview and give space to the oral evidence of some – in order to avoid unfairness to others – the puritanical historian fails to employ one of the richest sources of contemporary history. How different would Professor Hinsley's history of Intelligence have been had he availed himself of the testimony of the many surviving Intelligence practitioners and commanders – the 'customers' of Intelligence – of the Second World War! Fearing 'injustice', Professor Hinsley has confined himself to 'college history'. Though the sub-title of his work gives his subject as the *influence* of Intelligence on actual wartime operations, the study is in fact largely a work of speculation in this area, in sad contrast to the energy and resources being put into oral research programmes by most modern museums and archives concerned with the Second World War.

What of less puritanical historians, though? Are they influenced by biographers? I think there *is* continual cross-fertilization – even cross-disinfection! Until the biographer has done his job, historians are often very superficial in their judgement of historical personalities. Conversely, historians are often irritated by the exaggerated deference paid to certain historical individuals, and are spurred by this to restore balance and perspective – sometimes to an exaggerated degree. I remember seeing a copy of a letter written by Correlli Barnett, a contemporary historian, explaining to a correspondent his negative feelings about Montgomery, about whom he had written most disparagingly in his *Desert Generals*.[5] Like Professor Hinsley, Barnett felt Monty's fame to be unjust to the many who also deserved mention; moreover he abhorred Monty's character, his egoism and lack of magnanimity towards those he superseded or dismissed. Nor was Barnett alone. Other writers then entered the historical fray. Bit by bit Monty's desert reputation was eroded until it became almost *de rigueur* for historians to underrate Monty's military achievement.

Yet, in following this very natural distaste for an individual (and Monty was not a 'nice' man, let it be said), Barnett and other writers unwittingly distorted both evidence and the natural conclusions to be drawn from such evidence. Just as Professor Hinsley's puritanism resulted in history-by-speculation, so Barnett's determination to knock an individual off his historical pedestal resulted in history-by-manipulation. The evidence of one particular sacked brigadier was taken as gospel, and the history of the desert war rewritten accordingly, infecting a whole generation of historians and historical readers.

Can the biographer counter historical bias? Interestingly, I think he can. Just as certain contemporary historians are determined to attack what they see as the myths of certain individuals, and in doing so sometimes distort the history they write, so biographers are often concerned to restore balance and justice to an individual after historical overreaction or negativism. Put metaphorically, historians may be seen as jealous conductors: they often dislike individual players or soloists, claiming that they upset the orchestral sound with their virtuoso solos or cadenzas; and they sometimes sabotage their scores!

One task of the biographer, then, is to expose such conductorial humbug, and reveal the soloist's virtues. To do this convincingly the biographer must be a better historian than the historian, willing to tread where historians fear or are too indolent to tread. But whether historians will accept a reversal of their judgement is another matter. Certainly in my own case, Correlli Barnett refused to alter the text of his *Desert Generals* when republishing it twenty years later, and still clings to his theory that history has been unjust to the sacked generals of the desert in 1942. On the other hand, the Oxford Professor of Modern History, Michael Howard, has altered his judgement perceptibly over the years. In March 1976, on the day of Montgomery's death, he recorded in *The Times* the then fashionable view that it was 'doubtful whether he [Montgomery] will be regarded by posterity as one of the great Captains of history, or even one of the truly outstanding figures of the Second World War'.

Ten years later, in a broadcast following publication of the final volume of my 'Monty' trilogy, Professor Howard posed the question, 'Was he [Montgomery] really so much more significant in our history than his contemporaries – Alanbrooke, Alexander, Wavell, Slim? Is he really in the Wellington or Marlborough class?' He went on, 'A perusal of these three volumes gives a resoundingly positive answer to all these questions.'[6]

The reader can imagine who is now *my* historian hero!

Notes

1 F. H. Hinsley *et al. British Intelligence in the Second World War*, vol. III (HMSO, 984).
2 Ibid.
3 Ben Pimlott, *Hugh Dalton* (Jonathan Cape, 1985).
4 Nigel Hamilton, *The Brothers Mann* (Secker and Warburg, 1978).
5 Correlli Barnett, *The Desert Generals* (William Kimber, 1962).
6 Michael Howard, BBC Radio 3, 1987.

Contributors

John Barnes is a Lecturer in Government at the London School of Economics.

François Bédarida is Director of the Institut d'Histoire du Temps Présent, Paris.

Nicholas Cox is an archivist at the Public Record Office, Kew.

Dermot Englefield is Deputy Librarian of the House of Commons.

Norbert Frei is a researcher at the Institut für Zeitgeschichte in Munich.

Gaetano Grassi is a Director of the Istituto Nazionale per la Storia del Morimento di Liberazione in Italia.

Nigel Hamilton is a freelance author and official biographer of Field Marshal Montgomery.

Peter Hennessy is Co-Director of the Institute of Contemporary British History and a Visiting Fellow of the Policy Studies Institute, London.

Tom Nossiter is a Senior Lecturer in Government at the London School of Economics and Political Science.

Gillian Peele is Tutorial Fellow in Politics at Lady Margaret Hall, Oxford.

Angela Raspin is an archivist at the British Library of Political and Economic Science.

Anthony Seldon is Co-Director of the Institute of Contemporary British History, London.

A. J. Woodman is Head of the Latin Department at the University of Durham.

Index

Grigg Committee (Committee on
Departmental Records) 77–8
Guardian 19, 20, 21, 24, 31
*Guide to Current British Periodicals
in the Humanities and Social
Sciences* 32
Guide to Reference Material 32

Haines, Joe 27
Hakim, Catherine 64
Halévy, Elie 130
Hamilton, Nigel 165–9
Hankey, Lord 35, 42
Hansard 43, 103, 105, 106, 107, 109
Harris, Kenneth 54
Harrison, Martin 66
Hartley, T. C. 8
Hartman, Paul 66
Hastings, Max 3, 4, 24
Hazlehurst, Cameron 95
Healey, Denis 34
Heath, Edward 34, 35, 39
Hennessy, Peter 9, 17–27
Heraclitus 150, 154, 156
Heren, Louis 27
Herodian 153, 160
Herodotus 149–52, 156, 162
Himmelweit, Hilde 57
Hinsley, F. H. 165–6, 167–8
Historical Journal 49
historiography 133–7, 141, 149–63
history: and biography 39–40, 165–9;
instant 45–8; and journalists 19,
26–7, 143–4: official 44–5; and
politics 136–7; religious 142; *see
also* contemporary history; sources
History 49
Hitchens, Christopher 39
HMSO (HM Stationery Office) 43,
109, 110, 112–13
Hodson, H. V. 31
Holmes, Martin 48
Holroyd, Michael 5
Home, Lord 34
Homer 149–50
Hopkinson, Tom 27
Horace 159
Howard, Anthony 6

Howard, Michael 169
Howe, Geoffrey 34
Husband, Charles 66
Hutchinson, George 39
Hyde, H. Montgomery 10

*Imperial Calendar and Civil Service
List* 10
Imperial War Museum 14, 119
Independent 20, 21, 27, 31
Independent Broadcasting Authority
65; Independent Television 25–6, 60
India Office Library 14
Institut d'Histoire du Temps Présent
130–2
Institut für Zeitgeschichte 122, 124
Institute of Contemporary British
History 30, 50, 121
Institute of Historical Research 49, 95
*International Bibliography of
Historical Sciences* 49
interviews 3–15, 167; sampling 7,
56–7; United States 145
Isocrates 156
Italia contemporanea 49
Italy 117, 133–7

James, Robert Rhodes 6, 38, 42
Jenkins, Peter 21, 46
Jenkins, Roy 6, 34
Jenkins, Simon 4, 24, 25
Johnson, Paul 4
Jones, George W. 38
Josephus 153
Journal of Modern History 49
*Journal of the Royal Statistical
Society* 50
Julius Caesar 155

Keegan, William 46
Keesing's Contemporary Archives 31
Kellner, Peter 39
Kempton, Murray 26
King, Francis 8
Kinnear, Michael 60
Krock, Arthur 26
Kurti, Nicholas 5

Index by Gill Riordan